DEMOCRACY AND PROGRESS

THE MACMILLAN COMPANY
NEW YORK · BOSTON · CHICAGO
DALLAS · ATLANTA · SAN FRANCISCO

MACMILLAN AND CO., LIMITED
LONDON · BOMBAY · CALCUTTA
MADRAS · MELBOURNE

THE MACMILLAN COMPANY
OF CANADA, LIMITED
TORONTO

DEMOCRACY AND PROGRESS

BY

David McCord Wright

Professor of Economics and Lecturer in Law
University of Virginia

1948

THE MACMILLAN COMPANY

NEW YORK

THIS IS CAROLINE'S BOOK

Acknowledgments

It is difficult to acknowledge criticism without committing the critics to apparent acceptance of opinions which they may not share. None of those, therefore, whom I am about to mention should be taken as accepting all, or indeed any, of the points made in this book. They have each, however, given generously of time and interest, and they have all been encouraging even when they disagreed.

I wish first to thank Professor Horace Taylor of Columbia who introduced me to J. S. Gambs' "Beyond Supply and Demand"; and Professor Charles K. Davenport of Virginia from whom came my initial acquaintance with Alfred North Whitehead's "Science and the Modern World." These suggestions have profoundly colored my entire outlook.

My greatest debt in the preparation of the book is due to Professors L. M. Hammond and W. S. Weedon of the University of Virginia philosophy department who patiently criticized and discussed the entire work at nearly all its stages.

Others who read all or part of the manuscript and to whom I owe invaluable suggestions are Dr. R. D. Calkins of the General Education Board, Dean E. T. Grether and Dr. William Fellner of the University of California at Berkeley, Dr. Herbert Northrup of Columbia University, Dr. George Hildebrand, Dr. Armen Alchian, and Dr. Alfred Nicols of the University of California at Los Angeles, and Mr. John Cook Wyllie, Dr. Raymond F. Mikesell, and Dr. George T. Starnes of the University of Virginia.

I am also indebted to Professor James W. Angell of Columbia, Dean Harold Somers of the University of Buffalo, Professor Howard Ellis of the University of California at Berkeley, and Dr.

T. R. Snavely of the University of Virginia for stimulating discussion, criticism, and encouragement.

Dr. Wilson Gee, Director of the University of Virginia Institute for Research in the Social Sciences, provided indispensable assistance in many emergencies.

My debt to my Harvard professors and classmates in the Harvard graduate school of economics is so overwhelming that it would be futile to attempt to itemize it. Also, I should be most ungrateful not to mention those graduate and undergraduate students at Columbia, California, and the College and Law School of the University of Virginia, whose keen minds and eager search for truth have been a constant stimulus and incentive.

Finally, next to my wife, to whom this book is dedicated, I should express my debt to the memory of Thorstein Veblen—at once an opponent and an inspiration.

DAVID McCORD WRIGHT

Los Angeles, California
September 1, 1947

Contents

DEMOCRACY AND PROGRESS

Stating the Problem

SELDOM HAS greater physical power been combined with deeper moral uncertainty than in America today. It is almost as if we were suffering from a split personality. We hear constant talk of abundance; but in private life most of us find ourselves poor. We are still, for the most part, doing our work in the accustomed way; but in the minds of many lies the uneasy suspicion that the lives we lead cannot be reconciled with the values we profess. We are distressed not so much by the economic disorganization around us —great though that may be—as by a spiritual bewilderment which leaves us helpless among shouting prophets, not knowing where to turn.

Out of this desperate confusion has come a strong drive toward the discovery of new social techniques. An overwhelming mass of specialized knowledge has been accumulated, and we are now far better equipped than ever before to deal with mechanical problems of economic stability. But amid the very richness of our achievement we have found a great disappointment. The piling up of increasingly subtle theories and the elaboration of increasingly detailed programs have not reduced the confusion of tongues. Rather, it has magnified it.

Ten years ago the writer began the study of social problems by concentrating upon detailed analysis of a specific technical question: how to maintain income and employment. He must plead guilty to having thought such inquiries sufficient in themselves. But, over years of work and discussion, he has found that apparently minor initial differences ramify deeply. Nearly always a debate over policy has traced back to some more fundamental ethical or social judgment and he is now profoundly convinced that the man who wishes to avoid nonsense cannot study social policy on a technical level alone. There are many kinds of social stability, many types of full employment, many ways of reaching them, and we must make a choice. Still worse, most modern knowledge is "map" knowledge: it can show the way indifferently to one town or another, but it cannot choose our destination for us.

"The practical thing for the traveller to do who is uncertain of his path is not to proceed with the utmost rapidity in the wrong direction; it is to consider how to find the right one." The aim most prized in our civilization, avowedly at least, has been the achievement of a living democracy, and we shall use the search for this goal as our initial theme. Even if we did not already know it ourselves we have it on the word of Professor Gunnar Myrdal, a European socialist, that most Americans take their democracy seriously, are not hypocrites, and try to bring their professions and their practice into harmony. But in conversation with foreigners, or with extremists of this or that persuasion, how often have not Americans been confronted with some apparent contradiction: "How do you reconcile democracy with this—how with that?" Sometimes, indeed, they have had no answer.

Yet very often debates of this sort have been made on the assumption that democracy was a simple concept embodying one or perhaps two qualities or standards. Nothing could be more misleading. The sum of liberties and obligations that we call democratic freedom is not to be judged by any single standard but by a complex of standards. Worse yet, the individual qualities whose interpenetration produces a democratic culture are always to some extent in conflict. For example, it may be said that democracy is a matter of establishing electoral government. But if democracy were majority rule alone what could be more democratic than a lynching? We do not obtain democracy merely by holding an election. We obtain democracy, after setting up electoral government, when that government functions sufficiently justly and wisely and with respect for the individual personality. There is ballot-box democracy and there is ethical democracy, and the one is to be justified only in so far as it helps to achieve the other. The prime

purpose of this book is to discuss the social and economic requirements for such an achievement.

The analysis begins with an issue hotly debated today—the relationship between scientific progress and economic organization
—but soon more fundamental problems are encountered. We pass
from output per head to the ideal of a world free from rivalry and
conflict; and from that to the basic meaning of democratic progress.
Here the problem divides into two parts. First, we sketch the conditions necessary for democratic progress in the moral and artistic
sense. Next, we ask what economic system will best implement the
social ideals and standards just laid down. The remaining chapters
outline an approach toward general economic policy; and at the
end we try to look into the future of democracy.

Books like the present one have tended generally to fluctuate
between two equally unsatisfactory extremes. Writers like Hayek
have extolled the merits of the system while largely omitting its
problems. Opposing critics have elaborated the problems and
largely omitted the merits. The first group are unconvincing; the
second, superficial. It does no good to praise a system without
giving a reasonable idea of how it is to function. But neither does
it accomplish much to run over a long list of defects without
evaluating alternatives. Nor can we escape the dilemma simply
through "planning." You and I may both believe in planning,
but my plan may be to kill you. What is needed is first to determine the essential requirements of an economic democracy and
then to ask, In what way and for what purpose can we plan?

The problem which this book attacks is summed up in two
quotations from Alfred North Whitehead. The first stresses the
need for experiment and for adventure: "A race preserves its
vigour as long as it harbours a real contrast between what has been
and what may be; and so long as it is nerved by [that] vigour to
adventure beyond the safeties of the past. Without adventure
civilization is in full decay." Here is the key to the social philosophy
expounded in the present study. Nothing in it is meant to give the
impression that American democracy is a completed, or even a
nearly completed, achievement; and some of the most important
immediate tasks will be sketched as the theme unfolds.

But does the realization that our work is unfinished mean that we ought to accept any change simply for its own sake? Whitehead writes: "The deliberate aim at Peace easily passes into its bastard substitute Anaesthesia. In other words, in the place of the quality of life and motion there is substituted their destruction." Here is the modern dilemma. Uncritical and singleminded pursuit of some particular quality, without regard for other aspects of the case, often turns into the destruction of the very standard so ardently sought. Thus the forward-looking advocacy of change suddenly becomes intense conservatism if extended to include acceptance of a type of change which makes all further changes impossible. Conservatism, we should realize, is not a body of doctrine but a frame of mind, and not all the closed minds and closed systems are on the right.

In trying to synthesize problems of so broad a range as those presented here, it is obviously impossible to say everything at once. Grave danger of misunderstanding is consequently involved, and it must be stressed with the deepest earnestness that the message of this book cannot be understood unless it is read as a whole. Chapters on scientific progress, for example, must be read in connection with chapters on the ideal of a conflict-free world. Chapters on the distribution of wealth must be considered by the side of chapters on the business cycle and on foreign expansion; and so it goes—all the parts of the book are closely interdependent, and the impatient reader who on the strength of one or two chapters tries to classify the argument under some familiar label, will undoubtedly find himself mistaken. It should be realized from the start that the point of view here presented cuts squarely across current political and economic groupings in the United States.

A word should be said regarding the purpose of the quotations occasionally inserted. Almost without exception it is literary rather than authoritative. The writers quoted have expressed certain ideas particularly well; but they are not the sole authority for a given point of view—nor do I accept the entire philosophy of every author quoted. Most often, indeed, I do not.

Finally, this is a tract for the times and not a textbook. No obligation has been felt to labor the obvious, and emphasis has

been placed on those parts of the problem which seem most neglected and most important at the present time. So much that is
violently biased is published today that one would make no impression by presenting merely a spineless "on the one hand and
on the other." The aim here is, if anything, to give a needed counter-bias. But counter-bias does not mean caricature. The elements
of the problem relatively passed over here will be found to be
so prominent in the public mind that they run small danger of
being neglected. And I believe that the resulting final impression
is a balanced and a sound one.

The writer has long accepted his position as an illegitimate
child in any political family reunion. One who shares neither the
complacent acceptance of "laissez faire" nor yet the uncritical
"whole hog" attitude toward planning—both of which are so
popular today—is obliged to play a somewhat lonely role. Yet
the fact that the point of view here presented does not fit into
any usual political bracket may prove to be a strength rather than
a weakness. Democracy after all is a mimic warfare, conducted by
votes rather than by guns, in which the defeated minority accepts
the majority verdict with good humor. But such a form of government fails when the divisions become too deep: ballots give way to
guns and tanks, and the entire democratic fabric is torn apart.
Perhaps in setting up a scheme of values which takes elements
from both sides we may hope to point a common path to continued
achievement and renewed good feeling.

Science, Democracy, and Capitalism

CAPITALISM IS often thought of as a system which permits wealthy ladies to spend the winter in Miami—in other words as the mere existence of claims on property and a leisure class. So narrow a definition will hardly do. Claims on property of some sort are nearly as old as the human race, while leisure classes and "conspicuous consumption" were known before Babylon. The special cultural pattern of the last two hundred years cannot be entirely explained by phenomena found to a greater or less extent throughout the last two thousand. Some more detailed analysis is needed.

Our problem in this chapter is to discover the connection—if any—between science, capitalism, and the tremendous material progress of the last century and a half. But we must be careful how we place our emphasis. If it were "proved by twenty bishops" that capitalism, science, and material progress were inseparable, it still might not be true that capitalism was the best available social system. Many other questions need to be discussed before we reach a final choice. The problem of science is taken as a starting point not because scientific advance is a consideration which overrides all others, but because increased material well-being is the one goal common to nearly all factions in America today. Anyone who looks beneath the surface of modern controversy, however, soon finds that he must reckon with points of view which, consciously or unconsciously, wish to change the system not in order to smooth the way for science and material progress but in order to end them.

Another basic problem inevitably involved in the search for a connection between science, democracy, and capitalism is how far, in any case, we are justified in crediting the achievements of a period to its social system. Did the men of the nineteenth century, for example, do what they did because of their culture or in spite of it? Present-day philosophers would say that to dispute fiercely whether capitalism was the exclusive cause of science, or science of capitalism, is not only futile but lamentably old-fashioned. The modern point of view on the fundamental issue of determinism, implied, is a compromise. Modern science views the universe as a structure of interdependent evolving processes. A man may be depressed because he is sick; but he may equally be sick because he is depressed. At times the environment is too much for the mind but at other times the mind may twist the environment. In saying that there is a connection between science and capitalism, we do not need to say that scientific progress is altogether impossible in other systems. What we do mean to say is that special factors exist which make scientific progress particularly easy under capitalism. Our job in this chapter is to see what those factors are.

Many economists write as if the industrial revolution were to be explained simply by the rise of invention and not at all by the cultural features developing with it. The inference is that we may be able to retain and expand science while discarding the social framework within which it was born. This is reasonable as long as our regard is limited to the mere act of invention or of simple laboratory experimentation. There are no immediate grounds for expecting a socialist chemist, let us say, to be any less inventive than a capitalist one; and indeed it can be argued that more "facilities" would be extended to him, and therefore he would invent more. But such discussion tends to overlook the great gap between the making of an invention and its productive use.

Those who concentrate exclusively upon the laboratory side of things give no adequate weight to the innate conservatism and immobility of the human race and human customs. The word "conservatism" is not used in a political sense, but in the sense of love for old ways and old habits. Despite our modern gospel of progress, the fact that an idea is new is, in itself, quite enough to rouse opposition in the minds of many people; and this deeply seated hostility is reinforced and supplemented by the more mundane fact that the well-being and relative bargaining position of most of us depends, at any one time, upon the continued use of existing methods.

Not to prejudge the case between social systems, but simply to show our point, let us take a specific example. In 1910 the immediate prosperity of skilled coachmen, horse breeders, and livery stable keepers was dependent upon the continued use of horses. Some adaptable workers and industrialists might, and did, cross over into the new automotive business. But few men who have learned a trade have been so adaptable, and it is a fact well recognized that adjustment to technical change has usually been made in the next generation. Suppose, then, that there had been in 1910 a powerful horse monopoly, or a congress of united livery stable workers, using as a slogan protection of property, or prevention of unemployment, or "planning" of "security." Would we have been so certain of having automobiles today? Material and scientific progress do not depend on invention alone—they are also closely linked to a social environment which is hospitable to change. Just here lies the real issue—and like most issues it has a time dimension.

It is doubtful if there has ever been a day since the beginning of the industrial revolution in which a group of "experts"— whether appointed by a league of "big business," or by a congress of unions, or by a socialist congress—could not have planned a distribution of resources that would have made for a more "efficient" (in the sense of smoothly running) system than the existing one. Such a group could always have ended unemployment, always prevented "waste" (from its own point of view), and always given security. Furthermore, so far as any economic reasoning is concerned, it could have kept on doing this indefinitely. But, once the initial rearrangement had been made, could the group have planned a constantly rising standard of living?

Almost everybody believes in "planning" today in the sense that maladjustments cannot be allowed to get out of hand. What we need to discuss here, however, is the type of system, ardently advocated at present, in which the general over-all pattern of development is planned and licensed in advance by a unified group of "experts"—whether businessmen, bureau chiefs, or commissars is irrelevant to present purposes. Such a system we will call comprehensive planning. In judging comprehensive planning, it is important to remember that the great material progress of the last century was not a mere matter of "extension." It was not the endless heaping up of machinery of the same kind. On the contrary, our present standard of living is the outgrowth of constant, repeated, energetic, and unexpected change. In comparing, therefore, a comprehensively planned state and an unplanned one, we have to decide in advance how long a time period we are going to consider. In the short run the market economy is admittedly unstable and wasteful. Why this is so, and what can be done about it, will occupy a large part of this book. On the basis of things "as is," the planners can nearly always do better. But though in the short run the comprehensively planned state wins on smoothness of economic performance, and though in cases of extreme maladjustment—as now—over-all planning offers the possibility of a great immediate gain, we cannot stop there unless we are prepared to admit that we need no more discoveries. The real question is: Can such a comprehensively planned system be combined with the maintenance of an adequate continued future flow of useful new inventions? The importance of settling this issue is brought out by supposing that a program of comprehensive planning had been adopted in 1837 or 1873, or in some other year of great capitalist disturbance, which kept science and technique virtually at their existing level. What effect would its adoption have had on us today?

Over forty years ago Thorstein Veblen analyzed the activities of various businessmen attempting to thwart technical changes or increases in production which would threaten their private bargaining position. He gave the process the name "capitalistic sabotage," and it has been a stock slogan of the left wing ever since. But Veblen's phrase is too narrow. "Capitalistic" sabotage should rather be called "security" sabotage. It arises because in a changing system—any changing system—someone is likely to be hurt by change and that someone is likely to try to prevent it.

Socialist thinkers are apt to suppose that clashes of individual and general welfare would be avoided by the mere act of installing socialism. Admittedly, unemployment compensation, industrial reeducation, old-age benefits, and so forth can make the pinch of change less acutely felt. But in spite of this it still remains true that we have only to suppose a man's income bears some relationship to the value of his skills to society in order to have the possibility of a drive toward security sabotage even in a socialist state.

The commissar of automobiles, let us say, might derive much of his power and prestige from his special skill in that industry and the need for its product; the commissar of railroads, from the need for rail transport. How enthusiastic would they be to see the need for both virtually disappear with the rise of airplanes? Even if no money income differences are involved, there are valuable perquisites, or at least the secret sweets of power and the feeling of being a "big shot." All these incentives are lavishly used in Russia. What is the difference between going bankrupt, as a capitalist, and moving out of a former Tsarist palace into half a room? On a somewhat lower level of authority the simple "instinct of workmanship"—the pride of a man of, and in, his skill—may be offended by change which renders established methods out of date. Many an erstwhile happy man will be left stranded as a "back number," and no money salve is ever likely entirely to relieve his hurt. There are, to be sure, certain individuals who approximate the pure administrative type—who rejoice in the task of reorganization and welcome transference. They will object less to change than to the lack of it; but they form a relatively small minority, and cannot function except in a social system which welcomes their peculiar aptitude.

If then the mere fact of putting in socialism or comprehensive planning—even of a highly equalitarian type—fails to eliminate the clash of individual with general welfare, and the frictional opposition to change, we are obliged, in a study of the long-run outlook for science in a socialist or a comprehensively planned state, to ask whether such a system would contain any mechanism for overcoming the cumulative drag of nostalgic conservatism plus self-interest. We are also obliged to search out the secret which permitted the long-run industrial development of the nineteenth century so triumphantly to overcome barriers of this sort.

It is just here that what we may call democracy of aspiration or opportunity becomes important. The vital point to grasp in this problem of invention is that during the industrial revolution the existing social hierarchy was disintegrated and the doors of opportunity were thrown open in an unparalleled manner to individuals in all classes. Therein lay the special seeds of continued development. For the growing competitive economic system gave an extraordinary chance to the man with a new idea. No longer did he have to conform to the method prescribed by the guild, or have to ask the permission of some government official. Nor, on what we are inclined to view today as the debit side, did he have to worry much about the immediate consequences upon the social structure of the invention which he was exploiting. The result was an extraordinary outburst of scientific and technical change, accompanied by a tremendous increase in individual social opportunity. The introduction of new methods helped bring new families to the top, while the emergence of new families, by keeping society fluid, helped make things easier for still newer methods. Echoes of the process may be found in such apparently remote places as the calm chapters of *Pride and Prejudice* and the more stormy pages of *Jane Eyre*. Without saying that all this came about at once or that "equality" of opportunity was ever realized or even approximated, I follow Lord Keynes' summary of the nineteenth century, in England especially, that "the greater part of the population, it is true, worked hard and lived at a low standard of comfort—but escape was possible, for any man of capacity at all exceeding the average, into the middle and upper classes."

"A chance to rise on independent terms"—this was the strategic aspect of the nineteenth century's competitive framework which underwrote, encouraged, and made possible the tremendously rapid advance of applied as well as laboratory science. It has been said, "On the whole, the great ages have been unstable ages"; and, provided instability is not so great as to end in collapse rather than stimulation, the phrase certainly implies a profound truth. Our industrial revolution was by no means the first one. There have been other periods of tremendous constructive change. But sooner or later they have all run down. Explanation lies largely in the deterioration of self-perpetuating groups. Social upheaval, some-times for bad, but frequently for good, brings new minds and new ideas to the top, and the result is renewed development. That is the condition of Russia at present. But the new groups, unless again disrupted by circumstances, or forced to reorganize on fresh lines by outside competition, tend soon to freeze into oligarchies, aristocracies, and castes, and with this comes a progressive narrow-ing of the social framework. It is a fact well recognized that the "school," the "academy," tends to fall into increasingly rigid lines, and development increasingly must come from outside the "inner" circle.

The competitive order, on the other hand, as long as it survives, makes possible the emergence of new industrial and scientific leaders without asking the permission of an entrenched ruling group. The self-interest and the innate conservatism of such a group are not permitted to block the new idea, and, to the extent that the competitive order is approximated, the door is kept open for spontaneous and constant change. Here, however, lies the chal-lenge for the comprehensively planned state, in which the deter-mination of the industries that are to be permitted to expand almost inevitably determines the groups, and the individuals, that are to hold economic power. Suppose a national investment budget, care-fully drawn up with reference to a given structure of prices, tastes, and techniques. Then suppose that some manufacturer wishes to introduce an immensely productive new technical idea just brought forward by some scientist. This technique, we may further suppose, will, despite its productivity, upset the price structure of an indus-try, disrupt its investment plans, disorganize jobs, and cut across union rules. Under a regime desiring to maintain, let us say, 97 per cent security and employment, will the introduction of such an idea be allowed?

Some will say, "It will only be postponed for a while—the new idea will only be introduced more 'rationally.' " Will it? Seldom have the vested economic interests—which include the vested concern of the union in given rules, the vested concern of the bureau chief in given controls, the vested claim of the individual on his job, as well as the vested concern of the investor in his dividends—seldom have these vested interests been given a better argument against change than in the slogans of "security" and "planning." "Slow down," may be the initial slogan, "to avoid a slump," or "unemployment." But soon that slogan will be "Slow down"—unqualified. The interlacing forces of nostalgic conservatism and self-interest, present virtually in all societies, make it almost inevitable that further technical change will become more and more difficult. The laboratory scientist, finding his work cut off from practical, productive application, will either concern himself increasingly with metaphysical and abstract questions, or else turn his attention to perfecting still more dreadful weapons of war—in which there are fewer vested interests to oppose him.

Here, however, we must insert an important qualification and explain a factor which might appear to throw doubt upon our basic thesis. If a comprehensively planned and hence potentially stratified and immobile organization, or state, is located amidst others still competitive and developing, then it may come to exhibit a spurious and parasitic excellence in performance. For the developing and competitive states will be constantly breeding new techniques and ideas with all the incidental frictions and insecurities. But the comprehensively planned state need only blandly wait. After the superiority of the new techniques and new ideas has been so incontrovertibly established that even the most militant pressure group within the self-contained oligarchy cannot deny their value, comprehensive planning may be used to introduce them with a minimum of disturbance and a maximum of (short-run) efficiency. Thus, Imperial Germany was able to appropriate and apply the results of the English industrial revolution with a minimum of waste and friction. Even if (economically) conservative in-groups wish to delay change, the outside "pressure"—whether imagined or real—may force an imitative development, as in the forcible "opening" of Japan.

There are always many people who will mistake such imitative industrial rationalization for genuine superiority in technical progress. The fact that the comprehensively planned state sometimes furnishes after an interval the same results as competition, or "better" ones, and with less disturbance, will obscure the fact that such development might never have taken place without friction and competition somewhere. And though a comprehensively planned and stratified state, surrounded by competition, may well combine at times the best of both worlds so far as economic "stability" goes, we cannot stop there. The planned economic progress of Russia, for example, may benefit immensely from our competition, and seemingly avoid some of its wastes and friction. But without the spur of our outside emulation it is likely that the level of achievement in Russia would have been far lower.

Our argument must not be understood as meaning that we can do nothing except take disturbance on the chin. What is meant is rather that the line between stabilizing the economy and setting up an over-all direction of it is extremely tenuous, and that the two policies are insidiously easy to confuse. Those who feel that the difficulty has been overstated will do well to read carefully Lord Beveridge's *Full Employment in a Free Society*. Beginning with apparent advocacy of a mere policy of "filling in," or stabilization, Lord Beveridge's unflinching honesty and clear logic, plus the extraordinarily high standard of security which he seeks, lead him to control after control: "Stabilization of private investment through a National Investment Board, which would plan investment as a whole, using powers of control and loan and taxation policy," "a 'unified' wage policy . . . stable prices," "compulsory arbitration," "control of the location of industry." "Whether the use of the employment exchanges is made compulsory for all classes . . . it should be made compulsory in respect of all persons under eighteen, so that the flow of adaptable youth into industries may be wisely directed." And so on.

One need not suppose that Lord Beveridge did not see restrictive dangers. On the contrary, he recognized monopoly under many disguises, and was equally severe on excessive business demands and excessive union restrictions. But it is doubtful whether Beveridge, or any other advocate of the over-all planning of investment, has given adequate attention to the problem of obtaining continued change, or to the difficulties for a young man with a socially valuable new idea in the world of pensioned post-office clerks which his society could so easily become. Self-censorship is notoriously inadequate, and it seems highly doubtful that the comprehensively planned state—whatever its short-run achievements—would be compatible with a continued rapid development of science, especially applied science, or with a continued large-scale rise in the standard of living. When, therefore, "planning" passes beyond the vague and shifting boundary which separates "stabilization" from a general licensing of investment, democratic society is likely to pass from a regime of progress to a regime of slow stagnation. It is one of the greatest dangers of our time that neither this problem nor this boundary are at all recognized today.

· II ·

The Moral Dilemma of Progress

"Why," asked one professor, "should a man want to be better than his neighbors? Let him be thankful if he is no worse."

I ventured feebly to say that I did not see how progress could be made in any art or science, or indeed in anything at all, without more or less self seeking, and hence unamiability.

"Of course it cannot," said the professor, "and therefore, we are opposed to progress."

—SAMUEL BUTLER, Erewhon

THERE IS something peculiarly appealing to modern man in the contention that the evils of our present culture are all due to the "system" rather than to the shortcomings of the individuals who comprise it. In the first place, the idea is bound to have an element of truth. But in addition it relieves some of the chief nervous tensions of our day. No one ever encounters any bigger or more onerous problem than that of self-control. The urge for an alibi is entirely timeless. But, still more important, the questions which vex the modern world are so complicated, their ramifications so vast, that to understand them in detail appears impossible. How comforting, then, to be provided at one stroke both with an excuse for any personal misdeeds, and with an explanation of everything. Thus we find people insisting that the ugly vapid cheapness of modern life is all due to competition; that wars are the outgrowth of rivalry and competition; that unjustified strikes, however lamentable in themselves, are ultimately due, not to the greed of one side or the other, but to the bad mental climate engendered by competition; and that the way to solve everything is not to reduce, say, the strikes, but to end the competitive system.

11

If this point of view be accepted, the conclusions of the preceding chapter clearly lead us into a vicious circle: Material progress depends on competition—but competition keeps us from forming proper values. Is it not, then, obvious that material progress is futile? Few moderns are as clear-minded on this point as Samuel Butler, and as willing to abandon not merely competition but progress too. Yet I do not doubt that we shall soon see a rising trend in that direction. No more profound issue in the political, or the economic, life of mankind can be imagined. The ideal of self-abnegation has kindled the souls of men for centuries. But if we are not careful "self-sacrifice" may also be used to fasten fetters compared to which the restrictions of our present culture will seem almost trivial.

The argument can be broken down into several versions. First, objection may be made to any form of rivalry, as tending to call forth selfish, or at least combative, instincts. Next, certain kinds of rivalry may be frowned upon while others are thought permissible. For example, it may be considered wrong to compete with a man over the winning of a business order but right to compete with him over the winning of a political election. However, the modern anticompetitive gospel, in the more extreme forms, is turned against all types of struggle, rivalry, or desire for "success" —even, in some cases, a desire for attainment of a "worthy," "unselfish," or "noble" goal. For it may be held to be the fact of rivalry, rather than its goal, which explains ugly conduct.

In our present natural revulsion from all forms of conflict the extreme anticompetitive gospel is bound to have a special appeal; and we must examine it with care. Many people have talked of a new Utopia in which the scientist and the psychologist together will satisfy our wants and eliminate all sources of conflict. But relatively few have stopped to think what such an ideal means in terms of economic life. Nor, and more important, have many stopped to think what it may mean in terms of art, of science itself, and of democracy.

As long as our goal of social progress is a society in which there is no longer any strife, conflict, or unsatisfied desire, it is easy to show that we shall never reach it through material and scientific progress. A great deal has been said in the last few years about "ending the economic problem" through scientific discovery. The meaning of this concept is not easy to determine. To one man it may mean endless beer; to another, food. But if we consider the historical record no such naïve approach is possible. The belief that progress is good because it "satisfies" wants is easily shown to have little long-range validity. Even on the most practical plane the unchecked flow of human desires seems boundless. Yesterday's great advance is today's commonplace, and as old "needs" are satisfied new needs gradually come in to take their place.

In 1850 bathtubs and running-water plumbing were considered to be supreme luxury. By the 1930's they were so taken for granted that President Roosevelt cited as evidence of the "poverty" of the nation the fact that many people had no running water in their homes. Woodrow Wilson is said to have hailed the automobile in 1912 as an article of luxury which had done more to create "class feeling" than any other. We have not yet added universal automobiles to the "minimum" standard which separates wealth from poverty, but it will not be long. It has been truthfully said that the feeling of being wealthy is relative, and that, while some day everyone may be twice as well off as he is now, it will never be possible for everyone to be twice as well off as everyone else. The Emperor Charlemagne lived in a flea-haunted, stinking kennel which scarcely the poorest slum dweller would touch today. But the people of his time considered him rich and luxurious. The roof probably didn't leak very often! "Ending the economic problem" by material means can thus be made to appear as futile a goal as the donkey's carrot. If the line of thought we are pursuing is to make any sense at all, the concept must be given another meaning. No matter at what point we choose to stop, the economic problem can be "solved," with complete satisfaction and absence of strife, only by teaching people to limit their desires, not by working to satisfy them.

If, therefore, we wish to solve the economic problem along the lines of passivity and "satisfaction," removal of desire will be the first requisite; but there are economic requisites as well. These economic foundations are best seen in discussing that most drastic

of solutions now advocated for current problems, the "abandonment" of the machine and "return to the farm." There is something of the "noble savage" romanticism of the eighteenth century
in such an idea—not a little of Marie Antoinette being ever so
rustic in her dairy in the Petit Trianon. As for the telltale concession that we might possibly keep the machines which we "already"
have, such a dislike of new machines seems little more than
nostalgia for the "good old days." Is it not rather like the old lady
in *Punch* who wished only to travel on the "dear old railroad" the
way "God intended us to"?

If we want to make a genuine appraisal of the virtues of rural
life, in and of itself, we must not ask a week-end commuter to
Connecticut, nor a tourist traveling through picturesque Mexico,
nor a bondholder leading the "simple" life in Tahiti or Hawaii
with a radio, icebox, screens, and comfortable flow of dividends.
We must ask instead the drudging farmer's wife on the primitive
farm, bowed down and dulled with childbearing and heavy work;
the cripple embittered by injury incurable to rural medicine; the
anemic starving peasant children of India, and the famine-ridden
Chinese farmer. These are the real judges. Modern aesthetes and
philosophers of rural life tend to expect unconsciously both to
keep "in touch with nature" and to retain the advantages of machine technology. Some such combination may not be a bad idea—
but we cannot attain it and scrap the machine, nor must we overlook the link with modern civilization which acceptance of the
machine inevitably entails.

Our century of technical progress has enabled many of us
nearly to forget the two great problems of a purely agricultural
society: medicine and the birth rate. Can the person shaking with
malaria really lead the good life? Without modern medicine and
sanitation, may we always hope to avoid degenerative diseases? Of
course there have been primitive tribes which enjoyed good health
and a tolerable standard of living without much or any machinery.
But we must also remember the problem of population. Sometimes
an insufficient diet has left groups (including some American
Indians) so sterile that there was no population problem; or
material conditions have been too severe to permit much increase.

However, few of our back-to-the-land people advocate such a solution. Failing that, the evidence is convincing that purely agricultural societies with little machinery are likely to experience terrific population pressure, and that such pressure must be mitigated by birth control if slum conditions are to be avoided. Yet the humane and healthy forms of birth control are dependent upon modern science. Without the machine, the overwhelming majority of people must resort to infanticide or worse. Moving into a new continent, as our ancestors did, or living in a world of scientific progress, as we do, this dilemma may be forgotten. Our problem can become one of too few births rather than too many. But still an upper limit to the level of material progress is set by the race between the inventor and the stork. If we remove the inventor but give unqualified license to the stork it will not take many generations to bring a purely rural society close to the slum level. Let those who would dispute this study the history of China, India, and Japan.

One can, however, sketch a sample type of nonmechanical, rural society which would be relatively free from struggle, logically consistent, perfectly workable, and perfectly democratic—assuming that "excess" desires can be removed. In such a society everyone would be given an equally productive share of the land, and all citizens would be such philosophers that no one would have any desire for more. All machines save a few homemade tools would be scrapped. The inhabitants, still further endowed with stern philosophy, would accept illness with fatalistic resignation and contentedly forgo all medical aid except perhaps a few herbs. The standard of living would be maintained by ascetic continence, or (for those unable to reach such heights) killing all babies in the family after the third or fourth. I leave it to the reader to decide how desirable and possible a basis this is for the reorganization of the United States.

At first glance there appears to be a vast difference between those who want to end the economic problem through the machine and those who want to end it by abandoning it. Writers who feel that psychologists and scientists together could land us in a new Utopia where everyone will be happy, will indignantly repudiate the "caricature" I have just drawn. But little reflection is needed to make clear that the essentials of both solutions must be much the same. The mechanical Utopia, to be sure, will follow an epicurean rather than an ascetic philosophy. That is to say, people will not be conditioned to bare abstinence, but rather to some "common-sense" standard of living at which it will be judged well to stop. But "removal" of "excess" desire is fundamental, and still the problem remains of how this removal is to be managed and by whom.

In any likely circumstances, also, the mechanical Utopia will have to depend in the last analysis upon birth control. We have seen, in the preceding chapter, the conflicts of interest and the disappointments usually involved in large-scale technical change. But if large-scale technical change is avoided, in order to escape social conflict, a dangerous population problem immediately becomes possible. The real difference between the mechanical and the non-mechanical Utopia is that the psychologists, priests, leaders, or what-have-you who remove the spirit of emulation from the population will probably have a much harder time in the mechanical world.

In the Utopia without machines (once everyone is adequately "psychologized") there need be virtually no government. Each family is practically an independent unit, a mere loose occasional cooperation suffices, and the chief clashes of interest remaining are within the home. Nor has any one man the physical power suddenly to cut off another's bread. In the machine Utopia, however, the technological dependence of individuals upon one another will be matched by the need of a political-economic hierarchy to operate the machine. There must be a selection of administrative officials, or at any rate of technical operatives, who are to keep the wheels turning. But as soon as we speak of selection trouble begins. Were people born literally equal, it might be easier to eliminate rivalry and the resulting pain, for we could also eliminate selection. But equality, in its political application, must always be taken in a very sophisticated sense. Thus, R. H. Tawney, who cannot be accused of undue affection for the existing order, writes in his book *Equality:* " 'Equality' possesses more than one meaning. It may purport to state a fact or convey the expression of an ethical judgment . . . it may affirm that men are, on the whole, very similar in their natural endowments of character and intelligence. On the other hand . . . that while they differ profoundly . . . they are equally entitled as human beings to consideration and respect. . . . If made in the first sense the assertion of human equality is clearly untenable. It is a piece of mythology against which irresistible evidence has been accumulated." Tawney's concession, however, raises a serious problem for an integrated society which wishes to avoid all sources of disappointment. For if it is desirable to entrust at least some responsibility in certain fields to persons who are most competent in those fields we are unavoidably faced with the necessity of making a selection. Yet persons not selected may feel hurt.

Selection is not the only paradox of the ideal of utter lack of rivalry. It may, indeed, be asked whether a philosophy of complete nonassertion can be combined with any form of leadership. In the case of the ideal of pure passivity the combination seems definitely impossible. It is doubtful if the Yogi, deep in meditation, would feel justified in returning from a state of samadhi to stop a murder. At any rate he solves the problem by secluding himself where such issues cannot arise. On a less abstract plane some persons feel that "soul force" or "moral" persuasion is sufficient, and that the invasion of the Visigoths, let us say, could have been controlled had enough ancient Romans sat about in a disapproving manner. But even in the case of "soul force" we have shifted from eliminating rivalry to changing its form. For the attempt to exercise soul force against another implies assertion, possible rivalry, and frustration. Suppose two groups on opposite sides of a street exercising soul force against each other.

When we come to an integrated, machine-using society the conflict becomes even sharper. Must not the citizens retain enough ambition to want to be responsible officials? For example, the psychologists who are to remove excess desires in the mechanical Utopia must at least wish to be good psychologists. Suppose, however, that one psychologist sincerely believes that he has a better method of inculcating absence-of-self-assertion than another.

Should he not at least exercise enough assertion to assert new ways of teaching nonassertion? But is it right to show up the other fellow's shortcomings?

There is one conceivable moral state which might avoid the dilemma thus outlined. If the population were all so intelligent and adaptable that they would immediately recognize superior merit and a superior new idea, as soon as it developed, and if they were all so unselfish that they would cheerfully acquiesce in the disappointment of personal ambition, and renunciation of personal beliefs, then both the universal social problem of selection, and the more complicated problems added by the dynamic state regarding invention and change could all be overcome with a minimum of frustration and disappointment.

But simply to state the problem shows its difficulty and indicates the tremendous task faced by the psychologists. They have to inculcate in the same individual both ambition and renunciation: ambition, in order to lead the individual to assume responsible work for society; and renunciation (should a better man or idea appear), in order to avoid conflict or frustration. The simultaneous presence in the same man, however, of a determination to put over an idea believed to be valuable to the world, and of a cheerful acquiescence in the disappointment of that idea, is very nearly a contradiction in terms. And the argument must, therefore, shift its main emphasis from preventing disappointment to reconciling the individual to legitimate disappointment after it has occurred. Essentially our goal is not a society in which there are no winners and no differences of opinion, but a society whose less successful members are "good sports." Barring a very rare combination of intelligence, firmness, and energy, with ready self-abnegation, the potentiality of some degree of disappointment inheres in the idea of any standards at all of better and worse, or right and wrong.

It follows, in an imperfectly moral and imperfectly intelligent world, that the only way to avoid the generally inseparable association of the idea of assertion and potential conflict with the idea of value is to assert as our highest value that there shall not, under any circumstances, be any assertion. To do this one must value peace and passivity more than pity, more than love, more than justice, more than freedom, more than life. Rest or satisfaction has to be supplemented by other social concepts. "The riddle of the universe is not so simple. There are its aspects of struggle and of friendly help. But romantic self-abnegation is no nearer real politics than is romantic ruthlessness."

From these principles we deduce a basic requirement of social order: general acceptance of the method by which political and economic leaders shall reach their positions, and by which disputes shall be settled. We have seen that the psychological approach most relevant to the real world must run more in terms of therapy after disappointment than in terms of prevention of disappointment. Such an approach may be inculcated with fair success if there is a reasonably general agreement as to the means to success and methods of settlement. But if the fundamental basis of selection is challenged, then social chaos becomes well-nigh inevitable: the essence of economic peace is a generally accepted code of emulation and selection.

One must not, however, conclude that differences in quality and degree between various competitive codes are of no significance. The man who despises all differences of degree, and demands only absolute standards, immediately proclaims himself mentally adolescent. But an intelligent choice can scarcely be made unless we know what we are seeking. And certainly it is overwhelmingly important to know that we cannot abolish all selection and conflict, and can only change their forms. What we need is a code which, recognizing and regularizing the constructive conflicts inherent in creative activity, nevertheless restricts to a minimum conflicts and rivalry which are merely predatory and sterile.

· III ·

The Meaning and the Method of Democratic Progress

MODERN THINKING is perpetually confused by a tendency to consider democratic government as an automatic cure for our problems rather than an additional problem in itself. Yet the acceptance of democratic values inevitably carries certain limitations upon our field of action, and we are obliged to realize that the system is bound to imply its own special difficulties. The preceding chapter ended with the conclusion that we cannot abolish rivalry and can only choose among various forms. In the present chapter we must work out the democratic standards for such a choice. This implies an examination of alternatives. Side by side with the Anglo-American tradition of democracy there exists even among avowedly antifascist forces a formidable rival: the great Latin tradition of the "good" dictator. We in America have been so happily isolated from adverse currents that we have scarcely recognized such an idea as a real force. Yet from Caesar through Napoleon down to Salazar and even Perón, the ideal of the "good" ruler who will teach his people what is right has been potent. Under such an ideal, Hitler was not bad because he was a dictator. He was bad only because he did foolish or wicked things. The good dictator, on the other hand, is thought to encourage the people when they are right, wisely punish them when they are wrong, control their thoughts when they are foolish, wipe out their creations when they are mistaken, and, it is always said, do a better job than democracy itself of realizing the democratic values, protecting the human personality, and bringing about social progress.

The evaluation of the good-dictator principle brings us to one of the basic paradoxes of our system. The charge often brought by conscious or unconscious authoritarians against democracy and its usual economic companion, the pricing system, is that they make progress impossible. "If you give people what they want and they want filth," it is asserted, "nothing can be done." The majority of people, so runs the argument, are not very intelligent or very well educated, nor do they have very good taste. What is to be done with this masterless vulgar manswarm? How is it to be kept from weighing down the more farsighted or the more morally excellent man?

Here is a real problem. Although recent events have made the overt voicing of such questions unfashionable, they still exist, and will inevitably reappear. One solution of this dilemma is to deny it. There are doubtless people to whom *vox populi* is quite literally *vox dei*, and whatever is, is right. Happy are they, but their numbers are probably few. The intelligent man whether radical or conservative, is, like R. H. Tawney or Thomas Jefferson, soon forced to recognize values—both artistic and political—variations and inequalities in aptitudes and virtues, and the need for selection. Yet, if the more "able" (from whatever point of view one happens to be thinking) are outnumbered by the less "able," how can society make progress without compulsion? What is the method of democratic progress?

At first sight it would seem that one could decide upon the method of progress without committing oneself to particular ideas of its goal. Certainly the basic inhibitions of democratic rule apply to all methods, whatever the end in view. But we also have to decide whether we are willing to be democratic at all. This choice is largely influenced by our ideas of progress, and so there comes to be a close association between the acceptance of certain fundamental ideals regarding the aim of progress, and the acceptance of certain ways of obtaining it. We must discuss the goal before we come to the method.

At the present time there is a deeply seated, though largely unconscious, conflict between two basically different concepts of social betterment. One group looks upon the matter as the achievement of a fixed ideal static pattern of technical and social organization. Once this ideal is reached, or closely approximated, it need only be repeated endlessly thereafter. The other group looks upon life as a continual development. While usually admitting certain eternal values, it does not relate them to any fixed static cultural pattern. And the eternal values themselves are related more to the manner than to the direction of change. Emphasis shifts from an ideal final aim to an ideal process of variation.

In times of great and disastrous disturbance men are attracted to the ideal of the static pattern. Somewhere, they think, we must find permanence. The static pattern has, therefore, a special appeal for the weary, the bewildered, and the intellectually immature. It is from such elements as these that the authoritarian state has so often taken its birth. But when men are less hungry and less frightened they have time to be tolerant. When they are more vigorous they are less content with the endless repetition of a single form of creation. And when they are intellectually mature the prospect of change becomes less horrifying. Under these circumstances the ideal of continued development tends to gain.

The "solutions" of the economic problem in terms of "satisfaction" and "removal" of desire, discussed in the last chapter, clearly appeal to ideals of the static pattern rather than to ideals of constant change. True, various forms of the static state do not rule out all aspects of invention and creation. They may only rule out invention and creation which (for good or bad) cause important social change. Such civilizations are capable of high aesthetic achievement, of a limited sort. Architecture and the other arts and sciences which seriously affect social relationships cannot be allowed to vary greatly. But the energy which with us has gone into new scientific discoveries, the changing of techniques, and the application of abstract research to daily life could be drained off into writing sonnets, composing songs, or making relatively small individual works of art which would have virtually no repercussions upon social structure. In an extreme form the creative impulse might be said not to be destroyed but merely castrated by turning the scientist into the dilettante amateur.

Would modern man, however, be happy with such a limited scope of creation—even leaving aside the authoritarian features that would probably accompany it? An affirmative answer seems unlikely. The basic rule of such a society would be, "Of the fruit of the tree of knowledge thou shalt eat no further." Such a commandment violates some of the most fundamental impulses of the Western spirit, and indeed the human spirit. The points of view considered in the preceding chapter are essentially those of the pig and the hermit: the pig seeking satisfaction in a full stomach, the hermit in ascetic contemplation. The various epicurean lukewarm compromises contain the same craving for finality. But in choosing a social philosophy one cannot ignore other, equally important aspects of character. Of these, one of the most noteworthy is the full creative impulse. The most hopeful social spirit is not that of the pig or the hermit but that of the artist. The happiest man is neither the richest man nor the quietest man. He is the man who does the most interesting work. He does not spend eight hours a day in purgatory on the "job" working, and sixteen in paradise "consuming," but leads a rounded and integrated existence in which work and life are merged.

The social repercussions of such a criterion will be referred to throughout this study. For the present we need to call attention to a profound conflict between two "instincts of workmanship" or creative urges. There is, first, the man who, having learned an accepted skill, wishes to apply it continually, lovingly, and in much the same manner, indefinitely. There is, next, the man who finds an outlet for his creative spirit in improving old skills, and inventing or introducing new ones. A "professional" culture tends toward the first of these types. A "business" culture—if of the competitive type—facilitates the second.

Thorstein Veblen has written of a trinity of creative urges: the "family," "idle curiosity" (the fundamental drive of science), and the "instinct of workmanship." But he seldom realized explicitly the conflict between them. A tired and unhappy man, Veblen was an unconscious philosopher of the static state. His work is filled with an obvious longing to return to the Scandinavian peasant culture of his parents and to a glorification of its achievements. His attitude toward new machines is naïve and mixed, and his engineers seem more the tidy housekeepers of existing technology than the explorers of new landscapes. As a result he bequeathed to radical thought a legacy of reverence for the authoritarian technician, without adequate analysis or appreciation of the difficulties and clashes of interest inherent in the new idea.

Probably the social choice which these conflicts present will never be argued conclusively. We will assume, in this book, that the inventive-creative urge and the ideal of continued development are more likely to appeal to the democratic mind. Certainly we shall soon be able to demonstrate the closest possible connection between the institutions which make for inventive creation and those making for personal freedom and democracy of aspiration. We repudiate ideals of pure passivity and lack of assertion as incompatible with maintenance of any moral or artistic values; and we repudiate the static compromises as frustrating the creative spirit.

To holders of this point of view, the ideal of social progress becomes "not satisfactions but better wants." If the pessimist objects that social progress merely substitutes one desire for another, they can answer that there are better desires and worse desires. If he declares that change alters men's frustrations without ending them, they may reply, paradoxically but truly, that there are better ways and worse ways of being frustrated. And if he asks what is the end of all this creation the reply is simply that the aim of creation is the creation of a creative world—a world in which the loftiest and most satisfying creative impulses of the human being can be expressed.

But does not the aim of creation, and the repudiation of passivity, involve us in an opposite error? Is the choice only between an undiscriminating pity—leading to valueless negation—and the ruthlessness of the superman? Is there no middle ground between licking lepers' sores and exulting in the blond beast? Either extreme represents a perversion of democracy. Democracy is not antithetical to leadership—far from it; but it does impose inhibitions and limitations upon the leader.

The paradox of competitive struggle is not to be settled by ending the competitive game, but by improving the rules through education of the players. Not the ending of competitive acquisition should be our goal, but the competitive acquisition of nobler things in a nobler way. Putting the matter in a somewhat Chinese way: betterment comes by inculcating an increasingly superior and humane code of "good manners" of competition. Just as the victor in tennis does not win by smashing his opponent over the head with his racket, so, in the business "game," progress is achieved as we induce businessmen to refrain from winning through such methods as sweating child labor and adulterating goods. Nor should the good manners be all negative, nor should they be confined to the winner. The loser must accept the rules too. If after losing in legitimate competition he still seeks to obstruct desirable change he should, at the very least, receive no public encouragement under such delusive slogans as "passivity," "security," and "cooperation."

The view of progress just given entails that we do something from which the "scientific" point of view has been assiduously running away for the past century; namely, that we search for and proclaim values. The case for democratic and competitive development depends upon the answers to two questions: (1) Is there a group or class capable of developing and initiating good standards? (2) Will it be, has it been, listened to?

Democratic progress comes through the existence and effect of an active and influential "censor" class. By this I do not mean direct control, but criticism. With rare exceptions the most outstanding attribute of the successful parvenu is his frantic desire to conform to "nice" usage. The chief method of democratic progress lies, I submit, in the development of social codes which add to the present disapprobation of (overtly at least) becoming successful in certain ways—for example, brothel keeping—an equal disapprobation of other, more genuinely baneful lines of conduct, still often respectable.

In England the class whose ideas and standards have hitherto most greatly influenced the parvenu commercial magnate has been the "landed aristocracy." The results have not always been happy. Though the code of fair play and the ideal of the gentleman, in the ethical sense, contain much of the best of our civilization, there is a reverse side, and a deal of obsolete custom and snobbery with which we could well dispense. With all its achievements in political democracy England has known little of the social democracy, the middle-class good feeling, which so outstandingly characterizes the larger, especially the rural, part of the United States. This is a great loss. For, as implied at the beginning of the chapter, the spirit of social democracy and the brotherhood of man is far more precious than the ballot box, and the one is largely to be justified as a chief support of the other.

What is the censor class in the United States? It is to be found in the religious, professional, and intellectual groups, who without being organized and labeled like the English peerage, have exerted an immense influence over American life. From them comes the pressure toward higher codes of competitive conduct. This statement leads to an important conclusion regarding the horrors of the nineteenth century, and the existence of the pirate businessmen of the 1870's. May we not ascribe the excesses of early industrialism to a temporary abdication of the censor class under the influence of the popular interpreters of Adam Smith, Ricardo, Malthus, and Darwin?

While the ultimate standard of the public good was never entirely lost sight of, the combination of laissez faire economics and Calvinist theology produced a situation in which, for all practical purposes, the mere fact that a man was legally rich was supposed to guarantee his social desirability. The acquisition of personal wealth was virtually identified with the increase of public wealth and public welfare. It is this line of argument which is so effectively criticized by Tawney. In its later versions evolution and the survival of the "fittest" enter in, so that, in Brandeis' phrase, we were thought all to be bound for heaven in a perambulator labeled "Evolution." Under the influence of such ideas the majority of the American censor class temporarily abdicated, and the ugliness of the brownstone front reflects an almost equal ugliness of economic ideology. It goes without saying that there was a minority, but we are talking of the general tone. The abdication, however, did not last long, and today there can be no doubt that a large part—probably a majority—of the censor class is openly and actively critical of the competitive process, if not hostile toward it. From this fact a number of complications arise. For the issue now before us is whether the censor class itself should govern, and whether it is to be allowed to destroy the capitalist state entirely. We thus are brought back to the question of leadership in a democratic society and the limitations imposed upon it.

One answer to the suggestion that the censor class should govern is that, if it did, it would cease to be a censor class. For self-censorship, as we have earlier had occasion to remark, is not very effective. But there is more to the matter than that. Members of the professional classes doubtless feel that they, being "obviously" the best, should take over the direct control of society and impose "better" values. The same feeling exists in any other militant group. A man who believes that there is only one final "right" pattern of technical and political organization, which once achieved may be endlessly repeated, will find it hard to wait until the majority is convinced. Hence the association between philosophies of the static pattern and authoritarian rule. But the forceful compulsion of value, save in extreme cases, is essentially at variance with the standards and methods of democratic progress. It easily degenerates into "ordering people to be free" and violates the Great Refusal upon which democratic government is based. Thus a recent opinion of the Supreme Court:

Struggles to coerce uniformity of sentiment in support of some end thought essential to their time and country have been waged by many good as well as by evil men. Nationalism is a relatively recent phenomenon but at other times and places the ends have been racial or territorial security, support of a dynasty or regime, and particular plans for saving souls. As first and moderate methods to attain unity have failed, those bent on the accomplishment must resort to an ever-increasing severity. As governmental pressure toward unity becomes greater so strife becomes more bitter as to whose unity it shall be. Probably no deeper division of our people could proceed from any provocation than from finding it necessary to choose what doctrine and whose program of public education officials shall compel youth to unite in embracing. Ultimate futility of such efforts is seen from the Roman drive to stamp out Christianity as a disturber of its pagan unity, the Inquisition, as a means to religious and dynastic unity, the Siberian exiles as a means to Russian unity, down to the fast failing efforts of our present totalitarian enemies. Those who begin coercive elimination of dissent soon find themselves exterminating dissenters. Compulsory unification of opinion achieves only the unification of the graveyard.*

It follows that democracy imposes upon the leader and the superior man a peculiarly difficult task and demands of the led also a higher achievement. The democratic hero, if one may use the term, must have a higher character than the authoritarian hero. Democracy, properly understood, does not require that he surrender his values, but it limits his ways of enforcing them. To say that he must suffer fools gladly is too emphatic; but suffer fools to some extent, he must. The primary weapon of democratic progress must be persuasion.

Samuel Butler has said that any philosophy pushed to its logical extreme will end in contradiction or in nonsense. In the world which we know there must be some compulsion; but it is the essence of democratic doctrine that compulsion be kept to a minimum. The abnegation of personal power and the acceptance of equality of right which are essential in a democracy prevent the imposition of values by firing squad, torture, or other extraordinary methods; and, in the theory of the American state, there are limits even to the power of the 51 per cent. The personalities of the minority no less than those of the majority must receive a certain respect. For it may be said that with democracy the means are the ends.

Belief in democratic progress of the type we are discussing implies faith in the ability and willingness of the less brilliant, less moral, and less tasteful members of society to see and follow truth and the superior pattern when it is presented to them. Skeptics usually declare such an idea to be absurd, and as long as we stick to abstract argument they can make out a powerful case. Behind their arguments, also, will usually be found the impatience of the innovator who has not yet "sold" his pattern to the public. Nevertheless American history provides weighty reasons for rejecting

* *West Virginia Board of Education* v. *Barnette,* 319 U.S. 624 (June 14, 1943).

the skeptical view. The perfectionist is usually unwilling to consider problems in historical perspective. "Utopia today," is his cry. But if a man doubts the reality of democratic progress let him read the reports of travelers on the United States, from the early national periods down to the present, noting the earlier and later comments on American taste, political life, manners, architecture, and social conscience. Regarding the possibility of democratic progress I can only say that, difficult though it may be to expound abstractly, we have so far managed to make it work.

Yet it is foolish to suppose that so delicate a balance can take care of itself. Democratic control must be largely self-control. And even the greatest social achievements, if accompanied by a nibbling away of the structure which makes for self-control and responsibility in the individual, cannot prevent an eventual collapse of democratic society. It is plain that the system also involves, of its very nature, multiple short-run functional inefficiencies. Its equilibrium, as has been well said, is not that of a stone at rest but that of a spinning top. Surely it should be clear that so precarious an achievement must require very special conditions. The next chapter discusses the economic bases of political democracy, and the succeeding one passes on to its cultural weaknesses and necessities.

· IV ·

Political Democracy and the Alternatives
to Competition

ECONOMIC PEACE, we have seen, is the general acceptance of a
code or method of emulation and selection. But the believer in
democracy cannot accept just any code, any more than he can
accept just any peace. His code must conform to the standards of
democratic progress, grouped in the last chapter under three heads:
creativeness, tolerance, persuasion. Such values follow from the
basic democratic tenet of respect for the individual; and the task
of the present chapter is to determine the economic system and
economic code which will best implement the threefold standards
laid down.

The word "competition" immediately calls to mind a galaxy of
economic associations, and it is easy to forget that by itself it is
quite indeterminate. As we saw in discussing the ideal of a conflict-free world, competition is rivalry to excel, and the rivalry
could be in almost any field—from torture, bullying, murder to
poetry, "service," generosity. Our concern now, however, is a bit
more specific, and in this chapter on the relation of political
democracy to competition the word will denote economic competition in a comparatively "free" market.

There are several lines of criticism of the economic market,
discussion of which must be postponed to later chapters. It may
be said, for example, that the market is not "pure," or that it is
unstable, or that the emphasis upon "economic" goals warps the
cultural patterns of our time. Also competition may be taken as
meaning a market struggle in which "anything goes." The preceding chapter repudiated such concepts of unlimited struggle and
sketched the methods by which better ideas of competition might
be inculcated in a democracy. Cultural obstacles, however, and the

30

mechanical deficiencies of the system must be put off to later chapters. For the present, let us concentrate upon political and creative aspects alone. In choosing social systems it is, after all, not enough to show that a certain method of selection has disadvantages. Every method has disadvantages. The really important question is, Would the alternatives be any better? The theory of the American state has been that our political leaders were selected and controlled primarily by election, and our economic leaders by competition. That the system has never functioned ideally or perfectly is obvious. But let us see what the alternatives may be. The principal selective methods now urged as substitutes for economic competition are political election, seniority, and competitive examination. We will discuss them in turn and then appraise their joint effect upon social life.

Modern social thought is overwhelmingly characterized by an intense will to believe that we may change the economic organization of society without adverse effect on the quality of its political existence. Thus the first alternative usually proposed to hitherto accepted theories of dual action by competition and election is virtual abandonment of business competition, and extension of the elective method to economic affairs. Many economists write as if the holding of elections with universal suffrage were sufficient to protect the individual—no matter what our economic organization. For example, it may be said that as long as we elect the planners, or those who select them, we can control them; or that, if only the worker has a vote in the union (or in the management itself), he will be sufficiently protected.

Such extremely literal applications of political democracy to economic life make it necessary to remember the idea with which this book began—namely, that democracy is not a single simple standard but a complex of standards; and it is important to stress as background for our discussion a fact so evident that it is nearly always forgotten, that the competitive market in and of itself is already an application of the elective method to economic life. Viewed in the large, and with allowance for innumerable shortcomings, the competitive pricing system may be thought of as a perpetual election to decide what shall be produced. Money outlay forms the votes, advertising is the campaign literature, and the election returns—determining what goods shall be made and what not—are profit and loss. By this method we achieve such "democracy of choice" or of "preference" as we have secured. For it determines that virtually nothing gets produced long which the consumer is unwilling to buy.

Left-wing writers tend to protest analogies of this sort and to dwell upon the many defects of the process. But these defects are in themselves a valuable commentary upon the critics' own proposal—general reliance upon political election alone. Thus it may be said that advertising (the campaign literature of the economic election) is frequently silly, vicious, or untrue. But is absolute veracity or nobility an outstanding and characteristic quality of political campaign speeches? Or it may be said that the buyer (the economic "voter") does not really buy what he wants, since his personal expenditure is generally too small to compel products specially suited to his needs. His choice, therefore, is limited to the alternatives presented to him, and he may be said to have the "referendum" and the "recall" but not the "initiative." But how often in political life (even in the initiative) does a single voter pick his own candidate or proposal? Does he not also usually have to choose among alternatives put before him? As for the "impurity" or "imperfection" of the economic election—the "rigging of the market"—what of the purity of many political campaigns? Finally, some will object that in the economic election there are great discrepancies in "voting" power, because the man with a large income has many more "votes" (more money to spend) than the man with a small one. This point involves the distribution of income—a problem to which we return in later chapters. Nevertheless, granted that power in the economic election is unequally distributed, does the possession of an equal personal vote really give each voter equal political power?

The assumption that an equal vote gives equal power and hence equal protection underlies nearly all the writings of those who feel that business competition is no longer necessary or desirable. Of the advocates of such views one may ask: How much effective control of U.M.W. policy does a vote in the union election give to the individual miner in John L. Lewis's union? How much power did the possession of a vote give the individual voter in Mayor Hague's Jersey City? Anyone with political experience will recognize that past the town meeting, or other small assembly where the individual may have a direct hearing, and indeed often even then, what counts is not simply a vote but control of the organization or influence with its members. In the bad old days a city boss could say, "I care not who casts the votes of my city as long as I can count them." The more flagrant abuses have passed. But still the organization with an integrated program, and a well drilled vote which can be "gotten out" when needed, holds major control. There are more ways of killing a cat than choking it!

Here, however, lies the dilemma of those who wish to rely upon the election method alone. One may grant that in cases of enormous abuse of power the citizens may combine and "throw the rascals out." They have thus a residual veto. But the effectiveness of this veto, and the degree of abuse needed to call forth its exercise, largely rest upon the economic independence of the voter. The power of the organization to perpetuate itself largely depends upon its degree of control over his economic life. Anyone who has had anything to do with reform movements in politics knows that the fear of economic reprisal is one of the most important factors keeping people from independent political action. Men are notoriously reluctant to vote against their bread and butter. Yet if the alternative to support is great financial loss or even starvation—and a man's vote or sympathies do get around despite the most improved election machinery—it is increasingly difficult to have effective opposition. The really crucial point is that in a large electorate the other side must organize in order to be effective. And if you are in a position to pick off and neutralize the leaders of the opposition before they have completed organization, the chances for effective democratic political action against you become almost nil.

The most obvious way to neutralize the opposition is by terror and persecution. But the beauty of the comprehensively planned state for the "ins" is that it makes possible a far more suave but almost equally effective method. Even in states like Beveridge's or Dr. Mordecai Ezekiel's, in which the shell of both private property rights and political democracy is permitted to survive, we are already in sight of self-perpetuating oligarchy. For investment is "planned" in advance, or fitted into a national investment "budget," and this implies large-scale control over the flow of resources, over unions, and over management. The individual who will not "cooperate" in setting a "proper" price, or in ruling out a "bad" invention, the man who talks too specifically about the abuses of power which he has encountered, can find it mysteriously difficult to get materials; or strange legal obstacles will develop for him. Who that has worked in Washington can deny this possibility? And how difficult to establish undoubted proof of favoritism. So far as the entrepreneur goes, how hard to show that the sudden interest of the Bureau of Internal Revenue in his income tax or of the antitrust division in his trade contacts is not all pure routine altruism! Could any better method of picking off able incipient organizers be devised?

Most of us, however, are not heads of businesses. It might at first glance seem to be quite immaterial to us whether the business policy of the heads of companies was circumscribed, or if a relatively small group of wealthy people were treated unjustly—or even "liquidated." Particularly if we claim "not to believe" in technical progress, we can assume indifference. But there is more to the matter than that. For just as the role of the competitive market regarding the productive election is usually forgotten, so also there is another fundamental but neglected manner in which it serves to protect our basic personal freedom.

Earlier in this study we remarked regarding the purely rural Utopia, unlike the machine-using one, that no man would have the power (so far as mere technological organization goes) suddenly to cut off his neighbor's bread. But what was only a parenthesis in dealing with the abstract question of rivalry per se becomes a practical matter of the first importance in dealing with an actual machine civilization. The technological dependence of the modern city dweller, for example, is so great that it is doubtful if he could survive six hours the breakdown of his social environment. The water he drinks, the food he eats, come from hundreds and thousands of miles away, while even the air he breathes depends for health and purity upon complicated technical and social arrangements whose margin of safety is far narrower than most of us are ever willing to realize. Yet we have seen that leadership of some sort is unavoidable in any society. The question is, How, under such circumstances, can the leaders be controlled and selected? Here we have a society in which the throwing of a few switches can starve or freeze whole populations. Why then have the switches—so far—been relatively seldom thrown?

One answer would run in terms of character, self-restraint, humaneness, and certain instincts of workmanship. But the world has not yet, at least, been able to rely upon moral persuasion alone. In the background must be an additional factor: the fear of the consequences of reprisal. We are thus brought up against another problem of delicate balance in the task of achieving and maintaining democratic freedom. The state must be strong enough to punish a minority acting in an antisocial fashion. Yet no ruling group can be allowed to become so powerful as to be no longer adequately responsive to the public will. For such an unresponsive clique, possessing, in addition to political influence or control, the technological rule over the very basis of human life which modern science makes possible, would hold one of the most absolute powers known to history.

Let us run over again the problem of personal economic freedom in modern society. It is not hard to see how a self-sufficient farmer can be free—as long as he only wants to be a self-sufficient farmer. Provided merely that his property rights are respected, he can close his front gate and watch the "rest of the world go by." A man can also be independent in modern society by having an independent income—as long as he doesn't want to spend more than he gets—and he, too, need not fear economic oppression while his property rights are respected, and if he (or his trustee) has sense enough not to lose his money. But what about the great number of people who work for others? How can they be protected from oppression and bullying—especially when, in physical terms, they scarcely ever have more than a few hours' supply of food or even of water, and often very little more than that in terms of money?

The modern social thinker is inclined to believe that the prime hope for such people is in the trade union. Often this is the case. But we can no more depend upon unions alone for protection than we can depend upon elections alone. The essential guarantee —without which unions will rapidly degenerate—is alternative employment opportunities: a *bona fide* chance to get another job.

Left-wing writers make much of the differences in economic power which leave the individual worker unable to bargain effectively with a large concern. They seldom say anything about the differences in power which leave him unable to bargain effectively with a large union. But the energetic and ambitious young man who finds himself barred from the work he wishes by exorbitant fees and prolonged apprenticeships can tell a different story—as also can the worker, inside the union, who incurs the hostility of the leadership. Suppose a man works in a closed union in a closed-shop industry, with the check-off system. How can he protect himself from exploitation by the union? To impute to him any great power to protect himself is to be guilty of the cynical fallacy which led some of the popular writers on economics of the nineteenth century to say there could be no injustice because of "freedom of contract." To a union possessed of great funds for which there need be no accounting, with little effective control by the law, and with all the weapons of intimidation, fraud, and corruption at hand, the opportunity is wide for a tyranny from which there is no escape for the member save in a transfer to another industry.

The truth of the matter seems to be that unless the individual voter, in a union election just as in a political election, already possesses adequate independence, the election will almost inevitably become a farce. And in the last analysis this independence can be secured only through alternative employment opportunities of the kind which, though admittedly not perfect, the competitive system attempts to offer.

Yet it is precisely the transfer to other lines of employment which is increasingly limited by the trend of modern development. Let us suppose that the government embarks, as it has already partially done, upon a policy designed to give a more genuine democratic freedom to the worker. Let us assume a program of unemployment allowances, public employment agencies, dissemination of information regarding jobs, and schools for vocational reeducation. Are not these inadequate unless the worker is free to enter other fields without such things as exorbitant fees, fraudulent examinations, and unreasonable apprenticeships? There is no need to gild the lily. The right to "transfer" is a poor protection if there is not reasonably full employment—yet another problem which we must discuss later. But it is also a poor protection if "democracy of management" is used in such a way as to create a number of rival closed groups between which movement is almost impossible; or if "full employment" is obtained by giving the central directorate such far-reaching power over economic life, and hiring and firing units, that no man can escape their grasp.

As one reflects upon matters like these it becomes apparent once more how political and personal freedom as well as technological creativeness is bound up with the institutions which give rise to "democracy of opportunity or aspiration"—the chance to rise on independent terms. Through the competitive market we get at once the diffusion of authority and the alternative opportunities which are needed. And though the force of public opinion and even state action may exclude certain methods of reaching wealth and power, this influence cannot be carried so far—if democracy is to survive—as to leave most men dependent upon the personal whim of dominant individuals or groups. The problem has been summed up by saying that we do not want a society in which promotion comes through "pull" rather than "push." "Push," to be sure, may be an unsympathetic word; but substitute "superior energy and foresight," and the point is equally well made.

Yet on the basis of what we have seen regarding the fear of economic reprisal and its effect on political election—and also the weakness of the single voter, acting alone, in a large electorate —it is questionable how long effective democracy can survive removal of the restraint upon state action which substantial reliance upon the competitive market implies. Further it is hard to see how personal freedom may be protected in our modern machine civilization without the alternative job opportunities of the competitive system. Some critics of course will say that, however sound our argument may be, it is too late: competition cannot be ensured any more, and even if it were it would not work. I believe them to be wrong. While the "free" competitive system could not be simply left alone we could get reasonable competition and stability if we wanted to, without too much state action. We shall consider this further. But suppose the critics are right. Let them then ask themselves: Do these arguments mean merely the end of competitive capitalism—or do they not mean the end of democracy too?

Democracy of opportunity, we must emphasize again, is one of the fundamental guarantees of political freedom. But if men are inherently unequal in capacity, and if they are allowed to go as far as their ability can take them, the results are bound to be an unequal distribution of wealth or of power—whether as unequal as the present distribution may be debated, but certainly much more unequal than most left-wing writers are willing to admit. This is a basic issue which has run through the whole current of American political thought. Neither Thomas Jefferson nor Andrew Jackson believed in literal equality. Their ideas ran in terms of a "fair" chance and an "adequate" opportunity. Owen Wister sums up the matter in a passage which, though it reads naïvely now, yet expresses what has been the most deeply felt ideal of the American nation:

It was through the Declaration of Independence that we Americans acknowledged the *eternal inequality* of man. For by it we abolished a cut-and-dried aristocracy. We had seen little men artifically held up in high places, and great men artificially held down in low places, and our own justice-loving hearts abhorred this violence to human nature. Therefore we decreed that every man should thenceforth have equal liberty to find his own level. By this very decree we acknowledged and gave freedom to true aristocracy, saying, "Let the best man win, whoever he is." Let the best man win! That is America's word. That is true democracy. And true democracy and true aristocracy are one and the same thing. If anybody cannot see this, so much the worse for his eyesight.*

Such was the hope in the early days of our country. We wished to establish a country free from caste and permeated with that spirit of brotherhood—that feeling of good will and respect for the other fellow regardless of clothes, color, income, or ancestors —which is the true essence of democracy. It is this regard for the essential self-respect of every individual which separates our fundamental point of view from the Nazi's doctrine of the superman.

Yet it is important, in examining the alternatives to competition, that we realize that the ideal of equal opportunity requires unusual self-restraint, and that it is exposed to a special psychological instability. Nearly two centuries ago Dr. Johnson declaimed against the ideal of equality of opportunity. He argued that permitting ambition in everyone would greatly increase unhappiness, for only a few could be at the top in any generation. Following this line, it could be maintained that relatively equal opportunity is self-defeating. The more nearly it is attained, the less will those who do not rise be prepared to admit the inevitable implication regarding themselves, and the more fiercely will they blame the "system" for their personal failures. Furthermore, since absolute perfection in this as in other goals is never attainable, one will always find some degree of justified grievance upon which to rationalize.

Considerations like these come out most clearly where the election method and "democracy of management" are involved. Those who have served on collective bargaining committees, or assisted in drawing up wage scales and methods of promotion, will know the fierce conflicts of interest which almost immediately develop within the ranks of "labor" between the more experienced, energetic, or able workers on one hand and the rank and file on the other. In a country where the slogan is that everybody is "just as good as everybody else," resentment of the faster promotion or superior pay of the other fellow is almost inevitable, and the urge to rationalize his success as due to "graft," "pull," "bootlicking,"

* "The Virginian" by Owen Wister. Reprinted by permission of the Macmillan Company. Copyright, 1902, by the publishers.

"favoritism," "speed-ups," or "exploitation" is almost overwhelming. The union leadership, anxious to prevent splits, is apt to push for some objective standard which all will accept; many managers will agree for the sake of peace; and by a sort of hydraulic pressure the cry is apt to be "seniority"—which brings us to a second alternative to competition as a method of selection.

Three main questions are involved in seniority: the effect on technical creativeness and progress, the effect upon a man's happiness in his job, the effect upon his freedom to transfer. It goes almost without saying that a society generally organized upon seniority lines cannot hope for a rapid rate of technical or artistic change. The man with the new idea, if held down and promoted indifferently on a basis of age or service with anyone who meets an average standard, is usually so frustrated as either to run amuck or else to lose his original fire and energy by the time he reaches power. The few honorable exceptions but prove the rule. It is true that, if outside the self-perpetuating or static group there are other new competing organizations, then the old establishment may be forced to "move with the times" and re-organize itself. The appearance of continuous existence may remain, but what has really happened is that outside pressure has forced a deviation from former standards and a break-up of former points of view. There has been a fresh start. Furthermore the fresh start itself nearly always implies some disturbance of seniority relationships.

The second effect of seniority is upon a man's happiness in his work. A good deal has been said in modern times about the dull-ness and lack of interest of much industrial work. That much of this is correct is not to be doubted. But much of the work of the world has always been dull, and one wonders if some of the romantics—especially the enthusiasts for rural life—are not over-stressing the contrast between modern industrialism and earlier times. Furthermore there are some people who really prefer routine and monotony. Be that as it may, the seniority system, plus union opposition to incentive rates and other devices, does operate to take the interest out of life for the energetic and ambitious. With no possibility of advancement save the lapse of time, with no recognition of superior work, save the hostility of his associates, what pride or interest can a man take in his job? Granted that "incentives" may be abused, should not the attack be on abuses rather than on the idea itself?

Most liberal socialists of the English tradition expect to be able to put in comprehensive planning on a large scale without seriously impairing the adaptability and responsiveness of the market mechanism as a means of registering consumer's choice. Democracy of preference or choice is bound up with the productive "election" of which we have already spoken. The issue of how far comprehensive planning entails rationing is a profound one, which we shall encounter in many places. What must be stressed here, however, is that, if the promotion of individuals is increasingly dependent upon circumstances having little to do with the quality of service, the sensitiveness of the market mechanism is bound to be impaired. In this as in many other ways, what we may gain in democracy of management or status may be lost in democracy of choice.

What we are trying to do at this point is merely to review in the large some of the main defects of the elective and the seniority method. The many delicate problems of union organization require a special chapter and can only be glanced at here. There will probably always be some forms of activity in which seniority is thought desirable, and some people who will prefer that kind of organization, just as some people enjoy being post-office clerks. In a society with a really adequate transfer mechanism such people will naturally gravitate toward such industries. But the outlook for the happiness of the able and the farseeing, as well as for art and science, would be dim indeed if there were no frontier of unrestricted change where the new and ambitious man might find opportunity for his talents. Here too, however, the seniority system operates as an important brake. The man still relatively young— but with a family dependent upon him—may find it impossible to leave a job which he dislikes if in so doing he sacrifices a considerable seniority advantage. The cost of transfer—always important— may be greatly increased. All that the government can do in unemployment allowances will be neutralized if with each increase of state aid seniority requirements become more rigid.

One cannot close a review of alternatives to market competition without touching upon Bernard Shaw's idea that selection should be made by competitive examination. Philosophically at least, this would seem to be much the best method. Men are not forced into an artificial equality, yet "fair" and "impartial" criteria of selection are set up. But there are two defects: the reactions of the examiners themselves, and the inadequacies of the examination method as a test of many of the most valuable qualities of leadership. The examiners, even if they remain honest, will want correct answers, and they are the judges of what is correct. The man with an unorthodox opinion must either be a consummate hypocrite or liar, or else give up entirely. On the other hand, the examination method, as every good teacher knows, favors an industrious but uncreative mediocrity which concentrates upon "cramming" accepted prejudice rather than discovering new knowledge. So far, at least, we have failed to discover "objective" methods of examination which adequately test adaptability, imagination, and character.

Summing up then, we may say that there is a place for the elective method in economic life, and a place for the examination method, and there may be a place for the seniority method, but that no one of the three can be relied upon alone. For the greater part of economic activity and for most individuals the competitive market operates as the ultimate guarantee of individual and political freedom. It is at once the safety valve through which energy may escape in creative ways and the brake which protects the individual from the inertia and the possible tyranny of the majority. In the end those intellectuals who destroy business competition in the name of redistribution, security, and planning, because they hate Main Street, will find that they have destroyed the very diffusion of authority which protected them from Main Street.

It may, however, be charged that our argument envisages human society too much in terms of a rigid historical determinism. And since this attitude has already been repudiated in earlier chapters, fairness demands that we ask whether a sufficiently determined people might not conceivably retain their liberties despite the stratified hierarchic organization toward which modern left-wing ideas tend.

One way, of course, in which they might retain their liberty is by ending that type of organization. But for reasons already given it seems doubtful whether it would be possible to terminate the truly centralized state by political democratic action once it has been established for any length of time. The only chance for change would lie in a *coup d'état* or in still more violent and widespread revolution. Yet here we have to remind ourselves of the intense technological vulnerability of modern society. We quoted earlier the statement that "on the whole the great ages have been unstable ages"; but at the same time it was pointed out that not all unstable ages were great. Instability which merely creates a vigorous new ruling group and provides dominant culture with a valuable "cross" may be a great good; but disturbance which lowers the level of living below a certain point may well result not in progress, but in chaos. The transition to general economic centralization and planning, therefore, may well prove for political democracy an irreversible decision. Change may not be possible by peaceful democratic means, while the political convulsions brought on by the revolution could destroy the technical basis of modern life. We need to envisage not only slow stagnation and decline but also sudden fatal explosion.

Yet the view of cultural history presented in this book may be summed up quite briefly: the action and reaction of character upon institutions and environment. And, as in earlier chapters, one can outline a type of character which might enable democracy and science to survive in the centrally planned machine society. If all the citizens of such a society were possessed of a fierce spirit of independence, an acute and tense vigilance regarding the least arbitrary action against any fellow citizen, a profound knowledge of social problems, a deep spirit of tolerance for personal peculiarities and new ideas, a ready willingness to yield to the superior judgment and permit it superior success, and a quick and generous desire to subordinate selfish interest to change benefiting the social whole, then neither liberty nor science need end in the centrally planned economy. But these concessions only leave us with more questions: First, does the electorate today meet such a description? Secondly, if we are asked to accept a form of society which would be intensely dangerous without a specially noble type of character on the part of the citizenry, is it safe to adopt it before this special type of character has been developed? Finally, might not the effort necessary to keep the centralized machine state free—or even a far less heroic endeavor—give us even better results with much less danger, if applied to our present society?

· V ·

The Fundamental Weakness of Democratic Progress

IN IMPERIAL China high officers of state were often, nominally at least, selected by means of a poetry competition. The Jesuits are reported to have organized their missions in Paraguay upon the basis of a musical society. Granted that some form of competition and selection is necessary, why do we have to set up as our goal so "sordid" an aim as money profit? Is not this the basic weakness of our culture?

Proof that the competitive economic market furnishes overwhelmingly the most favorable organization for political democracy, should be a sufficient argument to believers in democracy for retaining competition. But the great stress placed by many modern writers on the evils of the "monetary bias" or "pecuniary calculus" makes it advisable to discuss the problems which it involves.

Many old-fashioned economists were so carried away with the beauty of their own logic that they seemed to confuse competition with perfection and capitalism with God. No such association is intended here. Economic competition is on balance the best general approach for a democratic culture; but that is not to say either that the actual world is "purely" competitive, or even that it is at all satisfying. What is meant is that many evils which now concern us result from forces deeper than competition, and further that removing the competitive order without dealing with these deeper forces will not make us better but a great deal worse. To reach the new world which we desire, we must know our true enemy and our true obstacle.

Why do we dislike our world today? A first set of reasons is "purely economic" or "functional." We dislike it because it is "too insecure," or too "poor," or because the economy "will not work." But there is more to the matter than that. Scratch the economic radical, and you will often find the social philosopher. A very slight study of the work of such men as Veblen, R. H. Tawney, and even Stuart Chase will show that they are not concerned just with occasional collapses of the system, but object to the whole pattern of modern culture. Even if capitalist society were as stable as the pyramids and as rich as Croesus, they would not be satisfied. Their real objection, and that of many other people, is not to "inefficiencies" but to modern life, which they find hectic, nerve-racking, callous, noisy, vulgar, and cheap.

The party which claims credit for the sunshine must take blame for the rain. The many apologists for capitalism who have attributed to it every success of our civilization cannot complain if their opponents burden it with every failure. But it is time to get beyond childish attitudes, and to separate what is due to "the system" as such from what is due to more fundamental currents in our culture —in other words, to determine whether capitalism is responsible for the ugly features of modern life or whether both capitalism and the ugly features are offshoots of a more deeply rooted force. We want to find ways of attacking this basic problem without destroying the competitive market, whose importance for art, science, and democracy has already been seen. Unless we can find them much generous indignation will be turned against the system which may eventually prove to have been entirely misdirected; and removal of the system, if the real problem lies elsewhere, will only prepare the way for inevitable frustration.

Probably the most eloquent and persuasive attack upon the idea of the market economy is that derived by R. H. Tawney from Neo-Platonic philosophy, and presented in his *Acquisitive Society*.* Platonic teaching gives no encouragement to ideas of literal equality, but it is none the less hostile to the usual concept of a competitive market. For the Platonists taught that in the ideal state each activity should be pursued for its own sake rather than for profit. Thus the shoemaker would concern himself not with profit but with shoes; the doctor, with healing rather than with salary;

* Published by Harcourt Brace and Company, Inc.

and so on. This point of view is reflected in the Socialist slogan "Production for use and not for profit," or in Tawney's plea for a "professional society."

As long as we confine ourselves to purely *a priori* reasoning the Platonic ideal certainly appears the best. Yet even here there are problems. For there is one function which societies organized on Platonic lines seem to have difficulty in including, and that is the function of altering functions. In other words the Platonic state as interpreted by Tawney—whatever its other merits—would probably be a static one. We have already seen that we can think of a society in which by definition Platonic organization and rapid creative or scientific change could be combined. In such a society everyone would be so intelligent as to recognize the superior idea or method immediately when it was explained, and so unselfish as to give way to it. But that society, I submit, would be the City of God.

On the other hand, attempts like Tawney's to implement literal Platonic standards in a less moral world seem always to involve a great deal of restriction. The elaborate structure of committees, shop committees, standards, and codes which Tawney sketches might, in a favorable atmosphere and for a generation or two, yield good static craftsmanship. But if our earlier arguments concerning the professional vested interest, the conflict of the static and the inventive instincts of workmanship, the security motive, and the decline of the self-perpetuating group have any validity at all, Tawney's society would offer little scope for the inventor, or for any important scientific development. Such a society might not even retain its initial level of technique; and, if we remember what has been said concerning the importance of the transfer mechanism and the inadequacies of the elective method, an increasingly hierarchic and feudal social structure seems almost inevitable—with all that this implies in the way of nepotism and *de facto* hereditary aristocracy.

However, a still more deeply seated psychological issue is at stake. Tawney wishes to set up a "functional" society, and he defines a function as an activity "which embodies and expresses the idea of social purpose." This definition displays a characteristic weakness of the insurgent intellectual: the tendency to judge an institution by its label, or nominal motives, rather than by its performance. For in testing various types of income by Tawney's standard it seems not sufficient if the incomes serve a social purpose in fact. He appears also to require that they "express" it. And by "expressing purpose" is apparently meant that each variety of income must carry some label. easily rationalized in terms of the ethical prejudices of the time. Every income, then, must be not merely functional (in a practical sense) but also plausible. The attitude resembles that of the scholar in Burton's translation of the *Arabian Nights,* who, seeing no rational explanation for having testes, began to remove his own with a razor.

Naïve nominalism of this sort is a very important social problem. The requirement that a social system be not merely rational but also. rationalizable puts the competitive order under a heavy but not necessarily justified handicap. If the decision is to be made on the basis of avowed motives alone, the businessman is defeated from the start: "I seek to cure the diseases of mankind," says the medical research worker. "I toil for the benefit of the whole nation," says the government official. "I try to probe the maladjustments of the social structure," says the economist. But "I am trying to make my flour business show a profit," says the businessman.

Yet surely we must know that the noblest individual in fact is not always he who has the noblest avowed purpose. And, just as there is such a thing as hypocrisy among individuals, there may also be hypocrisy among social systems—that is, the social system in which each man is provided with the noblest set of tags for his "function" may not be in fact the most just, the most effective, or the most merciful system. By their works we shall know them.

Tawney admires "energy and thought and the creative spirit." These, the competitive order has implemented to a degree unparalleled in history. But Tawney also yearns for a "complex and multiform society which is united by overmastering devotion to a common end," and holds that "such a combination of unity and diversity is possible only to a society which subordinates its activities to the principle of [avowed?] purpose." This conclusion does not follow. Granted an adequate principle of value criticism, it is the competitive economy which best displays unity in diversity—

"E pluribus unum." And the mere setting up of Tawney's specific economic proposals will avail no more than competition to give the basic value standards which are the real objects of his search. After all, his "professional society"—so far as mere form of social organization proves—could equally well be a society of "professional" murderers.

Ellery Sedgwick tells of going with his friend Jim the burglar to his club:

Our table . . . was perhaps two thirds of the way up the line. "See those lowest tables," he whispered. "Riffraff, second story men and such. Just above are the fellows in 'business,' 'pen men' like you and chaps like me. . . . There up beyond us are the real boys, cracksmen, and that top table, those are yeggs. They blow the banks."

It was a model of a well-ordered society. Nobody disputed authority. A man was content to wait until his talents were recognized and his turn came. Everyone knew his place and everyone understood the way that led up in the world.*

Probably the most trenchant criticism of the basic assumptions of eighteenth century liberalism is given by John Ruskin:

I may however anticipate future conclusions so far as to state that in a community regulated only by laws of demand and supply, and protected from open violence, the persons who become rich are, generally speaking, industrious, resolute, proud, covetous, prompt, methodical, sensible, unimaginative, insensitive, and ignorant. The persons who remain poor are the entirely foolish, the entirely wise, the humble, the thoughtful, the dull, the imaginative, the sensitive, the well informed, the improvident, the irregularly and impulsively wicked, the clumsy knave, the open thief, and the entirely just, merciful, and godly person.

Leaving aside whatever reservations one may have regarding Ruskin's adjectives, it is yet possible to paraphrase his argument on the basis of our analysis as follows: "I may, however, anticipate future conclusions so far as to state that in a society the major part of whose industrial investment is planned in advance by an offi-

---

* Reprinted from "The Happy Profession," by Ellery Sedgwick by permission of Little, Brown and Company and the Atlantic Monthly Press.

cially or unofficially organized, integrated, and licensed group, those who become powerful and direct the course of events will eventually be, generally speaking, affable, ingratiating, hypocritical, shy of open responsibility, avid for private power, opposed to change outside their own preconceptions, soft in manner, ruthless when secure. The persons who will remain without power and perquisites are the entirely foolish, the entirely wise, the diffident, the thoughtful, the self-respecting, the sensitive, the imaginative, the irregularly and impulsively wicked, the clumsy knave, the open thief, and the entirely just, merciful and godly person."

One might well concede that in the ideal state the sole motive should be the instinct of workmanship (recognizing, however, the peculiar difficulties of the inventor in such a system); but in any integrated society it has always been found necessary to supplement this instinct for the generality of men with other motives—the incentive of power, for example, or profit, or ambition. And since some supplement is always needed the pecuniary one is not fairly to be judged by comparing it with the ideal state, but with the most likely alternatives in fact available. What modern socialism will do, as I see it, will be to substitute for the incentive of profit the incentives of power, fame, and public honor. How great a gain *per se* is involved in such a substitution is not immediately evident. Is ambition—even the ambition to go a "good" job of "public service," as interpreted by the individual—necessarily less evil than profit? Remember: "Forbade to wade through slaughter to a throne, or shut the gates of mercy on mankind." That the profit motive has its victims, we know well. But what of Baber the conqueror, building pyramids of skulls, and what of Dachau, or the Inquisition, or Siberia? "Saul has slain his thousands; but David his ten thousands."

In the older "orthodox" economics a great deal of time was spent in showing how the competitive market could conceivably yield results exactly similar to hypothetical societies in which the "instinct of workmanship" ruled supreme. This argument of the older economists is valid as far as it goes; but it is based upon such abstract assumptions that it can seldom be literally applied (which does not mean that it is totally irrelevant). The better approach is to admit that the money calculus *per se* can give an adverse bias, and then first to show why the pecuniary bias may be preferable to some others, and next to ask whether the difficulties of the censor class in pressing for higher standards of wants and conduct are due to the economic market and profit motive as such, or to more deeply seated forces.

The truth is that the desire to shape all society around some single central goal is essentially authoritarian. Democracy is variety. Make men genuinely free and they will have various goals and various philosophies. The state-given goal, on the other hand, will inevitably be monist. The aim of the democratic state, therefore, is to make it possible for men to lead full and creative lives, without dictating the whole manner and purpose of those lives. If we grant this, many of the most criticized features of the economic market will be seen to be the product, not of its use of money, but of its democracy. Not only are discrepancies between ideals and practice more easily spotted in the case of the profit motive than in that of any other competitive supplement, but the motive is by far the freest and most flexible of available alternatives. If the people have a passion for music, large fortunes and large profits can be made from promoting music; if painting, then from painting; if many desires, then from many different activities. But the tone-deaf man in Paraguay and the unpoetical man in the Chinese court could not have had much fun.

The essential quarrel which the artistically disposed have with the profit motive is that it often leads businessmen to aim at the mass market. And the mass market, in our society, is not very aesthetic-minded. Yet, after all, is it not extremely democratic to aim at the mass market? Also, are we sure that the frequent vulgarity of that market is due simply to the use of money? Here we reach the basic problem. Democratic progress, we have said, comes through persuasion and criticism by an active censor class. But if there be no generally accepted community of values how can the censor class persuade? Granted that the money bias is a bias—just as the power bias is a bias—what is the fundamental obstacle encountered in trying to control them, and in trying to teach higher standards?

Cultural history is an unceasing drama that reflects the action and interaction of character upon environment. A strong, intelligent, and determined people may maintain its liberties and improve its ethical and aesthetic standards in the face of very hostile environment and cumbrous institutions. Conversely much less heroic efforts will suffice in a more favorable system. But, if the analysis of the preceding chapters means anything at all, the whole drift of modern policy is toward a type of social organization unfavorable to effective democracy; and we have got to see whether this development is offset by an improvement in the level of character. If it is not offset, the outlook is scarcely hopeful. Plato wrote that the ideal state would be approximated when kings became lovers of wisdom, and lovers of wisdom kings. But the democratic thinker must give a different emphasis. His goal is realized only to the extent that the citizens act as lovers of wisdom, and lovers of wisdom act as citizens.

The preceding chapter sketched the essentials of the democratic character. The qualities most needed are independence, responsibility, forbearance: independence in withstanding both direct oppression and subtle influence; responsibility for rather than to the state, and responsibility and care for one's own acts, and for helping others; forbearance toward the ideas and peculiarities of people who disagree with us. Parliaments come and go, but a people which has these three attributes need never lose hope—and a people which has lost them may count votes from morning till night without success. Yet we shall find at the very roots of our culture certain ideas and forces which constantly work against formation of the democratic character; and it is these forces that we may blame for most of the basic evils of our time.

Modern society is built upon foundations laid by the thinkers of the eighteenth century. Eighteenth century thought is the seed from which our tree has grown, and a search for the faults of the tree may begin with a study of the seed. I believe that the political thought of the enlightenment was characterized by a fundamental error. It tended to take for granted the preexistence of the type of character we have been talking of, and to assume men spontaneously "reasonable," and reasonably "equal." Through this assumption the value-creating institutions were slighted or ignored, and it was thought suffcient merely to appeal to "reason" through "education."

Democracy, however, cannot get along without values. Indeed it is itself a value. There can be no democracy, for example, if our dogma of sympathy and regard for the self-respect of every man is not accepted by the majority of the people. Democracy must be felt. It must be retaught in every generation; and, assuming that we want to keep democracy, our future stands or falls upon the success with which we transmit beliefs. We simply cannot avoid this conclusion.

Yet certain values contain an element of self-destruction, and democracy is one of them. Every religion has its heresies, every truth its likely perversions, every bit of sense its probable accompaniment of nonsense. There are various easy ways in which each gospel can be misunderstood, and the birth and rebirth of heresies from a given "orthodox" stem furnishes a fascinating study. I hold with the men of the eighteenth century that we must use reason, and that the primary weapon of democratic change must be persuasion. The slightest qualification of these principles is dangerous, for our natural intolerance and narrow-mindedness is such that the most reasonable and restricted concession opens the door to abuse. Nevertheless an honest liberal must realize that his doctrine like others, if pushed to an extreme, can result in contradiction or nonsense.

Examples are easily given. We wish for instance to work through persuasion. But persuasion of whom? Of the insane? Of an invading army? Where does one draw the line? Again, from our axiom of sympathy we draw our postulate of tolerance. But does tolerance imply tolerance of intolerance? Is it intolerant to try to persuade people not be intolerant?

American constitutional theory carries the concept of tolerance to the very verge. There is, in theory at least, complete freedom of discussion over an immense range of topics. A few personal rights are protected from majority action by the constitution—but the constitution can be amended. Attacks on the constitution, other than by amendment, or attacks on the elective method itself are viewed as attacks upon fundamental government, potentially traitorous, seditious, and criminal. But even in these cases our law grants in general a further latitude. As long as the attacks do not create an "immediate and pressing danger" they are not subject to criminal prosecution. We are, for example, entirely free to advocate violence —peaceably.

Yet the "immediate and pressing danger" doctrine, broad as it is, implies its own limit, and we do not carry our concept of tolerance to the point of tolerating our own destruction. Even Jefferson's magnificent sentence, "For here we are not afraid to follow truth wherever it may lead or to tolerate any error so long as reason is free to combat it," does not go so far. For Jefferson would not have said it if he had not been confident of the ultimate victory of truth in any nation having "free trade in ideas."

Just as tolerance, however, becomes its own opposite when turned into a tolerance for the destruction of tolerance, so there are many other ways in which the democratic analogies can be carried to absurdity. The fundamental contention of this chapter is that it is precisely such perversions, misunderstandings, and reductions to the absurd of democratic doctrine—undermining the value-creating institutions of modern society—that today threaten to bring the entire structure down. Two confusions may be mentioned: Democracy as a universal chance to make the best of oneself is confused with democracy as a compulsory equality with the worst. The democratic method as persuasion wherever possible, becomes confused with democracy as persuasion only.

The action of what might be called the democratic heresies is most clearly seen in the field of education. As the scope of planning becomes larger and larger, it is clear that more and more complicated questions will have to be submitted to the electorate. If, then, our faith in tolerance, in freedom, and in free discussion is to be justified it will be necessary constantly to improve the general level of public information. Furthermore, as the church and the home decline, education becomes the sole value-creating force in our society, and the public school finds the responsibility for developing social attitudes placed entirely on its shoulders. Yet, at the very time when the maintenance of democracy demands more and more of education, certain ideas derived from democracy work to make education less and less able to meet its task.

First of such caricatures of democratic thought is the twist which our equalitarian prejudice has given to the idea of universal schooling. Starting with the principle that the state must see to it that each of its citizens capable of absorbing instruction should receive a certain basic amount of information, our democratic prejudice against the idea of selection has in practice brought us perilously close to saying that each citizen shall get no more than the basic minimum of information. Properly understood, universal education should mean not merely helping the least fitted, but helping everyone. This implies that, within the limits set by administrative obstacles and available funds, instruction should be related to the caliber of the student. Of course there is a point beyond which it is undesirable to keep the "slow" student in school; but the decision should not be based on the private finances of the student alone, and we should try to bring him up to a basic level even if he is mentally slow. But this ought not to mean holding back one who is abler.

Jefferson thought of education as selective training. Translated into modern terms, his ideal would probably be as follows: From the broadest possible base an opportunity should be given every child to go as far and almost as quickly as his aptitudes will carry him. Large-scale state grants will enable poor boys to hold their own with boys of better fortune, and thus, in education at the least, there will be a genuine approach to "equality of opportunity" —but not literal equality.

We have obviously fallen far short of realizing this ideal. But no small part of our failure has been that Jefferson's concept has been confused with the equalitarian prejudices already spoken of. We are jealous of any special distinction. Is it a special distinction to go to college? Then everyone must go to college, whether he can profit by it or not. If a true college curriculum is too stiff for the crowds thus forced in, the answer is, Dilute it! It is undemocratic to select—however broad a base. We will shove the grammar school into the high school, the high school into the college, the college into the M.A., the beginning of graduate work into the

Ph.D., and we shall soon have to invent a Ph.Ph.D. to designate those who really do manage to obtain an education. And all this because our jealousy of special distinction keeps us from separating the instruction of the slower student from the instruction of the better one. As a result American public education becomes geared not merely to the average but to the subaverage or even the sub-subaverage, and there is a fearful waste of good brains and energy which democracy can ill afford. We tend to forget that few of the "founding fathers" were more than thirty years old. But today the man of thirty is often barely finishing his graduate course, and he is likely to carry through life the mark of the repressed years when, with all the vigor and energy of manhood, he was still in tutelage.

We are discussing the inadequacies of modern education as a means of democratic progress. Closely bound up with the effects of equalitarian prejudice are the results of yet another democratic analogy—education by persuasion only. The concept of modern education and child care which has reached the public is in effect that the child should not be "frustrated"; and by "prevention of frustration" is often understood simply that he (or she) should never be made to do anything which he does not wish. A more balanced approach, and the one probably intended by the best writers of the "progressive" school, concedes the necessity of teaching people to refrain from complete "self-expression" but hopes to induce proper social attitudes by "persuasion" rather than "discipline."

Thorough understanding of the problem requires that we begin with the crude interpretation. The basic trouble here is the one we encountered in trying to sketch an economy free from conflicts of interest. The truth is that, if frustration means having to do what one does not wish, then all civilized life, and democratic civilized life in particular, is one vast frustration. If I am to live and work with other people pleasantly and effectively there are a hundred things a day I must do which I dislike doing, and many more things I want to do which I cannot. Democratic tolerance for the self-respect of other people, for example, absolutely forbids me to ride rough-shod over others in pursuit of my own ideas.

It has been frequently debated in sociological literature whether man is a "naturally" social animal or antisocial one. The conclusion would seem to be that he is both. The tragedy of human life is that, if one wishes to have everything one's own way, one must live on a desert island. But then one will be frustrated because one is lonesome. This "imperfect sociability" which causes men to fluctuate between the desire to get along "well" with others and the desire to have their own way or, in a nobler sense, to inaugurate their own vision is probably one of the profoundest frustrations we know. Yet it is inherent in social life. Probably the happiest (in the sense of unfrustrated) life is that of a group of barbarian invaders who, recognizing bonds of sympathy and duty toward one another, may nevertheless inflict their smallest desire upon a captive population. But this is scarcely a pattern for democracy!

Yet not for the first time, and certainly not for the last, we find ourselves in a position where the excessive pursuit of one democratic analogy leads to the violation of another. What has just been said regarding "respect for the personality" of others easily leads to the idea of education by persuasion alone. The superficial analogy with political democracy is exact enough: freedom to "make one's own mistakes," "tolerance," "self-expression," "freedom of experiment" as opposed to the "iron rod of authority," and so on.

But before applying too literally to infants a technique that is by no means automatically self-fulfilling even with mature and educated adults, we have to ask a few questions. The first concerns the inadequacy of the persuasion method, if used alone; and this is closely tied up with the inadequacy of reason used alone. It is a sobering thought to reflect that not merely the progress but even the maintenance of civilization and democracy depends upon our ability to learn from the experience of others, and then to think further how many times we have ourselves committed utter folly despite explicit and repeated warnings. The truth is that the mind has to have information in order to act, and not all of it can be had in textbooks. This has particularly application to our notorious ability to persuade ourselves to believe what we want to believe.

A brilliant boy of eighteen, for example, may have a far better mind than his instructors—but does he, in most cases, have the experience of life upon which to base a completely valid judgment? His logic may be superb—but what of his promises? Discipline and punishment are ersatz experience. There are some experiments that cannot be repeated; for example, setting off dynamite while standing in the middle of an ammunition dump. The mistake (or experiment) of growing up a slovenly selfish sponger is equally fatal and irrevocable, but the consequences do not come so soon.

Another and more practical problem of the persuasion method concerns the immense amount of time and energy absorbed in wheedling reluctant youth. Can a democratic society operate a complicated modern economy on the basic level of information which the subaverage child can be cajoled into absorbing in the intervals of play?

The final difficulty of progressive education and the persuasion method may be put in somewhat paradoxical form: If we only use the so-called "democratic" education methods, shall we obtain the democratic character? In other words, is the child, or youth, who has almost never had to do anything except what he could be argued or bribed into doing, likely to have the regard for other people and the feeling of responsibility for his own acts which are essential to the democratic citizen? If the Victorian home was a dictatorship of the father, the "modern" home is a tyranny of the children. The ideal of democratic education should be one of reciprocal duties and reciprocal consideration, and it is hard to see how we are going to get it by overindulging either one party or the other.

The weakness of present-day education as a means to progress is thus easily seen. One aspect of this problem reflects the despair which hovers in the background of our culture. As a result of modern birth control children are usually no longer spontaneous happenings or "acts of God." In consequence many modern parents feel themselves morally responsible for creation of the child in a way which older people simply could not have understood. The modern parent thus often has a feeling of guilt for having called a being into the world to suffer. And in the last few years there has been no humor here! The result of this is that the modern parent tends to display an attitude of servile apology toward his children. Yet we ought to remember that the nature of social life is not set by us but by the nature of the world, and that even in socialism mutual self-respect and mutual duties must be learned for a successful or happy life. Sooner or later our children must leave us to go into a world which will not consider all their "feelings," and however we may yearn over them we can inflict no greater curse than to send them forth morally unprepared.

Summing up, then, democracy is a balance of a number of different qualities, not all of which are entirely consistent; and excessive pursuit of some one aspect leads to forgetfulness of the others. In modern public education the ideas of equality and persuasion carried to extremes leave us attempting to run a more and more complicated system on a lower and lower level of general basic information. Further, the use of the persuasion method virtually alone, and the almost total abandonment of discipline, lead to the development of an egotism and irresponsibility quite at variance with the requirements of democratic life. Thus the great technical achievements of the past fifty years have been accompanied by other outgrowths of democratic doctrine steadily nibbling away at the basis of self-control and of general knowledge.

Disquieting as the trends just sketched may be, we have not yet reached our basic difficulty. Let us take an American child who has just completed the usual public grammar school. Probably he has learned to read and write, but if the school is really "advanced" we cannot be too sure of this. It is certain that he has learned little or nothing about concentration, and, under the persuasion method, has slighted branches of study however valuable—for example, arithmetic—which require much drill or hard work. Further, the circumstances of his training probably have given him little idea of responsibility, or respect for others. Possibly at home or elsewhere he may pick up some values; but often, if he knows any standards at all, they are those of the leader and the gang. Yet for many such children society has a last chance in the college, and still more in the high school, to give needed information. Here too, however, we find another example of democratic doctrine carried to extreme.

The modern college or high school adopts the eighteenth century attitude that a "reasonable" man "spontaneously" knows all the really important things of life. It proceeds on the assumption that the student already is familiar with precisely those things which education is supposed to be teaching him. The largely unprepared youth in the college, for example, who may have no idea why he came to college or what college has to offer, is turned loose by the elective system to concentrate upon anything he chooses from bee keeping to hieroglyphics. In the public high school attention is increasingly distracted from basic studies to various forms of vocational education.

Those who stress the need of preparing the high-school student for a job have forgotten that one job for which he needs to be trained is bigger and more important than any other—namely, the job of being a citizen—and that to be a good citizen a man must possess the basic tools of his trade. Not merely must he be able to read, write, and figure, but he must have some knowledge of history, government, art, science, and the problems of democracy. Thomas Jefferson's elementary schools included instruction in history! Also a man must have the elements of the democratic character. Yet both in the college and in the high school any attempt to focus the curriculum on these subjects rouses extreme resentment. Why is this? An answer will bring us to the core of our problem.

The first, and subordinate, difficulty is one more example of democratic doctrine carried beyond reason: a concept of tolerance so broad as to amount to complete negation. Democratic education, we have seen, should be as free from authoritarian elements as possible. In the case of the college, "indoctrination" in the sense of propaganda is entirely out of place—a point to which we must return. Nevertheless, tolerance approaches self-defeating absurdity if it prevents us from acquainting students with the problems of democracy in an objective manner and with due attention to alternatives. If democracy means a tolerance so broad that it cannot even train its own citizens in its own problems, how on earth can it survive?

Anyone, however, who has worked with these problems soon finds that there is a more formidable obstacle than mere tolerance gone sour. We have said that the eighteenth century put its faith in "reason." But in general this was a special kind of reason: scientific reason. The only authority recognized in the chaotic intellectual life of today is the authority of science. But the scientific method, from its very nature, has almost nothing directly to say on any of the really vital problems of human life. For example, there is nothing in physics to tell one whether he should be true to his wife or his friends; whether he should die for his country; or whether he should be honest in his private trusts. These, however, are the real issues of life. We have set up a mute oracle in our temple and then become frantic because it does not answer! Yet the prestige of the scientific analogy is so great, and its ramifications so vast, that its influence often comes to constitute not merely a negative inadequacy, but a positive evil.

Many people complain of the difficulty of inculcating "proper" aesthetic and other values in modern civilization. The tendency is to lay this difficulty to the narrowness and selfishness of business culture. Veblen is a typical example of the trend when he explains the prime obstacle to artistic betterment in a "business world" as being that art is not a "business proposition." But Veblen is, as usual, allowing keen insight to be warped by intense anticapitalistic bias. What he should have said is that the prime obstacle to the inculcation of values is that they are not a "scientific" proposition.

By "scientific" we refer, of course, to the dominant "exact" sciences—physics and chemistry—which have given their tone to the whole trend of our thinking. Biology comes next in rank but save in the case of Darwin has not yet made so deep a mark in our culture. Also "scientific" must refer, for present purposes, not to modern science, but to the great materialistic science of the eighteenth and nineteenth centuries which swept aside nine-tenths of life in its doctrine of "secondary" (by inference unimportant) qualities, and proudly proclaimed that there was no reality save "matter" in "motion."

There is no need to detail here the manner in which this majestic structure of certainty has collapsed. "Matter" today, if it means anything, is viewed as a species of vibration, without our being at all sure what is vibrating—"a grin without a cat." Whitehead's work in the synthesis of biology and physics, in evolution and relativity, and his reemphasis upon value, is also growing in influence. But still the one final appeal recognized by the modern intellect is to the scientific, or experimental, method; and study of the qualities which this method is unable to touch remains in a state of anarchy.

We feel more and more today what has always been known; namely, that the dogma derived from materialist science that there is no reality save "matter in motion" is on a par with a statement by a color-blind man that there is no difference between red and green, or by a deaf man that a boiler factory is quiet. All that scientific method can possibly prove is that certain "realities" are the only "realities" which it can reach. It can never prove there are no others. The inadequacy of our criterion is thus obvious. But the lot of a musician in a world resolved to hear only through the deaf would not be enviable, and the plight of aesthetics in a world which tries to run all life by statistics is equally unhappy. The dominant scientific view of cultural values today is the theory of "the mores"—that is, that our ideas of morals, beauty, and good manners are for the most part mere fortuitous habits and survivals. With such a background how can ethics or aesthetics go far in a culture—any culture—which demands "scientific proof" for everything?

Not merely in the plight of values, however, do we find the influence of the scientific method. It is also responsible for producing a race of the most elaborately, expensively, and deliberately uneducated people on earth—the majority of the usual college faculty. For the technique of science is not only one of experiment, it is also a matter of specialization. We have spoken of democracy as a balance of qualities, and it is not surprising that there should be a growing tendency to concentrate upon some one quality or other at the expense of the rest. For, after all, the entire bias of knowledge in the past century has been to encourage each man to neglect the whole for the part. The tearing to pieces of the body politic by pressure groups is exactly reflected in the tearing to pieces of knowledge by college specialties. Life, however, is a "seamless garment." Even in physics there is recurrent need for an integration of the findings of specialized research, while in the "social sciences" excessive specialization often results not merely in inadequate knowledge but in pure nonsense. Thus we tend to accumulate a body of half-truths which not only never quite adds up to anything but is downright misleading. This does not mean that specialization should be abandoned. What is needed is that a man, before he specializes, should have a sufficiently broad training to understand related fields, and that constant critical pressure shall be placed upon him to keep up with those fields.

In our search for the obstacles to the inculcation of higher values in democracy, we pass from reason and science to applied science. This brings us to the opposite error from the elective system. Laboratory specialization is not the only way in which modern technique affects education. There is also the prestige of the factory method. When a commissar or a businessman intends to start a factory his first concern is the careful designing of a plant. Next the key administrative personnel is selected. Only thereafter are the rank and file considered; and the skill of the designers of the plant is far less important than the skill of the simple operatives. We find these steps precisely echoed in many modern American universities. Impressive buildings, "high-pressure" administrators —and an inferior faculty. Many a man who would hesitate before confiding his daughter's character to a prostitute has no qualms over entrusting his son's brains to a fool. It seems somehow thought that "ivy-mantled walls" and pseudo Gothic or Georgian architecture will work upon a youth's mind in the same way as exposure to a chemical process completes the product in a soap factory.

This factory analogy does not stop with overemphasis upon plant. Once a factory is completed, the aim of its operator is to "process" as much raw material, in as steady a stream, as possible. This too is reflected in modern thought and modern education. In the realm of thought an eminent philosopher and economist—

Dr. Ayres of the University of Texas—maintains that the highest value is "continuity," and that "the criterion of every economic judgment is keeping the machines running," while in the field of education we find a system of large classes, without discussion, and of lectures in which the student is "indoctrinated" with the prejudices of his instructors as relentlessly as a cake of soap is stamped out in an industrial plant. Such conveyor belt scheduling, however, which allows the student no time to catch his mental breath, and the method of indoctrination rather than discussion, are not democratic education. We do not want conditioned zombies but reasonable, self-controlled men. This implies presentation of the truth (as we see it) in an objective manner, with full opportunity for discussion, and with fair attention to alternatives. For such an education—the essence of democracy—there is no mechanical substitute for personal contact and the Socratic method.

Superficially speaking, it might appear that what has just been said contradicts earlier criticisms made of the elective system. The paradox, however, is easily solved. It is necessary for education to be somewhat authoritarian (in the sense of using discipline and deciding upon curriculum) in the earlier years, and while the student is learning the basic tool subjects which modern life requires. Democracy furthermore has the right to ask of its future citizens that they study the problems of citizenship. But authoritarian elements should relax as the student becomes more mature, and as he obtains a broader basis of knowledge. If the high schools did their job, the colleges would be able to use the elective system almost unmodified. But it should not be forgotten that Jefferson's proposals regarding the elective system were made for what we would now call a "graduate" institution. And if the colleges find students coming to them ignorant or one-sided this is no reason for letting them go out still more ignorant and still more one-sided. Doubtless required subjects confine a student's "freedom"; but if we grant excessive indulgence in infancy the penalty will be an otherwise unnecessary restraint in adolescence.

Brief mention must be made of certain other ideas derived from nineteenth century science and philosophy. First of these is determinism. Ours, it might be said, is the Alibi Age. If we murder our grandmothers it is because someone annoyed us when we were young. It would be difficult to find a doctrine better calculated to destroy the democratic requirement of responsibility.

Next we come to evolution and the "survival of the fittest." Though at present somewhat under a cloud this principle will sooner or later become popular again, and is easily perverted into a blanket indorsement of any struggle, and of whatever comes out on top. But the only thing proved by the survival of the "fittest" is that they are fit to survive. It does not prove that they "ought" to. Struggle as such, we cannot avoid; but there are many kinds of struggle, and the essence of progress lies in the constant selection of nobler struggles.

Finally one must mention an idea not strictly "scientific," but closely bound up with materialist science; namely, the utility calculus. The world view apparently taught by many nineteenth century thinkers was that everyone balanced a given amount of disagreeable "work" (disutility) against a certain amount of "pleasure" (utility). The idea often implied is that the end of life, "the pursuit of happiness," is best to be achieved by giving as little and taking as much as one possibly can. The influence of this idea in contemporary life has been both pernicious and important. Yet it is no monopoly of capitalism, and if it is found in some aspects of orthodox economics it also occurs in trade unionism and in much socialist thought. Crude applications of the utility calculus slur over all the joy of creation and the pride of work. Marriage, instead of being considered as a collaboration in a greater aim— the founding of a home—is viewed as an exchange of thrills, and the young man is encouraged to look for a soft job rather than an absorbing one. It is interesting to compare with this attitude the views of Justice Holmes: "Through our great good fortune in our youth our hearts were touched with fire. It was given to us to learn at the outset that life is a profound and passionate thing . . . above all we have learned that whether a man accepts from Fortune her spade . . . or from Aspiration her . . . cord . . . the one and only success which it is his to command is to bring to his work a mighty heart."

Holmes's sentence implies an idea concerning the weakness of modern life still better expressed by the philosopher Ortega. The fact is that the goods given us by the "Enlightenment" are secondary goods. Its freedom is freedom to go and find our own ends. It does not give us of itself a purpose in life, and the subordinate ideas accompanying it have, as we have just seen, gone far toward destroying the whole notion of purpose in personal lives. Yet, as we have seen in the case of Tawney, men must have some goals if they are to be happy, and if the personal goals are lost they will demand that their ultimate purposes be given by the state.

Thus, Ortega wrote in 1931, "to live is to live tensely"; "without a commandment obliging us to life after a certain fashion [value] our existence is that of the 'unemployed.' . . . Because to live means to have something definite to do—a mission to fulfil . . . Before long there will be heard throughout the planet a formidable cry, rising like the howling of innumerable dogs to the stars, asking for someone, or something . . . to impose an occupation, a duty." Again: "When Communism triumphed in Russia, there were many who thought that the whole of the West would be submerged by the Red torrent. I did not share that view . . . the European does not see in the Communistic organization an increase in human happiness." Yet "now indeed is the time when victorious, overwhelming Communism may spread over Europe . . . not for its own sake, rather in spite of what it is." For "whatever the content of Bolshevism may be, it represents a gigantic human enterprise. In it men have embraced a purpose of reform and live tensely under the discipline that such a faith instils in them." Consequently, "for the sake of serving something that will give a meaning to his existence, it is not impossible that the European may swallow his objections to Communism and feel himself carried away not by the substance of the faith, but by the fervour of conduct which it inspires." *

Thus, to sum up our argument, the years since the eighteenth century Enlightenment have lived upon the moral capital of the ages which preceded them. Democracy requires a stiffening or framework of values, yet the philosophy of democracy carried to

* *The Revolt of the Masses* by Jose Ortega y Gasset. Reprinted by permission of W. W. Norton & Company, Inc. Copyright, 1932, by the publishers.

extremes and the effects of eighteenth century philosophy, and subsequent scientific influences, have very nearly destroyed values, including the basic values of democracy itself. We have almost exhausted our moral capital. That is the basic weakness of modern democratic progress.

The reaction of most men to this situation is to run away from it. The life of the modern "man of action," and of the social reformer as well, is often one long frantic attempt to escape in action the haunting presence of the questions which he feels he cannot answer, but which, from his nature, he never wholly escapes asking. This daemonic energy of flight is never better seen than in the nihilism of Hitler; but it may also be observed in many places superficially far removed. The psychology of revolutionary activity is further reenforced by certain other factors. The life of the revolutionary—even if only in the realm of ideas—is often a thrilling one, giving full scope to impulses toward creation and leadership. Also the ordinary fields of activity offer less and less to the exceptional man as society becomes more hierarchic, stratified, and noncompetitive in organization. Thus we find the paradox, so common today, by which the genuine inquirer—the very type of man who would be most unhappy in a mature socialist state, with its static pattern and rigid orthodoxy—is the man who now finds most satisfaction in creating socialism.

The catharsis achieved by such an individual, however, is a nondemocratic and parasitic one, and its economic bases are temporary. The first generation of revolutionaries finds full outlet for its energy in the creation of the new state, as the first generation of planners does in the creation of the new plan. But they establish an order which will frustrate the creative impulses of many generations to come. It is ironically easy to associate the satisfaction which one gets in working toward an end, with the end itself. Yet in fact working toward almost any other end (or type of social change) might often have furnished precisely the same creative satisfaction, and escape from deeper thought. In the analysis of the preceding chapters I have tried to show that the idea of the competitive order is—on the lowest terms—no more hostile to the solution of the fundamental problem than any other; and I have tried to show further that it works in many ways to favor a democratic solution. So far as the problem of restless inquiry, for example, admits of any economic treatment, its amelioration is to be found in the maintenance of a frontier of change and a sufficiently open pattern. For this task the competitive order is peculiarly well fitted.

But it should be clear that the long-run problem of fundamental values, and basic inquiry, cannot be solved by going off on a tangent whether "heroic," scientific, or revolutionary. So far as democratic progress goes, even if we change systems we take with us materialistic science and its accompanying analogies; and we also take the democratic heresies, the factory organization, the theory of the mores, most of the utility calculus, and the denial or ignoring of value. But these are our real problems. The basic task lies in the evolving of a scheme of values and a sanction for them, which can either rank as a science, or at least persuade a scientific-minded generation. Those who look for an absorbing task in life may well find it here.

This book does not essay so lofty a mission. This is not a treatise on the philosophy of ethics. But, if we do not contribute to the problem directly, something at least is gained by showing the values which men must hold if they want democracy, even if no further reason is given for holding them. The basis of a democratic ethic must be consideration for the other man—not an absolute, undiscriminating lack of self-assertion whose paradoxes we have earlier explored, but a code of fair play. Such a code, I believe, finds its basis in sympathy. Some have argued that it is impossible to show why men should be taught sympathy. But perhaps men cannot avoid feeling it. Despite the imperfect nature of our sociability, a film of Dachau or Buchenwald would seem to me to offer more conclusive proof to most people of the need for the democratic ethic of consideration than all the labors of the metaphysicians. And once we begin with the idea of respect for the individual the rest can follow.

Again, on the problem of personal life, the emphasis, it seems to me, should lie not so much on the securing of "satisfaction" as on the performance of function. Yet there are many types of men and many types of function. The world has in it room for nearly all our skills. The task of this book is a subordinate one—an exposition of the problem of maintaining an economic society which will conform to the values we have sketched. We shall accordingly address ourselves hereafter to specifically economic problems. But one thing must not be forgotten. Men who change economic systems while retaining a philosophy essentially hostile to their fundamental aims are like men flying from a plague-stricken city. They only carry the germs of their own destruction with them.

· VI ·

Progress and Instability

THE PRECEDING chapter may seem merely to have raised a number of questions without answering them. Yet its arguments lead to a definite and important conclusion: The basic cultural problem is not economic, but democratic and scientific; and it cannot be handled by an economic remedy alone. Granted many subordinate evils, it is nevertheless true that the most criticized features of the basic ideal of the economic market are the products not so much of its use of money, but of its democracy. It follows that the American censor class, in turning against the competitive market on the ground that it is the prime obstacle to the realization of a higher culture, has mistaken its enemy. What is really needed is to come to grips with the relationship of values to the scientific spirit. How near Utopia we should all be if only the profit motive stood between us and the true and beautiful!

There is, however, another and, economically speaking, a more serious charge against the competitive order. The censor class, and indeed nearly all economists, are convinced that the basic causes of economic instability and insecurity are "planlessness" or "lack of control." This idea is accepted not only by the opponents of capitalist democracy, but also by many of its friends. All that is done in reply, for the most part, is to call attention to the political "freedom" which "planlessness" implies. But such freedom is easily ridiculed: "Our law in its majestic impartiality protects alike the rich and the poor in their right to beg in the street." If there were no more to the matter than that, it is doubtful whether the present system could long survive. Yet are we correct in placing the blame upon capitalist organization alone? Just how much shall we avoid if we change our social organization? May there not, here too, be some other and more deeply rooted force at work?

In judging social systems it should be remembered that most advocates of comprehensive planning claim not so much that their system will do a different economic job from capitalism as that it will do the capitalist job better. That is, they do not say, "Elect us, and we will ration for years, hold back inventions still longer, and in return give you—stability." Not at all. The promise usually made is to give and invent things for the consumer "bigger and better," and faster than capitalism—and still give stability. This promise, it seems to me, sets up contradictory standards which cannot all be met simultaneously by anticipatory planning, however perfect; and it is time to examine the real problems rather than the slogans by which they are debated.

In implying that the fundamental factors making for economic fluctuation are not so much due to the competitive order as to the liberal values, one does not need to say, as is so often insinuated, that we have to starve if we want to be free. Nor need one even declare that a perfectly stable society is impossible. What the idea does mean is that an industrial society without a stabilization problem is likely to be an industrial society without economic freedom; also that, though we may offset the forces making for instability so as to keep them within tolerable bounds, we cannot eliminate them without eliminating the liberal economic values as well. In other words, starvation may not be the price of our freedom, but using our heads is. Economic progress, security, and freedom—all good things—can never wholly be reconciled, and no automatic compromise is possible. If we want our liberty we must be willing to think for it.

What are the liberal standards within which the cycle is rooted? First, there is democracy of choice among goods and occupations. This means that within the limits set by whatever distribution of wealth we permit, we try to give the people what they want when they want it, and do not force them into specific occupations save in time of grave emergency. Next, there is democracy of aspiration and opportunity—a chance to rise on independent and honorable terms. Finally, there is a democracy of welfare—the desire to obtain an adequate general level of well-being. In other words a liberal economic system dislikes rationing and compulsion but values rising living standards and the technological changes which make them possible. On this basis it is not hard to show why such societies are unstable.

If one were asked to name the single idea which, more than any other, has confused our understanding of the problem of stability, it might well be the notion that all businesses are about equally prosperous or equally depressed at the same time. If only all lines of work reacted to the business cycle in about the same manner and degree, the problem of stabilization would be much simpler than it is. But there is hardly ever a depression so severe that no firms make any money, and never is there a boom in which all are equally prosperous.

Yet, whatever our social organization, if we wish to give people what they want when they want it we shall have to try to anticipate the spending patterns of consumers; otherwise there will be shortages, wastes, bottlenecks, or unemployment. Comprehensive planning does not avoid this task. It only changes the techniques by which it is approached. Still the fudamental difficulty remains to be overcome, and still there is a forecasting problem whose complexity is scarcely grasped in modern discussion.

Forecasting (and hence planning) would be comparatively simple in a world free from growth or invention. Once a satisfactory pattern were reached, it would be endlessly repeated. But a growing, technically progressive, but unrationed society is different. And since one of the main arguments for comprehensive planning is that it can handle growth and change better than capitalism, the case of the growing, changing world is the one which really concerns us here.

Yet in themselves increasing wealth and living standards make forecasting difficult. Suppose we try to predict the effects of a rise in income on a single individual. Say that he is very poor, and that he buys kerosene and kerosene lamps for light, sugar and salt for cooking, and sometimes, as a great treat, a glass of beer. Let him then have a sizable raise in pay. Will he only buy more of the same things? Certainly not. For light he will be almost sure to stop using kerosene and switch to electricity. Salt will probably not be much affected, for most people use about the same amount regardless of income. Sugar will be likely to increase. Beer, however, and similar expenditures furnish the real problem. For beer in our example is part of the "luxury" margin, and it is this which is most unpredictable. Perhaps our newly enriched individual will buy more beer; but he may change to more expensive drinks, or try something entirely different—better food, or concerts, or education. The main point is that his spending will respond to an increase in income in a very irregular and often unpredictable way. Furthermore what is true of this individual is true of society as a whole.

It may seem that the luxury margin is not very important, because it is such a small part of expenditure. But what is a luxury? Ideas on this point constantly change. Remember that in 1840 the height of luxury was a bathtub. The so-called luxury margin is often the forerunner of social progress, and to the consumer it is one of the most significant parts of his spending. The luxury of today is the necessity of tomorrow; and, in consequence, the effects of a rising income, for society as well as for the individual, will be very unevenly felt. In general, as output increases, rarities become luxuries, luxuries become "necessities," and many former necessities drop out altogether. This is the rule. But it would take a brave man indeed to predict exactly how each industry was going to be affected. Some mistakes are inevitable.

Invention adds the final complication. We may collect statistics carefully and make painstaking predictions; but a new product may upset the whole calculation. What value, for example, would consumption statistics collected before the First World War have had in the 1920's? The automobile had shaken up the whole pattern of tastes throughout our social life! Who is to say what will happen in the present postwar period? The over-all development we call economic growth is the product of hundreds of industrial movements: some industries rising, some falling; some virtually disappearing only to reemerge abruptly; others sweeping grandly upward and then dramatically vanishing. Like the flickering motions of a flame this rise and decline of individual products, in an

unrationed society, goes constantly forward, and only "on average"
—and occasionally not even then—can we trace any general trend.
Yet as long as the consumer is allowed any important freedom of
choice some such variation is unavoidable.

The consequences of this variability are twofold. First, even if
the socialist or capitalist society does a perfect job of forecasting,
and maintains full employment throughout, it will not avoid the
possibility of acute social strain. As we saw in Chapter II, socialism
does not, of itself, avoid the clash of individual and general welfare. The constant changes of an advancing science and an unrationed market raise some to power or to affluence, while relegat-
ing others to obscurity or to poverty; and leave one region stranded,
while raising others to great activity or wealth. Resulting social
disturbance may be profound. Yet the difficulty is not so much in
the type of society *per se* as in the rapidity of change and expansion, and the degree of choice permitted to the consumer.

How to obtain a fair degree of individual security in a changing world, is a problem which will absorb much space in this book.
However, we are now concerned with outlining the fundamentals
of economic stability, and must therefore pass on to the second
main type of disturbance which results from variable expansion:
"general" or "over-all" fluctuation. In other words we must discuss the business cycle itself—first as it is found in capitalism and
then as planning affects it.

We have seen that all businesses are not equally prosperous at
the same time. It follows that full employment will occur spontaneously only if about as many businesses happen to be expanding as happen to be on the decline. With such a fortunate balance
the economy could function fairly well. But there is no reason to
suppose that in the short run an adequate series of offsets must
always and inevitably spring up, and there are many reasons to feel
that they often will not. Theoretically, perhaps, human desires are
"boundless," and as fast as one industry reaches maturity another
will take its place. Practically, such symmetrical, frictionless performance does not occur. The net effects of change in a capitalist
society may be either overexpansion or underexpansion. Sometimes
demand conditions and expectations may be such that businessmen

will try to expand to more than "full" employment, and we are likely to get inflation. At other times spontaneous market demand may not add up to full employment at all, and then deflation will probably ensue.

It would look as if comprehensive planning could easily avoid fluctuations of this sort; but the matter is not so simple as that. So far as inflation goes, the chances are that rigid control would keep prices in hand. But even in this case it must be remembered that the first Russian Five Year Plan was not carried through without a great inflation. Also in most countries there has been a black market. Deflation, however, is the more complicated problem; and we will give it most of our attention.

In deciding whether comprehensive planning could avoid unemployment and income decline, we have to go back to the distinction already made between a program of "filling in" and a program of virtually complete planning in advance. To many people the various schemes of "deficit finance," public works and so on, are unworthy compromises—feeble crutches which barely enable the system to totter along despite the mistakes of the capitalist market. Their belief is justified only in a very special sense. Certainly some types of comprehensive planning could avoid the cycle entirely. Other, more moderate kinds could keep it within bounds. But liberal comprehensive planning, really tried, would retain many of the fundamental "wastes" now thought peculiar to capitalism, and could stabilize only by techniques already available under capitalism. In order to see why this is so let us put aside the whole idea of public works and "compensatory" finance, and see what problems the planners would have to meet if they followed the liberal economic values (that is, encouraged invention, and tried to give the consumer what he wanted when he wanted it), and attempted to stabilize solely through comprehensive licensing and *advance* planning.

We have talked thus far of economic disturbance as if it were found more or less at random throughout the economy. Pressures toward collapse, we have seen, could start almost anywhere. All economists, however, are agreed that, though expansion and decline are never symmetrical, there is one especially vulnerable sector of industry. Minor depressions sometimes develop from overaccumulation of inventories by retailers and others, but the highest proportional variations in employment occur in the so-called "durable goods" industries—the producers of plant, housing, machinery, and equipment. It is scarcely too much to say that a major boom is a time when durable goods are being made and a major slump is a time when they are not. If, then, comprehensive planning is to do a decisively better job than the "free" market, it must show its ability to do a better job of stabilizing the durable goods industries.

Most radical writers assume that the special instability of the durable goods industries is the result of some capitalist peculiarity: "mistakes" of businessmen, "planlessness," "useless" duplication, and so on. Undoubtedly all these could happen, and all could help to aggravate the cycle. One wonders, to be sure, just how much better a forecast really liberal planning could make; but the point which is almost wholly overlooked today is that we could well have instability and pressures toward general fluctuation even if there were no businessmen, and even if the planners made no mistakes whatever.

Let us take a very favorable case. Suppose the United States is governed by a politically omnipotent and economically omniscient planning board, possessed of every moral virtue. Assume that there is no failure of consumption to keep pace with consumers' goods output, that there are no monopolies, no pressure groups, no price rigidities, no inflation, no "hoarding," and, to give a perfectly clear field, no need of foreign trade or foreign investment. But suppose further that such an economy is confronted with the same problem with which we have been confronted since the war: a large, newly released labor force, considerable deferred demand, a huge potential rise in the output of consumers' goods. Does not the way seem open, then, for peaceful and uninterrupted expansion? Unfortunately, one further question remains: How fast shall consumers' demand be satisfied?

It can be shown that even in such an ideal state it will be impossible to increase the output of consumers' goods rapidly without distorting the structure of industry, "overbuilding" the durable goods industries, and eventually entailing waste or unemployment. Take housing as an example. Suppose that the population is increasing fairly evenly. The chances would be that about the same number of additional houses would be needed every year. If we wanted a really stable housing industry, we should have to gear it to this steady demand, and fluctuations in either direction would be most undesirable. Say that the normal output for a given general situation, and distribution of wealth, would be ten thousand units per year. But now suppose that for four or five years—during, say, a war—no houses are built, and a "backlog" of accumulated demand piles up. In our example, this comes to about fifty thousand houses. Can the planning board, using careful advance planning alone, satisfy this backlog promptly—and still stabilize the private industry? Unfortunately it cannot. The task is impossible—no matter what the form of government.

Suppose we decide to satisfy this housing demand right away. Thousands of young architects, foremen, and skilled workers are trained. A huge increase in plant is undertaken. The industry suddenly raises its capacity from ten thousand units a year to fifty thousand units. The "backlog" is satisfied. But then will come the tragedy: We shall not want fifty thousand new houses every year. We only want fifty thousand houses now. Once the "backlog" is satisfied, demand drops to the old level of ten thousand, and about four-fifths of the men whom we have induced to go into the housing business are out of jobs. Yet there has been no "overproduction." Not one house "too many" has been built. It is simply that (from the point of view of stability) we have built them "too fast." The planners face an insoluble conflict between giving people what they want when they want it, and stabilizing the industry.

The case would not be quite so bad if other industries could be relied upon to take over when the housing industry slacked off. In fact, however, there are likely to be not one but many shortages, so that a good many durable goods industries will be expanding at the same time. The result of this simultaneous expansion will be such a tremendous (but temporary) rise in the demand for steel, coal, iron, and other construction materials that the economy will be well-nigh hopelessly distorted. Sudden appearance of a new industry capable of absorbing all the resources left idle by the satisfaction of the backlog right away would be quite unlikely.

The final complication, under capitalism, is furnished by deflation. Many people believe that, if only a little time is allowed, sufficient new industries and new wants will be forthcoming. The community will become adjusted to its new level of wealth and can begin upon a renewed expansion. There is a good deal of evidence to support this view. But unless some measures are taken to prevent demand from falling too far, during the interval of adjustment, depression will not be confined to the single industry or group in which it began. Far from it. A general drop in income ensues which spreads rapidly, though with varying severity, over the whole economy. Before adjustment has a chance to take place, the community may be plunged into prolonged and unnecessary depression. Businessmen will be afraid to start the new projects which might otherwise have been shortly begun. Instead inventions will be postponed to the beginning of the new boom, and, by swelling the size of the new backlog, will only serve to make the next boom worse.

We have already implied that the planners, by holding off the market certain government welfare projects and beginning work upon them when a serious drop in income was threatened, could keep deflation within bounds, and make possible a more even spacing of inventions. But much the same sort of thing can be done in capitalism. Furthermore the planners, if they really try to meet the liberal values, cannot avoid the basic distortion upon which disturbance is founded.

The account given in these pages is of course much simplified. Those who wish to find the problem presented in full complexity are referred to the writer's *Economics of Disturbance*. Suffice it to say that, applying our analysis to society as a whole, the reader will find no solution to the problem consistent with perfect stability which does not involve waste and "excess" capacity, or else denial of consumers, or else sabotage of various commodities and techniques. Capitalism is unstable today after the war precisely because, working through the profit motive, it still tries to give the consumer all the things he wants when he wants them. But the same would be true of a socialism with similar values. Omnipotent, omniscient planning eliminates many subordinate difficulties; but a basic dilemma remains.

So far we have used wartime shortages as an example. Suppose, instead, that a radically new type of house is invented which is so desirable and so economical that everyone rushes to buy it. We shall immediately have the same backlog problem. The same rush to build a large number of new-type houses will be followed by the same relapse to long-run demand and the same risk of eventual slump. Unless the planners are prepared to "kill off," or "hold back," new inventions through comprehensive licensing and planning, they will find all their problems recurring. For the evidence is overwhelming that, even without deflation, major inventions do not come in a steady stream.

Comprehensive planning is often advocated as a means of arriving at some given plane of abundance where controls may be relaxed. But in fact, as long as we allow the inventors to function, there can be no end to the process of control. Introduction of a highly desired new product will be likely to re-create immediately all the former difficulties, and reinaugurate the necessity for all sorts of rationing and restrictions. Mere anticipatory direction, however complete, can never reconcile the conflicting virtues of progress and stability.

Let us put this postwar, post-invention problem in more concrete terms. During the war we accumulated a mass of unfilled wants. How numerous those wants are may be disputable; but that they are acutely felt cannot be denied. Also, returning from the war and released by war industry, are great numbers of young men eager to establish themselves. Yet it is said we cannot allow business to expand too fast because, if we do, "there will be a slump."

What does this "eventual slump" argument lead to? It is doubtful if most of those who use it have any idea of what is really implied. It means more than an understandable protest against letting expansion turn into runaway inflation. It means that, if we insist on "planning" for perfect stability, we shall have to refuse to satisfy the consumer's wants even though rapid expansion might soon be possible, and it means that we shall have to prevent the absorption of young men into private industry even though jobs are present. Instead a mass of unemployed will have to be supported on public works; rationing will have to be continued; and industry will be permitted to expand only bit by bit, over a period of maybe fifteen or sixteen years, in the hope of obtaining an eventual stability. Moreover, even should such stability be attained (and the complications of the problem are tremendous), it could be preserved only by the most drastic sabotage and retardation of new invention and investment. The fact is that under these circumstances any politically possible rate of industrial expansion will inevitably lead to some "overexpansion." But this would be no truer of capitalism than of a socialist society attempting to solve the same problems. The essential conflict is not socialism versus capitalism but rationing versus speed.

The conclusion which our analysis yields is a mixed one, so far as the performance of the competitive capitalist order is concerned. It may be said in essence that the system is "bad" because it is "good," and "good" because it is "bad." From the scientific discoveries and expansions which are our pride come the insecurities which are our curse. The system, in the very act of rapid growth, almost inevitably distorts itself, and it is doubtful if there is any perfect solution for this problem. Certainly, if we want even a tolerable general level of security we cannot expect always to be able to let "nature take its course." But, on the other hand, is the solution a complete general regimentation of all social life? Two general lines of approach are indicated. The first is the policy of "filling in" already spoken of. This has been so egregiously overpraised and oversimplified in recent years that it is deservedly suspect. Furthermore it can never give the perfect stability and repose for which so many of us yearn. The other policy is rationing and sabotage: "Slow down" invention; "We have had enough progress anyhow"; and so on.

Those who concentrate upon the mere mechanical problem of obtaining stability are apt to favor the second policy and wish to "slow down" invention. Indeed, if there were no urges toward security sabotage (analyzed in Chapter II) and if we overlooked the effects upon democracy (Chapter V), there could be no doubt that the "slow down" policy was the right one. But if we believe in technical progress, and in democracy, no such solution is possible. The far more difficult and dangerous policy of offsets is the only one consistent with our values. The movement to "plan" growth and change is, in many of its forms, no more than a movement to end them. If we cannot overcome the blind urge for security, and if we cannot at the same time find some method of easing pressures toward restriction by keeping disturbance within bounds, future historians may well write the epitaph of our civilization as follows:

From freedom and science came rapid growth and change.
From rapid growth and change came insecurity.
From insecurity came demands which ended growth and change.
Ending growth and change ended science and freedom.

Some psychologists have said that it is harder to dissociate ideas than to associate them. Many readers of the summary just given will immediately reduce it to an antithesis between planning, socialism, restriction, and stagnation on the one side, and competition, conservatism, capitalism, and progress on the other. No such simple dichotomy is possible. In studying the barriers to a genuine democratic progress we shall find, paradoxical as it may sound, almost as many anticapitalist and restrictive ideas among certain "capitalist" groups as among certain radicals. It is time, therefore, to give more specific definition to our economic goal, and then to discuss in terms of facts, rather than labels, the obstacles to its realization.

· VII ·

Economic Goals and the Distribution of Wealth

IN OUTLINING AN economic goal for democracy the sincere ad-
herent of democratic values soon discovers a basic dilemma. The
competitive order is one of the major economic bases of political
democracy. Yet, left to itself, it seems to produce spontaneously
a pattern of income distribution grossly different from that which
our democratic preconceptions would lead us to expect. Since
economic peace is the acceptance of a given scheme of distribution,
and since widespread questioning of the basic distributory habits of
a society is an almost inevitable precursor of general revolution, it
follows that we shall have to examine this paradox of economic
inequality in an "equal" society, and see what arguments can be
made for and against it.

Attacks upon existing methods of wealth and income distribution cover an immense range of points of view. Some simply
object to the fact of inequality, or to "so much" inequality, on
political or moral grounds alone. Others purport to show by
"pure" mathematics that the world would be happiest if all incomes were equal. A third group reserves its criticism for special
kinds of income such as "rent," or interest, or profits. Another
voices a protest against "functionless" property and the "acquisitive society." Less lofty arguments center around the technical
problem of economic stability. Thus it may be said that we have
business cycles because the rich invest too much, or that we have
unemployment because they invest too little. Finally there is the
doctrine of "increasing misery." We must "end the system," it is
said, because the "rich are getting richer and the poor poorer."

We have already examined in detail the basic political and
philosophical arguments against the competitive market. Now we

must discuss more specific criticisms of various types of incomes actually found in the present distribution of wealth. As in the case of basic theory, Tawney's *Acquisitive Society* again represents the most persuasive and eloquent attack; and we will once more use it as our point of departure.

In so far as Tawney merely argues that the possession of wealth should not in itself be a sufficient proof of the worth of the possessor, or the desirability of the particular wealth-getting activity involved, he says no more than has been said by almost every leading economist for generations. It is now some hundred and twenty years since Ricardo began his attacks upon what economists call "rent"—in the special sense of the unearned incomes of the great English landlords of his time. The concept has been broadened almost in each decade. But there are several factors to be remembered: first, difficulties of administration; second, the fact that rights to draw socially "unearned" income may have been paid for from income earned in a socially desirable way; and finally, and most important, the fact that it is precisely the *dynamic* incomes, the incomes resulting from and associated with inventive-creation, which are most difficult to rationalize by criteria which insist that everything must have a plausible label.

The static frame of reference within which Tawney's proposals are drawn up is easily shown. For example, he writes, "Though a coal mine is a speculative investment, coal mining is not"—as if there were no such thing as oil. Or again he ridicules the idea that "ships will not go to and fro unless ship-owners can earn fifty per cent upon their capital."

This last statement brings out a crucial problem and leads to the examination of certain special kinds of income often attacked, notably interest and profits. Today we hear a great deal about "reasonable" profit. The implication usually is that all profits should conform to some average figure—for example, 5 or 10 per cent. Such an idea is too facile. Every responsible person believes in reasonable profit—but what is "reasonable"? The consideration usually forgotten is that reasonableness is relative to risk, and that risk is frequently proportional to novelty. Ships of a sort would undoubtedly go to and fro at less than 50 per cent profit, and indeed (temporarily at least) for no profit at all. But this does not mean that a man will fight all the pressures of vested interests (bureaucratic, and trade union, as well as capitalist), and even sometimes of social obloquy, involved in putting over the *new* idea—merely for the sake of a reward designed to keep the average at work.

Modern theories of monopolistic competition indicate strongly that the apparently "unreasonable" rates of return are more often associated with rapidly developing new business, and changing technique than with "entrenched monopoly." Indeed the whole concept of reasonable profit, in the sense in which we are discussing it, is derived from public utility (monopoly) regulation. In return for substantial freedom from competition, the right to earn a reasonable figure (but no more) is conceded. However, in the theory of the competitive economy one may well find three groups: "new" firms or techniques earning high profits; middle-aged ones earning "reasonable" profits, and older ones making no profit at all. This theory, like all theories, is never realized in perfection; but the reality of economic life comes much nearer to it than many opponents of the system are willing to admit. If, in the name of redistribution, we cut off all high rates of return indiscriminately, we may find ourselves cutting off the very sector of risky novel investment through which the economy makes its major growth.

In a profound little book, *The Theory of Economic Development*—unfortunately almost unknown to the general public—Professor Schumpeter makes the vital distinction between the businessman in the sense of "captain of industry" or "promoter" or "entrepreneur" on the one hand and the businessman as mere manager on the other. The distinction is not one of authority or legal right. The president of a large but static firm is, in Schumpeter's language, a mere manager; whereas the moving spirit of the rapidly growing new concern may be an "entrepreneur" or "promoter" though he be nominally only the fifth vice president. The difference lies in the degree of imagination and energy called for, and in the novelty of the line of conduct followed. It is noteworthy that, though Tawney frequently mentions the functions of the manager, he nowhere recognizes the special problems of the entrepreneur. It may be, as he puts it, a "robust *non sequitur*" to say that the constructive energy of the "manager" would be lost if private property were further "attenuated"; but it is not a robust *non sequitur*, or even a *non sequitur* at all, to say that the energy of the innovator would lack adequate constructive expression if the competitive system were further attenuated.

As it is with profit, so it is with interest. So long as the growth of the economy is not unduly handicapped, there are likely on average to be more would-be borrowers than lenders; and those who have money to lend may command a price for it. Under such circumstances, saving—the "provision of capital"—is, as even Tawney concedes, a useful social function. But if the process of saving, investment, and resulting growth is successful, and if the national income rises, there inevitably will come to be certain individuals who can live "on their income." This does not in practice, however, mean that the proportion of "idle" to "workers" will indefinitely increase, for, as we saw in discussing ideals of progress, the "minimum" thought "necessary" to retirement is also increasing. Nor does it mean that production is retarded— quite the contrary; and it is hard to see why we should destroy a useful institution simply because it is so successful! Of course if we cut off incentives for investment, and if we give such authority to a multitude of vested interests—both "conservative" and "radical"—that growth can no longer take place, and long-range stagnation ensues—then interest becomes a "rent," a "survival," a "tribute"; and any other hard names may be applied that chance to be available. But, before the epithets begin to fly too fast, should we not ask ourselves why it is that saving is no longer "desirable"?

As one considers matters such as these the conclusion is increasingly brought home that the chief *prima facie* objection to the competitive system of distribution is the bald fact of inequality itself. To this may be added the conviction of many that the mechanical instabilities of the system are somehow linked up with the distribution of wealth. We shall therefore consider inequality *per se* and follow with an examination of its relationship to economic cycles and unemployment.

Economic inequality cannot be evaluated without reference to some moral standard. Those economists who have attempted to prove by "purely scientific" mathematics that the total of "satisfaction" would be "maximized" by equal distribution—in effect, that the rich get less "satisfaction" from their money than the poor— have been forced to surround their argument with so many concessions as to make it virtually meaningless. The basic assumption needed is that all men have similar desires and capacities for enjoyment. But this assumption is not self-evident, and the fact that most people's wants change and increase with increases in income cannot be brushed aside. As Mr. Tawney observes, "There can be no finality in the mere addition of increments of income any more than the gratification of any other desire for material goods." We may and do say that, from the point of view of ethical value judgments, certain "needs" are more "important" than others; but already we shall have left mathematics far behind.

The basic objection to inequality of income and wealth lies in its apparently self-perpetuating character. Even granted that men are inherently very unequal in aptitude, and hence that inequality between individuals is unavoidable, there still remains a problem. For it will be asked: "How can we possibly talk of 'equality of opportunity' when the mere fact of having well-to-do parents gives a man such great advantages of medical care, of nourishment, of social and business contacts and even (sometimes) of manners?"

The answer to this question cannot be made in a simple yes or no. It is not sufficient to ask, "Do you believe in economic inequality?" One must also specify what type of economic inequality in what type of society is involved. Certainly the existence of any economic inequality among parents inevitably involves some opportunity for privilege among the children. We shall return to this problem shortly. But before we decide whether the evil is overwhelming, and whether the disadvantages of wealth may not also be considerable, we have to know more about the social environment involved. Inequality in the sense of feudal privilege transmitted automatically, without regard to the abilities of either father or son, is one thing. Inequality as an incentive in a competitive framework is quite another. The writer would not lift a finger for a capitalism of the vested interest; but the capitalism of creative competition may validly command loyalty.

Yet even competition or lack of competition does not tell us enough for a final verdict. We must also know something of the social attitudes and customs which are at stake. In this connection American thinkers should remember that much European social criticism, or social criticisms by Europeans, is aimed less at capitalism as we know it than at peculiarities of European or English social structure. For example when Tawney writes, "What is prized most is not riches obtained in return for labor, but riches the economic origin of which, *being regarded as sordid*, is concealed," or "So wealth becomes the foundation of public esteem, and the mass of men who labor, but who do not acquire wealth, are thought to be vulgar and meaningless and insignificant," he is protesting against an English point of view more than an American. The survival of feudal titles and social distinctions in England may appear immaterial when combined with the fact of political democracy. But such relics are (or, at least, were) far more important than might be thought. Existence of the panoply of feudalism tends to make the parvenu industrialist ashamed of the legitimate achievements "in trade" which are the real and valid sanction for his position, and encourages him to masquerade as an hereditary idler as quickly as possible. The attitude implies both an undue contempt for legitimate work and an undue reverence for the mere fact of wealth once it is achieved. The tradition, and to some extent the fact, of a special body of hereditary privilege attainable only by birth is kept alive; and the many who take such pretensions at face value are proportionately embittered. In America, however, it is not the man who works that is looked down upon so much as the man who does not work. Nor is hereditary idleness respected. A few people may read seriously the pitiful vulgarity of our social columns and our "exclusive" resorts; but the economic origin of most wealthy families in this country is too recent and too well known to convince any man of sense—barring the eternal blot of the race question—that there are any social or economic doors from which he need feel himself inevitably barred.

The question of social attitudes toward the new rich is fundamental, and brings to light a serious paradox. On the one hand, the existence of a class of newly wealthy should be viewed as one of the principal achievements of democracy. On the other hand, it is a prime requirement for democratic progress that a blanket indorsement shall not be given to the vulgarian. Here again true democracy depends upon a balance of qualities. The proper democratic attitude toward the successful parvenu should be censorship for sharp dealing, ridicule for grossness—and respect for legitimate achievement.

The modern intellectual finds it difficult to maintain this attitude. He has trouble in disentangling a dislike of certain people who are rich, or of certain ways of getting rich, from opposition to the existence of any wealthy at all. The truth is that the new-rich industrialist is not *prima facie* a very sympathetic type to the scholar trained in admiration of the Platonic philosopher-king. While it is a gratuitous insult to suppose that the man of plain origin must also be common, the insurgent intellectual even if of very simple antecedents has been educated to distrust money as such, and may be repelled by social crudities and lack of information. He concentrates his fire upon easy accusations of profiteering, and sharp dealing; and a justified dislike of bad qualities obscures his respect for the good.

But it is the contention of this book that literal attempts to inaugurate the reign of the philosopher-king are in practice the inevitable forerunners of the torturer and the book burner; whereas the appearance of the new-rich industrialist has been in practice the forerunner of the growth of freedom of thought and a rising trend of living standards for the masses. Did not Hitler claim to be following Platonic ideas! We must beware of treating a philosophic parable as a literal blueprint. The methods by which the new-rich industrialist has achieved his fortune may not be quite those which the Academy would commend. But are they not on balance often better than many which have been invoked in hierarchic despotism? Is the court favorite making his way by intrigue, poison, and prostitution an admirable figure? Is the catamite of a philosopher exactly the type of person we wish to encourage?

The clue to democratic progress, we may again repeat, is found in an adequate public criticism of all citizens, so as to induce a higher code of wealth-getting. The prime obstacle to such criticism is not social structure, but our modern distrust of all value standards. The basic problem is philosophic rather than social. But let us not be too despairing of our own country. The horrors of the General Grant period of the 1870's must not be forgotten. But there is deeply embedded in the American mind an eminently sound respect for legitimate achievement plus a healthy skepticism toward the mere possession of wealth. And we are certainly the last people in the world to be accused of despising the fact of work.

Reflections such as these have led Tawney in his book *Equality* to draw a significant and very valuable distinction between mere economic leveling and the true democratic goal: the reduction of snobbishness, as distinguished from insistence upon values. He writes: "A community marked by a low degree of economic differentiation may yet possess a class system . . . rigidly defined . . . it may be marked by a high degree of economic differentiation and yet appear . . . comparatively classless." Bearing in mind, then, that our aim will be to establish a fluid, relatively classless society in a competitive framework and to obtain the maximum equality of opportunity consistent with economic freedom, we may proceed to a discussion of the advantages and disadvantages of inequality *per se*.

The first decision we have to make in dealing with economic inequality is whether our goal is to be a "fair" start, or an "equal" start. If we say that our goal is a literally equal start, we are plunged into a mass of difficulties. In the first place, what is an equal start? Unless "equal" be taken to mean "identical," we shall find it impossible to give the concept any very accurate definition. Certainly the degree of equality or inequality of opportunity cannot be measured by a mere comparison of the incomes of the parents. To give an obvious example, will the fact that a boy is likely to inherit wealth really give a "better" start to the spoiled son of a diseased and dissipated father? Even if parents are equally healthy and intelligent, the advantages of the wealthy boy over the poor one are not necessarily so great as they may seem—if only because of the fact observed by Thurman Arnold that "the individual for whom all struggle and conflict has been carefully ironed out generally develops into a jellyfish."

The next objection to the ideal of literal equality is that it is virtually impossible of attainment—impossible, that is, without the destruction of the family. For a literally equal economic start demands, we have already seen, literal equality of position among parents. But this is impossible. Furthermore inequalities of power or strategic position may be transmitted as well as inequalities of wealth. To give a very mild example, the names Roosevelt and Taft have a certain political value quite independent of monetary inheritance, and difficult to "redistribute" by law. In more despotic societies very important and genuine privilege may be transmitted. And since abolishing inequality of wealth does not abolish inequality of power, and may even increase it, a literally equal start is forever unobtainable as long as parents can identify their children.

We might perhaps adopt Plato's suggestion and raise all our children in identical state orphanages. But again, so long as the children's parentage is known, fathers appear to have some tendency to favor their sons and the children of the "guardians" would in practice tend to receive special treatment. We might carry the argument one step further and remove all traces of family identification. But in that case how are we to prevent degenerative incest? Though the evils of incest may have been overstated at times, still I doubt whether anyone would advocate the removal of all barriers in this connection. However unwelcome and unsavory such reflections may seem, they cannot be avoided, and force us to the adoption of an ideal of a "fair" rather than an equal start. The problem becomes not a choice between absolute equality and inequality but determinations of the degree of (economic) inequality we think tolerable.

The ideal of a fair start has two aspects. First, it is necessary for the state to intervene in the case of the poor and provide such services of health, housing, and education as the community believes necessary to prevent individuals from being unduly handicapped. Next, the people must see to it that cumulative advantages of birth are not allowed to pile up indefinitely. These two standards will scarcely be disputed by any sincere American; but in agreeing upon them we have no more than begun our problem. Who is to bear the burden of the public expenditures? How far need we, or should we, penalize by law the accumulation of wealth? What are some of the disadvantages as well as advantages of an extreme redistributive policy?

Facts regarding the distribution of wealth in our society can easily be stated. The distribution of income is highly concentrated; the distribution of property, still more so. But though, at any given time, property and income are highly concentrated the turnover of individual possessors is very great. The upper (and lower) income brackets of a competitive capitalist society have been compared to hotels, which are indeed always full, but filled with different people. Furthermore, despite many allegations to the contrary, no trend toward "increasing misery" can be established. During the cycle there are swings of considerable importance in either direction; but the average pattern of wealth and income distribution appears to have been extraordinarily stable over the whole period of which we have knowledge. Yet the average national income per head has been rising, and it follows that, even if the relative share of the poor has not substantially changed, their absolute income has on average been constantly rising. In addition to this, as Professor Schumpeter shows, there has been an immense qualitative shift in favor of the poor. That is to say, technical progress has meant far less to the wealthy than to the masses; for, given enough wealth and command over labor, the very rich have always been able to obtain luxury.

It might be asked why, if this is the case, so many people are convinced that the "poor" are "getting poorer." The answer is twofold. First, there is the habit of thinking in terms of absolutes rather than proportions. Because there are some enormous fortunes, many people tend to forget the rest of the distribution. The second reason is an important change in the character of property as distinguished from its distribution. An older middle class of owners has been largely supplanted by a newer group of salaried men. It is true that the vice president of some modern corporation may have as large a (relative) income as the owner of a farm or small factory had a hundred years ago. But it may be that the vice president does not have so strong a sense of possession or achievement. In the same way the vice president may hold shares of stock relatively equal in value with the property of the small industrialist of his great-grandfather's time; but the same feeling of security and permanence is not involved. Yet the distribution is the same, nor need the process even imply, as we shall see in a chaper on monopoly, any necessary diminution of the "purity" of competition.

It is important also to remember that, though the modern type of property and position may be less satisfying, it is in a sense more democratic. For modern capitalist wealth is far more easily competed away than the claims upon rich land, or the strategic industrial positions, of a static economy. Tawney writes: "For talent and energy can create opportunity. But property need only wait for it." This, however, is better as rhetoric than as sociology. True, the possession of property does help one to wait. But wise investment is not an automatic process. There is no claim on wealth in our society which can be left to take care of itself. Even government bonds may be confiscated by inflation. Corporate trusteeships appear to be a way out for the incompetent; but those who remember the experiences of 1929 will know how disappointing they can be. In short there is no brand of privilege more vulnerable, or less likely to survive the loss of energy and intelligence beyond a generation or so, than capitalist financial wealth. It is peculiarly open to attack, and in a dynamic economy its base is constantly being nibbled away. This is the most potent method of redistribution.

The background we have sketched enables us to evaluate far more justly the head-on collision which at first appears between the institution of the family and the ideals of democracy. For the institution of the family, with its emphasis upon creative parental love, leads to a desire to work to give one's children a "better start"—both in the sense of bequeathing them a "good name" and in that of providing them special economic advantages. If there were no forces automatically operating as a brake upon accumulations resulting from this motive, the results would eventually be an intolerable degree of intrenched privilege. But a dynamic competitive system constantly tends to undermine any given large fortune, and to redistribute inherited wealth. Even though the rise of new fortunes keeps the shape of the distribution curve unchanged, the same families no longer hold undisputed position. And if we supplement the erosive effects of competition upon wealth by state expenditures designed to give an adequate start to the less privileged it is most unlikely that any family will enjoy "unearned" wealth indefinitely. "Three generations from shirt sleeves to shirt sleeves." True, our policy will never give absolute equality—but absolute equality is unobtainable anyhow. And the family motive in a competitive democratic environment is both humane and useful. It is, at worst, a more unselfish form of selfishness than the mere desire for personal fame.

We reach therefore a final question: How should the funds be raised to meet state expenditures needed to give the less privileged an adequate opportunity? In much radical literature the problem is viewed simply as one of diverting resources which would otherwise be "wasted" by the rich into helping the poor. Champagne money, let us say, would be converted into milk funds. Unfortunately the problem is not so simple as that. As has been shown by Professors Hicks and Hart and many others, the resources actually used by the rich in "conspicuous consumption" are a mere drop in the bucket compared with the wants of the poor. For example, if in 1941 we had decided that no one should have an income over $5,000 a year, and had reduced all incomes to that limit, we should have reduced total consumption by only 5 per cent. That is to say, we should have had available for distribution among the 78 per cent of all American families who had incomes below $5,000 only 5 per cent of extra consumption. "Equalizing" wealth distribution, in our society, does not reduce consumption greatly. What it does is to reduce saving. And the amount which could be taken without making the economy run backward amounts on average to only about 10 per cent of the gross national product!

Many people will ask: "What harm is there in reducing saving? We can't invest all our savings today anyhow." Quite possibly so. But, as earlier pointed out, it is not enough to say that "savings" are in fact "going to waste." The real question is, "Why?" The answer requires a consideration of many forces, and in listing them we are brought up against one of the most profound and little realized paradoxes of a redistributive program: *The redistribution of income and wealth is not the same thing as the redistribution of opportunity.* A high progressive tax on large incomes may not increase either the opportunities or the well-being of the remainder of society. Worse yet, it may even decrease the well-being and opportunities of the remainder of society.

One is apt to visualize a process of wealth and income redistribution as taking money from rich people and giving it to poor people. But this is true only in a very sophisticated sense. Money yielded by high progressive taxation does not go directly to the poor—it goes to the government. It does not directly build up the poor—it builds up the government. The poor do not get purchasing power which they can spend in any way they wish, so often as government services which they may not want; and they do not get the full benefit of the taxes but the taxes minus deductions (and possible wastage) for government service. It may be said, and often truly, that it is better to give "the poor" free maternity clinics, let us say, and education than to give them money to spend "on liquor." But there is an authoritarian element in such a program which, if we are not careful, can easily be a source of real oppression. Here too we find a conflict of standards between helping people in spite of themselves and giving them democratic freedom of choice.

An adequate approach to equality of opportunity undoubtedly requires great government outlay. "If every individual were reared in conditions as favorable to health as science can make them," writes Tawney, "received an equally thorough and stimulating education up to sixteen, and knew on reaching manhood that, given a reasonable measure of hard work and good fortune, he and his family could face the risks of life without being crushed by them, the most shocking of existing inequalities would be on the way to disappear." Patently such a goal implies large-scale government action. But government action is not restricted to such fields, and it is time that we began to evaluate more fully the immense possible amount of nonpecuniary privilege and resource consumption which can be made available to those in control. Nor can we evaluate educational equality, for example, by such easy measures as outlay per pupil. The chief advantage of the private schools is not money but the fact that they have been less corrupted by the equalitarian and other trends sketched in Chapter VI.

Liberals, particularly in this country, have advocated high progressive income taxes with the largely unconscious, or unexpressed, mental assumption that that is the way to get a nation of many middle-sized independent businesses and many middle-class independent people. But this assumption does not automatically fulfill itself. We may well get instead a nation whose economic life is carried on by the state, or by a few corporations owned or controlled by the state; and a population not of independent middle-class owners, but dependent clerks and government employees. The flow of money into government hands, and hence the power of the state, is directly increased without our being at all sure that any reciprocal, or proportionately reciprocal, benefits will be forthcoming to the individual.

Mention of such possibilities leads to the second aspect of the problem—the fact that high progressive taxes may actually reduce the opportunities of the individual. Our argument in this book has been that any measure which disproportionately hampers the rise on independent terms of the new man and the new enterprise strikes directly at the democracy and the technological creativeness of our society. Yet it can easily be shown that income taxation, even at a uniform proportion, may well favor the man who is already rich at the expense of the man who is trying to better his economic status, the established old firm at the expense of the enterprising new one. The addition of high progressive rates, under usual tax laws, makes things even worse, and the result is frequently a policy for those "already there"—a policy which helps monopoly and increases social stratification.

Most people, when they think at all about the reasoning behind high progressive income taxes, suppose that if a man is making a large income he must have a large fortune. From this it is an easy step to the notion that imposing a heavy income tax will redistribute a large fortune. Neither idea is correct. The size of a man's income in any given year may have very little relationship to the amount of capital he has managed to accumulate, while even very heavy income taxation does not *per se* redistribute capital.

A firm which has already accumulated enough capital can afford to pay more than half of its income in taxes. Not so the firm with little capital which is endeavoring to retain funds for expansion. And in a dynamic capitalism the income of active, and relatively small, new businesses may be nearly as large, in absolute terms, and hence taxed at nearly as high a rate, as the income of older static firms. In the same way the beneficiary of a trust fund can well afford to pay three-fourths of his income in taxes. There may be "plenty"—as one often hears—left for him. But if he, or his trustee, invests wisely, his income comes in, year in and year out. Not so that of the active business or professional man. Furthermore, inheritance and estate taxes, granted ordinary care in drawing of wills and preparation of trusts, may take a century to level down a large fortune, barring the effects of competition—a force which redistributive taxation itself discourages. But very few new fortunes can be made. Our tax laws thus accomplish the distinguished result of making things easier for the second generation beneficiary than for the active founder—easier for the descendant than for the ancestor.

When we begin to study the effects of high progressive income taxes the problem becomes even worse. We have said that high progressive income taxes usually discourage competition. This apparently paradoxical statement can be easily explained. It must be remembered that our income-tax laws have been for the most part drawn up and enacted by people on steady salaries for the benefit of people on steady salaries. Very little effective notice has been taken of the difficulties of the active business—especially the active new business—the income of which may be constantly fluctuating.

In the first place, no adequate deductions are permitted for losses. If a man makes money, he pays a high tax on it. If he loses it, that is largely his affair. It is a "Heads I win, tails you lose" policy. Again income taxes have been for the most part figured on the income for each year, standing alone, and, save recently in special instances, little or no account has been taken of losses in previous years. But when income is averaged over a period of years it may be found that there has been no net income at all. In some recorded cases the income tax has amounted to over 400 per cent of actual income. In other words a high tax has been paid on the income of a single year. But during the preceding and ensuing years the business made losses. And over say a five-year period the tax paid to the government in the one good year has amounted to over four times the net income earned for the whole period.

Losses aside, a high progressive tax may impose an unfair burden when considered over several years. Suppose a man has inherited a small fortune and invested it in government bonds. His steady income thereafter might be say $5,000 a year. Suppose another individual is an active and self-made businessman struggling to establish a new concern. His business brings him in $10,000 in some years and little or nothing in others. Suppose that it also averages $5,000 a year. But say incomes at $5,000 are taxed at 5 per cent and incomes at $10,000 at 10 per cent. The man with a steady income will pay $250 a year right along. But the man who makes a $10,000 income, every other year, will pay $1,000 in each good year, and even though he pays no income in his bad years his income tax will nevertheless average $500 a year—twice that of the coupon clipper—though their actual average income is exactly the same.

When we remember that it is precisely the vigorous new business—the business which gives the new opportunity—which is most likely to have a fluctuating income, we see how the American income tax frequently works against the very people it is trying to help, and how it discourages competition. Furthermore the durable goods industries—the industries in which both cyclical and long-range unemployment are concentrated—have a highly fluctuating income. Thus our redistributive taxes also work against one of the very sections of industry we ought to be encouraging. And finally there are a number of professions—for example, architecture, engineering, and authorship—which have very unstable incomes, and they too are unfairly penalized. Had the American people deliberately set out to impose the maximum burden on opportunity, activity, and democracy, they could scarcely have done a better job.

The conclusion to which our analysis leads is that our income-tax laws should be amended to allow more generous deductions for losses, and that carry-over provisions should be inserted enabling businesses and individuals to average their incomes over several years. One authoritative study concludes that a carry-over period of at least five years is needed to give risky new business, or fluctuating business, and professions an adequate chance. Even, however, if we make the adjustments named, and even if we return to the idea of a flat proportion rather than a progressive income tax, it must still be remembered that a tax calculated on incomes alone burdens unduly the *new* man—the man who is trying to accumulate a fortune as opposed to the man who already has one. It follows that, to give a more adequate equalization of opportunity, we must also explore the possibility of setting rates which will take into account the resources as well as the incomes of firms and individuals. In the case of the individual the earned income credit, now abolished, was a step—though a most inadequate step —in the right direction. In the case of two corporations with equal income, the one with the smaller invested capital might be taxed at the lower rate. In that way the two concerns would be put more nearly on an equality as far as ability to expand is concerned. Merely to state the problem, however, shows its administrative difficulty, and it is doubtful if any perfectly satisfactory solution is possible.

One further question remains to be answered. Suppose that someone is ingenious enough to work out a way by which the effective burden of the income tax can be equalized between the old and the new firm, and the established and the new man. Should we then be justified in making our rates so heavy as to flatten out tremendously the distribution of wealth and income and set an absolute limit upon accumulation? How much inequality are we going to admit, anyhow? The answer compels an examination of the absolute price of business enterprise.

Fashionable modern doctrine would have it that businessmen work chiefly for fun and prestige. They are said to bring home a profit as a hunter brings home a duck, and the chance of bagging even a very small one is thought to be sufficient to get them out on the windiest day. Thus it is frequently maintained that, if adequate tax deductions and so forth are permitted, the businessman will do "just as good" work if limited to a net possible gain of only 1 or 2 per cent. In the same way some quite responsible and relatively conservative writers have suggested that inheritance taxes should be made so drastic that only enough money to take care of the bare "necessities" of life would be permitted to pass to the heirs. These extreme measures, furthermore, are advocated not simply on the ground of democracy or morality, but on the ground that such rigorous taxation will "make no difference," even under capitalism, and that we do not need to permit large incomes or large fortunes in order to get sufficient investment.

The importance of the creative and prestige features is not to be denied. But there are other motives also. The businessman does not merely have a choice between profit and loss. He has a choice between activity and leisure. In some cases a man may work harder to overcome the effects of a high profit and income tax; in others, not. The greater the extent to which leisure and cultivated hobbies are preferred, the more likely the tax is to discourage activity. To put the argument at lowest terms, there would seem, at least, to be a margin of possible productive action concerning which income- and inheritance-tax laws, by making it more difficult to accumulate and transmit an estate, cast the balance in favor of leisure.

A writer, let us say, might write one book for fun, two books for support, three books for the sake of his children. Confronted with a contract for a fourth book, 90 per cent of the proceeds of which would be taken by the government, he might prefer to go fishing. In the same way a businessman might make one venture for fun, two for support, and so on. In the hunting example, it might well be asked if a professional hunter would bring in quite so many ducks if he knew that nine of every ten would be taken away. And the evidence overwhelmingly suggests that the "steadiest" capitalist motives have been as follows: The corporation still in the active expanding stage is more interested in retaining earnings to pay off debts and expand operations than in paying out dividends. The usual capitalist individual is more interested in the accumulation of a fortune than in the enjoyment of income. Furthermore, he is interested in the accumulation of a fortune largely to transmit it to his children.

We might perhaps, by appropriate modifications of income-tax law, give the new corporation a fairer chance to accumulate capital. But even here an absolute limit upon size would serve to discourage endeavor. And if we follow the trend of modern ideas and permit corporations to expand unequally while severely limiting personal income differences the problem remains of personal incentive, and we are too apt to forget that enterprises are initiated and corporations managed by people. No corporation ever did anything. The people in corporations do whatever it does. If they have no incentive to act as good corporate officers, the corporation has no incentive. So far as the professions go, there can be little question that the income tax has had serious effects on incentive. Why not the profession of being an executive?

We have here a fundamental issue which many people are unwilling to face: The opportunity both to obtain and to transmit important relative economic advantages has been one of the chief incentives in competitive democratic capitalism. Viewed from a standpoint of literal equalitarianism, such an incentive is, of course, "undemocratic." But by the same line of reasoning any desire to excel in any line of endeavor would be equally undemocratic. The modern liberal with his tendency to underestimate the importance of risk, and to overestimate the automatic nature of growth, fails to see the need for large prizes in the economic lottery; but if we expect the continuance of the creative growth which we have enjoyed in the past an adequate relative incentive both of income and of inheritance must remain. Whatever our predilections, simple honesty requires us to disentangle the idea that inequality of income and inheritance is immoral, from the idea that it is unnecessary in the competitive society. The real basis for income and inheritance taxation, in the minds of many people, is not the "economic" generalizations so loosely made today but ethical dislike of capitalist incentives. Such hostility may be valid, but it is not honest to present as reform what it is in fact, with the magnitude of the changes necessitated, revolution.

"Liberal" political and economic thought for fifty years has been increasingly impregnated with the idea that we can rip the prime motive power out of capitalism without impairing its power to function. During the past fifteen years the argument has been carried one step further, and it has been said that equalitarian taxation, by reducing saving, actually makes the system work better. Thus many writers today enthusiastically maintain that the only way to save "free enterprise" is to adopt a tax system which will deprive it of its main incentives—and, in its usual form, will encourage monopoly and reduce opportunity. A prime oversight in all such programs is the unconscious assumption that demand automatically satisfies itself. But this is far from true. We may undoubtedly increase demand by "soaking the rich"; but, as long as we rely on capitalist and competitive incentives, no increase in supply may be forthcoming; indeed, supply may actually be decreased. It is the government that will have to bridge the gap under these circumstances, and we are left with the choice between a gradual socialization of the economy and a complete breakdown.

In the light of this discussion we can much better evaluate the idea that "saving" is "excessive," or that it is the cause of our economic insecurity. So far as the business cycle goes, we have already seen that it cannot be attributed to the general distribution of wealth. It is true that during a slump redistribution could "increase demand" and (if it did not hamstring supply) might help a recovery. But, once recovery were under way, the need for saving and investment would again arise. What would be needed, then, in the case of the cycle, is not high saving nor low saving but variable saving, and a redistributive program does not take effect quickly enough to serve this purpose.

The idea that saving is at fault is more plausible in dealing with "long-range" unemployment. In such a state of affairs the economy even at the top of a boom (for example, in 1937) does not reach a satisfactory level of employment, and saving is *prima facie* excessive. But yet again we ask, "Why?" The answer lies in a multitude of restrictions placed upon the competitive economy by various forces, both conservative and radical. And though we shall see in the next few chapters that drastic and undiscriminating redistributive taxation is only one of many such forces, it is nevertheless a very important one. The argument that we must tax the well-to-do because there are no adequate "investment outlets" is thus in considerable degree a self-verifying one. For the taxes themselves will help to prevent investment from being made.

It follows, therefore, that if we genuinely wish to maintain the competitive order, with all that it implies in the way of democracy and opportunity, the funds needed to give the less privileged an adequate start should be raised by taxation more nearly proportional than progressive. Certainly the present American rates on sizable incomes and fortunes are absurd if we expect to continue to have large-scale risky private investment. Furthermore the funds actually yielded by such taxation are relatively small compared to the needs which it is expected to satisfy. Their effect in discouraging the growth of the national income is out of all proportion to their immediate return. It is not so much champagne money as beer money which must be diverted into milk funds. There simply is not enough champagne money to do the job.

We are now in a position to outline more concretely the economic goals appropriate to a society which wishes to give maximum encouragement to the creative spirit, maximum democracy of life, and maximum equality of opportunity consistent with democratic freedom. The program which such a society must follow falls into three heads: (1) adequate encouragement to competition and prevention of monopolies, whether radical or conservative; (2) a well planned stabilization program designed to keep the cycle within bounds; (3) state expenditure to give an adequate start to the underprivileged in health, housing, and education. So far there is little ground for opposition. But in addition to this the tax program must be adjusted to give a better chance to risky new ventures, as against established old ones, and to people attempting to accumulate some capital, as compared with those who already have it. Finally, if we want the dynamic risky new investment upon which so much depends in opportunity, competition, and continued technical change, we have to permit adequate incentives of inheritance and income. Equalitarian taxation in America today is working against its own aims rather than promoting them.

The problem, as we have found so often before, is one of undue emphasis upon a single aspect of democracy at the expense of all others. In a search for literal economic equality we destroy all the spontaneity and freedom of development which has underlain our achievements in the past. How much nearer equality are we if, in reducing inequality of wealth, we increase inequality of power? Why should we object to the passing on of an income of $10,000 or even $100,000 a year to descendants, if in the process the national income has been increased by millions annually? True, there are the offensive playboys of the Harry Thaw and Tommy Manville type. But the evidence is overwhelming that these are rare exceptions. The opponents of competitive distribution have to make up their minds which way they want it. They cannot say that we must have a drastic redistribution of wealth both because the rich are "wasters" and because they "save" too much.

The real decision turns on two questions: Can the national life be kept sufficiently competitive to maintain an adequate turnover in the possessors of wealth? Can we usefully employ the savings which our distribution of wealth makes possible? The capitalist distributory structure, unlike many other forms of power, automatically destroys itself if not allowed to be useful. Thus continued restriction produces continued unemployment, produces constant unrest. But is the world today really so rich that saving is not needed? Do we really no longer need growth? To answer these questions, we must study the forces which are choking off economic progress in modern democracy. They may be grouped under three heads: business monopoly, union sabotage, international restriction. When we have examined these three forces we shall be able to offer a more specific policy approach.

· VIII ·

The Problems of Competition

THE FIRST destructive force which we have listed is "business monopoly." But in order to understand this force we must have an idea of why it has arisen. Nothing could be easier than to prepare an apparently overwhelming case for economic competition by stating all its merits and omitting its defects. Yet if we only do that we shall not have accomplished a great deal. This book obviously expresses a point of view and is a plea for that point of view. But we are not interested merely in explaining a certain attitude. What equally concerns us is getting an idea of the problems which our point of view implies. We can do little more here than sketch an approach to the problem. Nevertheless, without some knowledge of the seamy side of competition we cannot hope either to defend the competitive order convincingly, or to understand its development, or to influence its future. An argument is not finally refuted unless it is refuted in its most plausible and persuasive form.

At present one constantly hears that "competition has failed," and that the world is becoming more "monopolistic." "Therefore," it is said, "we must have comprehensive state planning." But a great deal more needs to be asked before we can take such ideas at face value. What are the reasons for the present situation? Is it really as bad as we think? What is a monopoly, anyhow? Admittedly there is a serious industrial problem today. But are we sure that we are looking for it either in the right place, or with the right equipment?

The Federal Council of Churches of Christ has recently passed a resolution condemning "monopolies" of business and labor. The intention of such a measure would correspond closely with

104

the point of view of this book. But one wonders whether any of the delegates who voted for the resolution could have given even a tolerably clear idea of what a "monopoly" is. The truth is that "monopoly," like "socialism" or "inflation," has become a smear word capable of so many interpretations as to be virtually meaningless. If our thinking on the subject is to be anything more than a confused blur of disorderly prejudice, we have to adopt some clearer terminology.

One of the commonest mistakes in economics is confusing the history of economic thought with the history of the economic system—the changes in our attitudes toward a process with changes in the process itself. When modern society and modern economics were emerging from centuries of planned social life or feudal custom, the economists of the eighteenth century put their whole emphasis upon the virtues of "free" competition. And they defined "free" with reference to the freedom which most impressed them at that time—freedom from government control. Later writers carried praise of competition (or competitive praise) to absurd lengths, and it was often implied that free (meaning merely nongovernment) competition would automatically give us a near "Platonic" world in which almost the sole motive of industrial action would be the search for technological efficiency. If a man made a "better mousetrap" the world would beat its way to his door.

It has remained for modern thought to achieve an almost equal absurdity. Taking at face value the claims of the earlier writers for the competition of their times, many people today have discovered (naturally enough) that no such Utopian conditions now exist. Thereupon and without further ado, they jump to the idea that society has somehow declined from a supposed competitive golden age. Such reasoning is totally inconclusive. The mere fact that modern competition is not "pure" proves nothing in itself. A great part of competition never was pure, and, as we shall see, it is very unlikely that it ever could be.

Equally open to objection is the statement that lack of competition means that we must scrap capitalism. The real question is not whether the capitalist market fails to attain a mathematical ideal of "optimum" production, but whether a socialist government would come any nearer to doing so. Furthermore, even if we did achieve the mathematical optimum but created more despotisms in the process, the social gain would be, to say the least, questionable. Since, so far as economic theory goes, we have no way of judging relative administrative efficiency, mathematics alone can never dictate the choice between social systems.

Despite these facts a great part of the energy of economists for seventy years has gone into developing, with ever increasing refinement, concepts of competition which would justify the glowing optimism of earlier writers. And it is such super-refined concepts that many people are now trying to apply today to the problems of the real world. Yet even on its own terms it is not hard to show that the mathematical competitive ideal would never function adequately in any likely society.

Modern mathematical standards of competition outline a state of affairs in which the old-fashioned claims would be almost literally true. Every concern would be such a small part of an industry that it would, by itself, have no influence on prices. Prices therefore would be entirely set by the "impersonal laws of supply and demand." Since everyone had only a tiny fraction of the field, no one would find it worth while to do extensive advertising. And with advertising ruled out, together with price strategy, almost the only remaining concern of the businessman would be technical efficiency. Such an apparently idyllic state of affairs the economist calls "pure" competition. It is usually thought to have been approximated in the case of farm products before the Agricultural Adjustment Administration, and there are a few sections of industry which come near having similar conditions. But it does not take long to see that "pure" competition on these terms is not very common.

On the other hand, if "pure" competition is rare, "pure" monopoly would be even rarer. Indeed, under modern ideas it would be almost impossible. A pure monopoly would be a business with no competitors. But what sort of business? Under the National Industrial Recovery Act "industries" tried to organize themselves into "codes." Almost at once terrific snarls were encountered over what was an "industry." Are oil, gas, and coal one industry? They all produce heat. What about electric and gas refrigerators? Many concerns found themselves operating under eight or ten different codes at the same time. The truth is that much indiscriminate modern discussion of "monopoly" takes no adequate account of competition between products. Suppose John L. Lewis obtained entire control of every coal mine. Even then he would not have a complete monopoly, for, as is becoming more and more obvious, there are numerous substitutes for coal. Before 1941 the Aluminum Company of America had no competitors at all—in its aluminum business. But that does not mean that it did not have competitors. There were substitute metals. All this must not be taken as proving that we do not have a monopoly problem; but it does prove that the problem is not one of black versus white, but one of innumerable shades of gray. Our adolescent habit of overlooking all distinctions of degree is indefensible. We cannot fire off a blunderbuss labeled "Monopoly" and be at all sure what we are going to hit.

If, however, we are really to understand movements away from the competitive ideal, we must grasp a further point; and that is that the concept of "pure" competition even on its own terms is often unworkable in a developing world. There are several deficiencies—some concerning broad questions of social policy and others more specifically economic.

The most important oversight involved is the frequent ignoring of any necessity for standards of social value and conduct. Without adequate social standards pure competition in production easily becomes competitive production of pure garbage. John Ruskin described the misdirection of social wealth as the production of "illth"; and no sensitive person needs to have the reality of this problem explained to him. But in our present scientific culture the difficulty of maintaining and inculcating values is well-nigh insuperable. This, however, is no fault of competition. We do not blame an automobile because it is wrecked by a drunk. What we should criticize, however, is the modern idea that giving the drunk enough automobiles will somehow make him sober.

Outside the field of moral policy, probably the most glaring inadequacy of pure competition concerns social waste, and the destruction of natural resources. There are, for example, numerous costs which for one reason or another do not show up in the business balance sheet but must be borne by the community. In a world regulated only by pure competition, individual producers would be able to pour smoke and soot into the air, polluting the homes and destroying the health of an entire community. Yet this cost, which should be borne by those who are really at fault, or should be at least deliberately apportioned by the community, is shifted over willy-nilly to the budgets of hundreds of innocent people, many of whom are quite unable to meet it, and consequently live in disease and dirt. The "purest" of "pure" competition could not overcome this evil.

Again, in the case of many natural resources such as commercial fishing, unregulated pure competition gives every encouragement to complete destruction. If future generations are to eat, say salmon, the salmon must be allowed to spawn sufficiently. But a small producer—alone among thousands—has no motive for self-restraint. Suppose a single producer thinks the rivers are being "fished out" and decides not to catch as many. Will he help the fish, or only make an unnecessary present to his competitors? Conditions being what they are, there is nothing for him to do but go on fishing, whether he thinks it unwise or not.

This problem of natural resources stresses once more the ambiguity of the word "planning." One frequently gets the impression today that all "planners" want the same thing. This is absurd. Planning only refers to method. The real question is, What kind of planning—and for what end? Simply because unregulated pure competition sometimes fails to protect natural resources, we must not jump to the idea that the only alternative is a choice between state ownership and a single fish "monopoly." Instead, the state may often intervene to set up "rules of the game" within which competition can still take place. The establishment of closed seasons and various other regulations can protect the public interest without monopoly, self-perpetuating groups, the dead hand, and so forth. Of course such regulation would not be automatic or easy, and must be watched to prevent its being manipulated for special interests. Nevertheless it can be made to work, and this type of planning to "help competition" offers a broad field endorsed even by such conservative writers as Professor Hayek.

Natural resources and value standards do not, however, reach to the heart of the economic monopoly problem. The basic difficulty is more complicated. We have seen that competition makes for rapid growth, and that rapid growth in turn makes for the business cycle. But we cannot stop there. Rapid growth and the business cycle together make for what is called "cutthroat" competition, and "cutthroat" competition is the businessman's chief reason and alibi for monopoly.

Radicals and "monopolists" alike have combined in rare and surprising agreement to impregnate the public mind with the idea that large-scale units are "more efficient," and that we must therefore have either "monopoly" (usually sugar-coated as "cooperation" or "rationalization") or government control or ownership. This argument does not stand examination too well. While maximum technical efficiency probably does call for fewer units than are consistent with the "pure competition" we have been talking about, it also falls far short of requiring a single great "monopoly" or government bureau for each "industry." Probably the most important reason for "monopoly"—in the sense of one great producer absorbing an entire field—is not so much technical efficiency as superior ability to stabilize the market. And if we want to prevent or retard this trend toward centralization we must understand how the unstabilizing factors work themselves out.

In discussing the relationship of progress and instability, we saw that important business booms are the outgrowth of a tremendous "wave" in the installation of durable equipment. But when the industries initiating the boom have saturated their market and "leveled off" the result is usually a collapse of the durable goods industries—steel, coal, machinery, construction, and so on. That would be bad enough, but the problem does not stop there. The Achilles heel of an exchange economy is the fact that depression spreads from industries immediately affected over the whole system. Unemployment and deflation in the steel mills, for example, may mean fewer sales for the furniture business, and that in turn may mean less demand for lumber. Adam Smith thought that when one industry made losses people would simply "transfer" to other more prosperous lines. But the trouble is that, when one large industry goes under, we may not find other products expanding quickly enough to take its place, and so depression and unemployment become general.

Under such circumstances the producer in a field approximating abstract ideals of pure competition is almost helpless. In time of prosperity price reduction may increase sales and even make for larger profits. But in depression—though there are some circumstances in which price reduction can help—the chances are that, once income has begun to fall rapidly, price cutting will not increase profits or turnover at all. Furthermore, no one can tell when panic price cuts, once begun, will stop, and the small producer alone among a crowd of similar competitors is peculiarly vulnerable. Individual businessmen may know that things are going too far, but they can do nothing. As in the case of a small fish-packing plant, refusal to follow the crowd will not remedy the basic evil—it will only give temporary help to competitors.

The chances are, therefore, that in a more or less purely competitive field price cuts during a depression will be carried beyond reason. Prices will sink to a level far below long-run costs of production, and in order to salvage something from the wreck the owner of the business will keep it in operation as long as minimum pay-roll and other day-by-day expenses can be met—even though depreciation, profit, interest, all are in default. Continued operation is possible in the case of industry, particularly just after a boom, because a quantity of durable new equipment has been freshly installed and hence, even though creditors take over the plant, and prices are exceedingly low, the factory can still be kept going. In agriculture, on the other hand, production is maintained by exhausting, or "mining," the soil. No adequate fertilization or conservation can be managed, but the starved land continues to yield crops of a sort.

Conditions like these may justly be called "cutthroat" competition, and, though businessmen constantly use the expression as a smear word against anyone who ever reduces a price, no one who remembers what happened after 1929 should deny that the phrase can sometimes describe both a real and a serious evil. Nor can it be entirely confined to depression. Whenever we find the combination of a great deal of durable equipment and a product whose sales do not react quickly to price reductions, pure competition is likely to be unstable and may be disastrous. It should be noted, however, that, save in the case of occasional suicidal competitive frenzy, both slow sales response and durable equipment are necessary for a disastrous price war. For if price reduction brought a quick increase in sales there would be no need for wholesale cutting, and if a price war began at a time in which there was a great deal of plant about to wear out, firms with decrepit equipment would simply shut down. Supply would then be cut, and (barring general depression) prices would soon rise or stabilize themselves. Nevertheless we have here a paradox: The competitive order, precisely because it is competitive, tends to rush ahead to satisfy demand. But in so doing it produces a jerky installation of durable plant which may start both depressions and unwise price cutting. We find ourselves in a vicious circle not unfairly (though unconsciously) satirized by the student who remarked that competition is bad because it gives rise to monopoly!

Here is the core of the monopoly problem. It is not so much superior technical efficiency that furnishes the drive to "monopoly." Technical efficiency only furnishes a drive to large-scale business— and that, as we shall shortly see, is quite a different thing. The real advantage of monopolistic restriction, so far at least as survival is concerned, is its power to steady the market during a deflation, enabling the industry to prevent or minimize cutthroat competition. Whenever it is proposed to decentralize an industry by antitrust action the cry is always raised that decentralization will lead to cutthroat conditions; and no defense of the competitive order which overlooks this problem can have any real validity. The question is: What to do?

The type policy most discussed today, in theory anyhow, might be called the "Damn the torpedoes—full speed ahead" approach. It is said, with apparent plausibility, that the bankruptcy of individual producers makes no difference as long as the public is benefited, and therefore price (and wage?) cutting ought to be encouraged, because it will "bring about a new adjustment." The policy is further justified by pointing out that unemployment during a depression is greatest in the fields where prices are kept stable (for example, steel) and least in those where prices are "flexible" (for example, farming). From this it is an easy step to assert that, if only all industries were forcibly pulverized and made equally "purely" competitive and "flexible," all would be well. And many writers draw the further conclusion that the business cycle itself is merely the "result" of "monopoly."

Politics is not the only field which makes strange bedfellows. Economic theory frequently does the same. There is a curious parallelism between the basic assumptions of some "liberal" policies of enforced pure competition, and the logic underlying many arguments for rigid adherence to the gold standard and the balanced budget. The common denominator linking both is the tendency to put the full burden of economic adjustment upon price reduction alone, and the tacit assumption by both that if only there were enough competition there would be virtually no business cycle.

Unfortunately, economic stability depends on many more things than "monopoly" or competition. Even if every industry in the United States were split into a thousand purely competitive units there might still be depression, and, conversely, though every business were monopolized or were "planned," there might still be unemployment. The paradox is easily grasped with the help of a bit of economic language. We must realize that even when competition is "pure" it still may not be "perfect." Pure competition simply refers to the numbers, and the attitudes of mind, of buyers and sellers. But perfect competition refers to the speed and accuracy with which those same buyers and sellers can come to an adjustment. In a "perfect" market every buyer or seller has all the necessary information. He knows what people want to buy and how much they have to sell, and so on. Everyone, furthermore, has a perfect power of adjustment. Coal heavers can become brain surgeons overnight. The Empire State Building may be transmuted into six battleships in the twinkling of an eye, and so on. Only by combining both pure and perfect competition would a perfectly "automatic" system be possible, more or less literally justifying the various highly colored Utopian claims of certain of the earlier economists.

But it is easily seen that, if pure competition is unlikely, perfect competition is impossible. Even in a socialist state it would be impossible to get perfect knowledge of everything—including what people are going to think next week; and always it takes time to bring about an adjustment. Men and machines cannot instantaneously be whirled about in a dizzy dance. Yet it is precisely these "frictions" of adjustment that give rise to the business cycle. A major problem of the cycle is in the more or less periodic recurrence of "backlog" problems due to fairly sudden changes in inventions and in the wants of buyers. There is little in pure competition to guarantee either that "wants" will change smoothly, or that inventions will be introduced in steady stream. These, however, are the essential requirements for stability in a changing world. Competition is to be justified as helping to keep social and economic life democratic and creative. But no type of competition conceivable in the real world can be relied upon, left to itself alone, to ensure a constant, smooth, and automatic adjustment.

On this basis it is not surprising that the durable goods industries, such as steel, are among those in which "administered" prices are most common. For one of the prime causes, and main characteristics, of a depression is that the private demand for durable goods has been temporarily saturated. Sales would not increase rapidly even if there were a most drastic price reduction, and measures to prevent cutthroat competition are quite understandable though not necessarily desirable. On the other hand the fact that there is more unemployment in steel plants than among farmers is due not merely to the nature of pure competition, but also to the fact that the durable goods industries deal with postponable wants. People have to eat almost every day, but the old car and the old house can be made to do for many a year. One must concede that if farming were a monopoly depressions would probably be much worse all round. For the "purely competitive" farmer, though losing much in depression, still eats after a fashion, and the industrial population eats too—at the farmer's loss. But even if agriculture and durable goods were equally "monopolized," or equally competitive, output and employment would probably still decline less in agriculture. The essential difference is not the "flexibility" of the agricultural price, but the durability of the industrial product.

France and Germany in the 1930's gave us a grim and devastating object lesson in the results of a policy of adjustment by forcible price reduction alone. Refusing to adjust their currencies to world depression, they found themselves undersold even in their own markets. Price cut followed price cut, and wages fell with almost equal rapidity. Bankruptcy and unemployment increased, and the social structure was shaken to its foundations. By a single decree all rents in Germany were cut in half, and the prices of all "branded" articles reduced. Still there was no relief. The frantic masses turned to Hitler. France, which had had almost no aggressive trade union movement of importance in 1929 and was still prosperous in 1930, was by 1936 governed by a Socialist premier. Various elaborate sequences spun by academic economists show that wages may fall faster than prices, or prices faster than wages—whichever the particular theorist believes will cure depression. Or it may be argued that, if prices and wages fall fast enough, those who still have some money left will find such bargains that they will feel obliged to take a chance and buy. We must not assume that every depression will necessarily follow the disastrous history of 1929. Some price or wage reduction, if combined with other measures, may help greatly. But, once a really violent decline has got under way, it is almost impossible to tell when it will stop; and the policy which relies on reduction *alone* will needlessly aggravate every social friction. Though the mathematician may prove "by definition" that price reduction must stop a depression "some day," such a statement to the homeless is more likely to produce revolution than reassurance.

> I am sure that we all are a debtor for
> Mr. Hoover's delectable metaphor
> When he said that three years
> Would bring balm to our fears—
> Which the starving no doubt feel much better for.

Our discussion of the inadequacies of compulsory price reduction as a cure for unemployment may seem to have wandered from the monopoly problem, but the connection is easily explained. For the most that a policy of forcible "pure" competition *alone* could hope to contribute during deflation would be price and wage reductions as far-reaching as those which were deliberately planned by the Brüning government in Germany and attempted by the French. The German policy was, indeed, deliberately shaped to approximate the results which it was thought pure competition would have yielded; and the conclusion is irresistible that successful application of such a Spartan policy is impossible within the framework of democratic government. While some price and wage reduction may be desirable in connection with other policies the "Damn the torpedoes" approach, used alone as a means of combating depressions, is more likely to dynamite the state than save it.

There is a further objection to the forcible and uncritical pulverization of business. Many who advocate it do not expect to rely upon the policy, unaided, as a cure for depression. They expect to associate decentralization of control with some method of maintaining or increasing national income in depression. Such an approach is far more constructive and realistic; but, so far as theories of pure competition are concerned, it still encounters the objection that, though technological efficiency would probably not be affected by much more decentralization than we have, it is doubtful that it could ever be carried so far as to approximate any of the mathematical ideals of pure competition without great technical loss. Thus the academic competitive standard not only is inadequate as a socially tolerable means of stabilization, but is an impossibility. Something less rigid and more practical must be worked out.

After devoting seven chapters to a defense of the competitive order it may seem strange that we should now take so much space exposing its deficiencies. But the answer is easily given. Despite the many glaring inadequacies already detailed, the competitive order can be justified as a general social approach. But in order to defend it convincingly, and to frame a policy which will really enable such an order to work, we are obliged to know both how much competition it is reasonable to expect, and what results we may reasonably expect of competition. The true friend of democratic and competitive capitalism does not try to claim for his system a smoothness of performance which is in the nature of things impossible. Such claims may be made with apparent impunity during good times, but they have an unpleasant habit of backfiring later. By encouraging unjustified optimism they pave the way for an inordinate despair. The person who uncritically accepts all-out competition as a universal panacea will be likely, after grasping its deficiencies, to switch with equally unjustified vehemence to all-out planning. "Damn the torpedoes" gives place to "Three cheers for the commissar."

The policy toward which our values point is clearly one combining monetary stabilization policies with decentralization and "workable" rather than "pure" competition. But in order to sketch an approach toward a 'workable" competitive standard we must first discuss those policies which try to remedy the deficiencies of competition in a cyclical world by changes in industrial organization alone. Monetary stabilization is (or has been) so far removed from most people's normal ideas and experience as to seem entirely theoretical. The man in the street, whether radical or conservative, is almost sure to attribute depression to business policy or some part of the structure of ownership rather than to the fundamental frictions of change. Monetary measures, if understood at all, are dismissed as superficial. Thus businessmen tend to lay the depression to price cuts rather than to the decline in demand which underlies them; and radicals lay depression to high profits rather than to the disorganizing inventions and changes in wants which underlie them. And so it works out that, no matter how many subordinate problems remain, the normal, reasonable, obvious solution to everyone—left or right—comes to be some sort of cooperative industrial planning designed to freeze or adjust prices, wages, and profits in various ways. Though bitter conflicts over the distribution of income survive and are, indeed, aggravated, the basic "planning" approach commands the assent of all parties; and the person who suggests that the whole method of attack is wrong in its emphasis finds himself treated as a perverse lunatic.

If we rule out compensatory finance the schemes of industrial organization usually suggested during depression fall under three heads. The first is "democratic" cooperative planning of the National Industrial Recovery Act type. "Business," labor, government, and "the consumer" get together to "plan" output. It may be noted that a similar policy was the underlying economic ideal of Fascism and Nazism, in so far as they may be said to have had one. The next system is that adopted in England in the twenties and thirties and furnishes a curious example of the meeting of extremes. There the Conservative government gave big business free rein to merge, and freedom of competition became freedom to end competition. In the name of laissez faire the country was handed over to private planning. The final type of plan is wholesale government ownership or control.

Of the three plans the first, the NIRA type, has the strongest appeal to Americans. Its political seductiveness is especially striking. Existing property rights are not threatened, they are even protected, while the inevitable drift toward sabotage helps to increase individual "security." In January, 1938, a few months after the crash of 1937, President Roosevelt gave a press conference on the causes of depression which is one of the more interesting political documents known to the writer. Unfortunately, it cannot be given in full; but the following excerpts put the case for the NIRA type of plan as persuasively as one can find it:

Q.: How can the Government do anything to prevent this type of unintelligent business operation? Can you give us any idea of how you would go about it, what can be done?

THE PRESIDENT: Oh, yes; I think so. Let us take an example: Don't write the story that I am advocating the immediate reenactment of NRA. But the fact remains that in quite a number of the code industries under NRA it was perfectly legal for the heads of all the companies in a given industry to sit down around a table with the Government, and, from their own statistics and the statistics of their own trade associations and the statistics given them by the Government, figure out much more clearly than they ever had before, as an industry, what the probable demand of the country would be for a period of six months or a year ahead. In other words, they could make a more intelligent group estimate as to the purchasing power of the country and the inventories of the particular article necessary for the immediate future.

Now, done that way, it is a perfectly legitimate thing for them to do— sitting there, with the Government, and trying honestly to find out what the needs are going to be for the next six months or a year, so that they won't overproduce. It is legitimate just so long as it is done without any attempts at price-fixing or driving competitors out of business or things like that as a result of the conference.

There is a question today whether a meeting of that kind, around a table, is legal under the anti-trust laws. A lot of people are afraid of it. I would very much favor making it a completely legal thing to do: to meet around a table to find out, with the help of the Government, what the demands are, what the purchasing power of the country is, what the inventories are.

Q.: How would the estimated annual production be allocated among the units of the industry?

THE PRESIDENT: Don't do that—keep competition . . .

Both the surface plausibility and the basic confusion of such an approach are striking. What possible sort of competition would be "kept" under such an arrangement? How could the "competitors" possibly adjust their individual production to the general "estimate" without some sort of tacit quota system? And what chance would the man with a new method have? In view of the analysis given in the earlier part of this book there seems to be little doubt that such a regime would be one of slow stagnation. But there is a further defect. Our savings habits, plus the size of our investment industries, and hence the continuation of full employment, are all geared to the maintenance of investment outlets through constant, active, and unexpected change. If private industry is to be allowed to log-roll itself into a stalemate in the manner indicated, then this "margin of change" needed for full employment will be cut off, and satisfactory employment can only be reached by government investment. But if government investment takes over most of the margin of change it will only be a matter of time before the system is substantially socialized. Here is another means of "saving the system" which in fact only cushions its death.

Strangely enough, there is probably, in the short run, more to be said for the English policy of the single great firm—so far as mere volume of output and lower prices are concerned—than for the more "democratic" National Recovery Administration plan. Remember that by Roosevelt's account the type of policy he favored was "legitimate" only as long as it was done "without price fixing" or "driving competitors out of business." It is nevertheless almost inescapable that tacit price fixing would be implied; and the proviso that no competitors be ousted has, as its inevitable consequence, the result that prices must be set high enough to take care of the most inefficient firm rather than more efficient ones. The plan offers a field day for restrictive vested interests. But the single great firm, if under vigorous management and with enough surviving interproduct competition, will be far less subject to restriction of this sort, and will probably give, for a time at least, both larger output and lower cost, and also be more hospitable to change.

It must be realized that the textbook picture of a "monopolist" as an Ebenezer Scrooge squeezing the last possible dollar out of the consumer by high prices and exploitation cannot be uncritically applied to modern large-scale business in the democratic countries. The textbook monopolist is without private conscience or the fear of government, or of public opinion. The actual businessman has all three. The tendency of American large-scale business is to set a price somewhat higher than the "purely competitive" theoretical ideal, but not nearly as high as the theory of pure monopoly would lead us to expect. If in slump the price does not drop greatly, in boom it does not rise as it could. Just how much would actually be gained in cheapness by direct public control is highly questionable. The record of the concern which, before 1941, was the most notorious example of a great single firm without direct competitors in its own line—the Aluminum Company of America—should dispose, once for all, of some of the more hysterical attitudes toward this problem. Over a period of forty years prices were reduced by some 88 per cent, and output increased about 3,000 per cent. Perhaps prices could have gone still lower, and output have increased still more; but the record is convincing that large-scale American private "monopolists" are far indeed from conforming to any Scrooge pattern. Liberals would do well to read Lord Keynes's account of how large-scale business tends to "socialize itself" even while remaining in entirely private control.

Having thus given the devil his due, we nevertheless question whether the record of the Aluminum Company or any other great American business justifies a "world of monopolies" on the English pattern. Quite the contrary. The behavior of a few great firms, surrounded by a largely competitive environment and culture and acting under a suspicious, if not hostile, public scrutiny, gives no fair indication of what would be done without competitive surroundings and under a complacent government. Given the latter conditions, it is only too likely that even interproduct competition would be "rationalized"; and business is no more exempt than government from the tendencies toward deterioration of the self-perpetuating group we have already stressed. Without the spur of outside competition the original energtic management of big business will inevitably decline. Keynes's compliments regarding the "self-socialization" of big business are distinctly double-edged. For a part of the process of "self-socialization" may also be self-bureaucratization. Furthermore the world of monopolies, like the world of trade institutes of the NRA type, cannot solve the problem of full employment. For it too will tend to choke off the margin of change. Historically, it is significant that neither in England nor in America was the employment problem solved in the thirties save by recourse to war industries. The liberal or conservative planner may hope to "fill the gap" left by hamstringing private industry with a vast "welfare" program, but he must remember that that is not the only possible outcome.

The so-called conservative of the English type, furthermore, who sees in private cooperating monopoly the answer to left-wing clamor for security and stability must realize that, even if he does temporarily solve the problem of employment and security by combining monopoly with welfare projects or (more likely) armaments, this restrictive policy is but the prelude to his own industrial suicide. Indeed, liberals, conservatives, and believers in democracy alike should beware of laying excessive stress on personal security. For if they set up personal economic security as the highest value there can be no doubt that the greatest degree of such security would be reached under totalitarian dictatorship! And the unwary masses thus encouraged may well yield security from persecution in order to obtain "security" from economic fluctuation. The liberal democratic state can give a reasonable minimum of economic security. It cannot give more than that and remain democratic.

But there is a further fatal psychological weakness in the world of private monopolies, or, as it has been called, the "conservative corporative state." The business head, in order to justify his system, must talk the language of competition. But if competition is obviously absent his words carry little conviction. In the ideological debate he is foredoomed to defeat. Thus it may be said that English capitalism, in cartelizing and monopolizing itself so thoroughly, both bought its own coffin and donned its own shroud. Having thus taken its place by the grave, it pressed the pistol to its forehead and said to socialism, "Fire when ready."

Adherents of comprehensive planning will doubtless hail the foregoing paragraphs with glee as indicating the inevitable doom of capitalism and the inevitable rise of a new industrial Utopia. The writer, however, dissents from both these points of view. In the first place we shall shortly see that the drift toward monopoly need not be overwhelming; and in the second it is by no means obvious that government control or ownership will be any more democratic or more creative than private large-scale business.

One of the strangest and most incurable habits of the human race seems to be the tendency to hail the utmost possible extension of an evil as its cure. Thus we "preserve" old buildings by tearing them down and putting bad copies in their place, and we take as the cure for partial private monopoly by industry universal monopoly by government. But just how much have we accomplished in the change?

There are certain points in which government monopoly does seem pretty clearly to score. Chief of these is false obsolescence and excessive advertising. When private large-scale business (not necessarily monopoly) has substantially saturated its "backlog" in the manner we have already seen, there is a temptation to keep people buying by changing styles, high pressure salesmanship, installment buying, hectic advertising, and occasionally (in a highly "organized" field) deliberate reduction in life of the product. *Prima facie* the socialist state trust would indulge in no such high-pressure tactics. But on the other hand a multitude of restrictive tactics are attributed to large-scale business which the socialist state trust would almost certainly employ, and if the private competition of large-scale units is sometimes hyperthyroid, socialist activity is likely to be oppressively subnormal.

There is a serious latent paradox in the modern theory of socialism. Many socialist writers, such as Dr. Lange, now Polish Ambassador, have admitted that if goods are to be manufactured to suit the buyer's tastes it will be necessary to set up a market, rather like the capitalist one, in which the socialist state trusts will "play at competition." If this is not done the socialist regime will be likely to be one both of rationing and of a labor draft. In other words, democracy of choice or preference demands some sort of market competition. But this concession confronts the socialist with a serious paradox. If his state trusts really compete against one another for men and materials, and if the power (or possibly the wealth) of the competing commissars depends upon the relative importance of their industries (how else measured, in most cases, than by sales volume?), will they not, in a rich system, be tempted to advertise, and indeed do many other things, to increase revenue? Russian state socialism furnishes no adequate guide in this connection, for the important difference between Russian industry and American is that Russia is a poor country. And the consumer there, under recent conditions anyhow, will usually take anything. But in a mature, liberal, American socialism the case might be very different.

On the other hand, if the socialist indignantly repudiates the idea of competitive advertising, it is fair to ask whether his commissar would really compete at all, and whether the whole system might not be much more likely to ossify. We have already seen that the basic "superiority" of comprehensive planning, as far as cyclical stability is concerned, would have to rest upon a willingness to sabotage or hold back new inventions, and to refuse to satisfy wants promptly. A great deal is made of the tendency of private "monopoly" to hold new inventions off the market. But a socialist state trust would have almost the same incentives. There would be, first, the desire to "plan" the flow of capital installation so as to prevent humps and bumps in the durable goods industries; and there would be, next, all the pressure group, vested interest, simple inertia obstacles which we have already analyzed. If the planners have, with immense effort, just finished the Dneprostroi dam, how kindly will they look upon the inventor who suggests starting all over on something new? Yet it is precisely the same desire not to destroy newly created durable values too quickly that underlies the reluctance of private monopoly to introduce new inventions at once. And it is the same pressure group problem that creates the danger in a "self-socialized," "bureaucratized" private business that the new invention may never be introduced at all. Thus we conclude that if the state trusts really compete they run the risk of competing "wastefully" as American large-scale business sometimes does. And if they do not have genuine competition they will probably be even more tempted to sabotage than private monopoly now is. Finally, if the socialist points out that there may be a middle ground between extremes, may we not reply that we can also look for that under capitalism?

The consideration which finally casts the balance in favor of attempting a capitalist solution is the effect of comprehensive monopoly upon personal and political freedom. We have already seen that, where the individual is unable to transfer beyond the reach of the ruling group, his political independence is endangered; but there is another problem of large-scale units which is almost as important from the point of view of human happiness. For lack of a better word I will call it the "contacts" problem.

In working in large units of business and government I have often been impressed by the apparent hopelessness of the position of the ambitious young man in a subordinate position. Suppose he is a clerk in some regional office, without connections "higher up." How on earth can he bring his ability to the attention of those really in control? It can be done; but it is very difficult, and always the president's secretary has a better chance than the man behind the adding machine. How many a "mute inglorious" insurance genius has been left to "rest" in the bureaucratic red tape of some large office!

This problem is the real objection to size; but it is a matter of size, not capitalism. And big business as well as big socialism is, or should be, always looking for ability. Discovering and advancing brains is just as simple and just as difficult in one case as in the other, and I can see little practical difference between being the boss's nephew or secretary and being the commissar's nephew or secretary. But at least, under capitalism, the energetic young man who finds himself frustrated has a better chance to shift over to a line in which he can find greater opportunity for advancement—especially if depression is kept within bounds.

We have stressed the difficulties and shortcomings of socialist monopoly because it is important to realize that modern industrial socialism is not so much a remedy for the disease of bigness as an aggravation of it. Our efforts at decentralization today are often enfeebled because many people hold them inadequate and prefer the more drastic, and, in theory, far simpler solution of government control. But once we see comprehensive planning and government control for what it is—the highest degree of monopoly rather than its cure—then our attitude will be very different.

We have reached the point at which we may begin to suggest constructive ideas of "workable" competition. The first thing needed is to realize that changes in the size of individual businesses do not necessarily tell us anything about the changes in the "purity" or the "perfection" of their competition. Confusing bigness with monopoly and smallness with competition is a mistake made in a good many suggested antitrust programs at the present time, but there is little warrant for it. For example, it was said that government should lease war plants to "little business." In so far as this is an attempt to help the new man, it corresponds closely with our point of view. But the scheme is easily perverted into covert introduction of centralized planning. When a little businessman leases his plant from a government bureau and gets a loan from a government bank, under loan and lease terms which compel him to submit to comprehensive wage, price, and production control, he is scarcely the independent industrial pioneer we are looking for. This is especially the case if he also pays taxes which prevent him from adequate expansion with internal funds. He is no more than a foreman or hired manager for the government who is allowed to flatter himself by saying he "owns" the plant. The little business that counts is the little business that has a chance to grow into big business. Survival of a few limited property rights is not survival of capitalism.

On the other hand, if "little business" need not mean competition, neither need "big business" mean "monopoly." To determine whether a business is a "monopoly," we must ask not only how big it is but also over how big a field it competes. It is, for example, a far cry from selling buggies at the county seat to selling automobiles over the whole world. But who is to say that competition is less keen in one condition than in the other? The truth is that when the size of the market is taken into account the modern myth of decline from a supposed golden age of competition receives little or no support either from economic history or from statistics. The village economy, to which we look back so fondly, was in reality a highly restricted, inflexible, and "monopolistic" one.

Yet, though large units competing over the whole world may still be relatively competitive, in comparison with many governments they are far larger than what has usually gone before. This is not entirely the case, for both the Bank of the United States and the British East India Company were very large in comparison with the governments of their time. Nevertheless many small countries today are impotent to deal with their economic problems, and the contrast between, say, the "sovereign" power of Guatemala and the businesses with which it deals is striking. The one chance such a country has of retaining its *de facto* independence is to play off the competing big firms against one another. Here is certainly a case for regional federation and regional antitrust action. The United States, today, is about as small as a community can be, and yet be sure of maintaining real economic power.

In the same way, though big businesses competing in the world market may be as relatively competitive as village businesses competing in the village market, it is harder for an individual to get started independently in the world market than in the village market. Here too the distinction must not be overemphasized, for the plow hand wishing to break into the village flour-milling business, let us say, would be just about as much at a disadvantage. Without the aid of credit from someone, there would be little chance. What gave the nineteenth century village worker his real opportunity was the possibility of moving into industry, or migrating westward, and it is the problem of preserving a similar frontier of change that really confronts us today.

Mention of the frontier of change gives the clue to our basic problem. Suppose that, for all the reasons indicated, we decide to try to maintain the maximum of decentralization and competition possible in the modern world. What should be the real aim of such a program? Merely to maintain "reasonably" low prices and high output from existing facilities? Much technical economic theory reads that way, but it is not enough. For if we merely stress prices and output we shall soon encounter all the "good monopoly" arguments.

Again, is the aim of antitrust enforcement to realize the abstract purely competitive ideal? We have seen that that is impossible. Nor can we expect to achieve by decentralization such "perfection" of competition as will, in itself, take care of the cyclical problem.

Finally, may we hope by antitrust action to create willy-nilly a world of relatively small businesses? We could do so, by paying the price; but compulsory pulverization of business involves a great technical loss, and may also be the complete antithesis of the policy of independent development and relative equality of opportunity for which we have pleaded.

The real aim of antitrust policy is not any of the standards just listed, but the preservation of the economic democracy and the technological creativeness of our society. By seeing to it that there is always, on average, enough smaller active and independent business, and enough interproduct competition to keep large-scale business from becoming either stagnant or oppressive, and that there is a sufficient frontier of unregimented change to give an outlet to the restless spirit of inquiry, we may hope to maintain an adequate transfer mechanism and an adequate spur toward overcoming restriction and thus to keep our country free. That is our real aim, and it may be substantially achieved despite the survival of many theoretical "impurities."

Outlines of such a policy may be briefly sketched. First of all, because we cannot hope for an automatically self-adjusting world, monetary policies designed to maintain maximum employment and to keep fluctuation within bounds are essential. Such measures will also greatly mitigate the pressures toward wholesale cutthroat competition which are the chief argument for monopolistic restriction. In addition, specific credit policy is needed to give small business a chance. Credit is one of the most important factors in the democratization of opportunity in our society, for by it the man without capital is able to get a start. Whatever the arguments of the "rationalizing" type may be for a merger of banks, no democratic society can tolerate a monopoly or even near-monopoly of credit; and we must consider carefully the impact of some of our theories of commercial banking upon small business before we adopt them too literally.

What is our policy to be regarding size? In so far as size *per se* is considered, the aim should be to get a sufficient number of smaller firms in addition to big ones, rather than to penalize bigness in itself. But we should also see that these smaller firms really are able to act independently, and that they are not merely timorous dependents.

In this connection it should be remembered that business is not the only thing that can compete, and that we do not necessarily kill competition by laying down rules of the game. Thus false obsolescence and excessive advertising may be handled by a combination of legal restraint and public education. Again private business competition may be supplemented by cooperative movements, and even by occasional government operation of the "yardstick" type. But such measures, while valuable as auxiliaries to private competition, are not adequate substitutes. Given sole possession of the field, they would themselves soon take on most of the qualities of monopoly.

In the pursuit of our policy all the conventional weapons of antitrust policy may be employed. In addition there is probable need for reexamination of our patent laws regarding "improvements," and for restrictions upon merger by purchase. This chapter, however, is not a technical treatise on the antitrust act. Our aim is merely to give a general approach.

But is not our policy hopeless? I do not think so. Big business is itself subject to certain self-limiting tendencies. The United States Steel Corporation, for example, at the time of its founding contained 60 per cent of all the capacity of the industry. It certainly appeared to be an overwhelming "monopoly." Yet United States Steel today has only approximately 30 per cent of the industry, and it has several times been forced by the competition of "Little Steel" into the adoption of technical changes sooner than it wished.

The real obstacle to our policy is the feeling of many that the idea is futile—either futile in aim or futile in performance. Regarding aim, we have tried to show the importance of competition to democracy. Regarding performance, we have sought to set up a possible and practical goal which may be pursued without inevitable disappointment. Antitrust policy is futile only if we expect it to bear the whole weight of economic adjustment.

Liberals today must learn to distinguish their friends from their enemies. Just because a communist, let us say, believes in "planning" he is not necessarily a "fellow traveler" toward the same goal but with a more drastic remedy. Communism with its subordination of means to ends is the antithesis of true democracy. The real fellow traveler of communism is the private monopolist who wishes to relax the anti-trust law, and the real monopoly problem today is that the slogan of "planning" has made the fact of monopoly respectable. Until we disentangle our ideas on this point there will be little safety for our democracy.

· IX ·

Cooperation Unlimited?

"LABOR MONOPOLY" is no more the result of mere chance, or human perversity, than its conservative counterpart. Both are the outgrowth of deeply seated forces, and both represent a response to concrete needs. If we want to mitigate restrictive pressures, whether from one side or from the other, we must know why such pressures have arisen.

The union movement may be considered as any one of at least five things: a protective organization to secure "fair" treatment within the framework of competitive democracy; a means of approaching certain psychological problems of modern technology; a first step in the establishment of a new "cooperative" or "conflict-free" mode of economic life; a producers' pressure group; a vehicle for the will to power of certain individuals. To treat such a complex of forces as a mere wage-hour-profit problem is clearly to fall far short of real understanding.

Some of the needs finding expression in the union movement have grown out of the general moral vacuum in our civilization already mentioned. Others spring from the special problem of labor itself. Concerning the latter, many people will feel that the basic point of view toward progress expressed in this book contains a serious latent contradiction. We have said that the happiest man is neither the richest man nor the quietest man, but the man who does the most interesting work; also that the end of creation is the creation of a creative world. Yet it will immediately be charged that modern large-scale plant and assembly-line technique make for a peculiarly dull routine in which the creative instinct is almost wholly frustrated.

"Arts and crafts" criticism of this type has always seemed to the writer to be far more searching, logically at least, than the usual "surplus value" "exploitation" line of approach. This is not to deny the existence of conditions which, given a chance, could sometimes produce sweatshops, or to dispute that labor does not always get everything to which it is entitled even under orthodox economic theory. But the rapid rise of the standard of living of the worker under capitalism would certainly indicate that the masses have, on balance, benefited from "the system." Furthermore, mere underpayment can be remedied by a type of unionism much more limited in scope than many modern leaders, even those "believing" in "capitalism," are willing to accept. Perhaps a glance at the statistical record is in order. Professor John T. Dunlop writes:

The level of average hourly earning in industry as a whole increased approximately thirteen times in the period 1820–1945. From less than 8 cents an hour the average wage during these 125 years increased to over $1.00 an hour. At the same time the prices entering into the budget of wage-earner families doubled. As a consequence what an hour of work would buy increased over six times in this period. . . . From 1919 to date the level of money wages has more than doubled, while the cost of living is approximately the same. There are striking figures. The first simple fact about the wage level then is that it is an inclined plane. Alexis de Tocqueville, that shrewd observer of American democracy, asserted over a hundred years ago "that a slow and gradual rise of wages is one of the general laws of democratic communities."

The role of trade union influence on this rising wage rate level was probably relatively minor in the 125 year period as a whole. No question is more fundamental to the economy of the next generation than whether the historical relation of wages and prices is to be continued under strong unions.*

But numerous writers, such as G. K. Chesterton, or Ruskin, hold that all that modern technical progress has been able to accomplish in "standards of living" is useless, for what men have gained in "satisfaction" as consumers they have lost in creativeness as producers. Ever cheaper toothbrushes, in their opinion, are

* "Wage Determination and the Economics of Liberalism," U. S. Chamber of Commerce. Quoted by permission.

a poor compensation for ever duller work. To them the struggle over wages and hours is not so much concerned with its avowed objects as it is a rationalization of deeply seated subconscious dissatisfaction with the technological conditions of modern life.

It is difficult to say, *a priori*, how much of this line of thought is objectively true, and how much is a self-verifying argument. As one recent critic has remarked, the worker's instinct of workmanship is being "talked out of him" by the intellectual. So much of the dislike of new machinery is mere nostalgia for the "good old days" of childhood that the ideas of a man like Ruskin, for example, whose Oedipus complex was so great that he could never proceed to physical consummation of his marriage, must be taken with a large discount. Yet, tell a man every day, and three times a day, that he is unhappy because his work is dull (or that he is being defrauded), and he is quite likely to come to believe it himself. However, this does not prove that the idea was initially correct. For, first, there are unquestionably people who enjoy monotony and routine, and resent change; and, next, though much of the work of the world is dull, much of it always has been dull. If machinery has destroyed many satisfying occupations it has created many others. What the total effect on balance has been, is highly debatable. There is considerable inconsistency in left-wing attitudes on this point. For it is scarcely reasonable to accept Veblen's idea that the machine makes the worker less "combative," and at the same time maintain that it makes him more dissatisfied because it frustrates his instinct of workmanship.

Yet it cannot be denied that large-scale technical organization creates numerous difficult psychological problems. There are the feeling of being "lost," the "contacts" problem already spoken of, and the lack of a satisfying sense of personal ownership or achievement. As one psychologist has said, "The feeling of belonging to the right group seems to be more important than making a few extra cents per hour. The workers' strongest complaint is the lack of recognition of their dignity as human beings." Yet a feeling of loyalty, of enthusiasm, of "belonging" can be created and has often been created within the realm of business, even large business. One of the main problems of the union organizer moving into new and obdurate territory is how to break this up. And the real question to ask is whether the union *per se* has, in this respect, anything much more to offer.

The psychological problem, as I see it (leaving aside, for the moment, wages, hours, and "security"), does not spring so much from capitalism as from size and technique. A worker can feel and be just as lost in a large union, and can be just as much exploited by it, as with a large company. If close comradeship were really the prime goal, then the logic of the situation would seem to call for the autonomous or at least semi-autonomous small local union which is so frequently attacked today. To be sure, in the earlier and more enthusiastic phases of union organization, or of political collectivism, a man may get a special "kick" out of feeling himself one of the "workers of the world." But the object of loyalty is so diffused and abstract that retention of enthusiasm soon becomes largely a problem of recurrent propaganda and semantic hypnosis—which, after all, is the worst that can be said about company efforts to meet the same problem.

Certain suggestions regarding the psychological problems of size will be made at the end of this chapter. What is important to realize here is that we must frequently look beyond wages and hours for the fundamental sources of dissatisfaction. One glance at the appalling ugliness of the typical coal-mining town, for example, will tell more about the United Mine Workers than a thousand volumes of statistics. How can people fail to be dissatisfied in such surroundings! Yet frequently the union either is not the best organ to reach the basic difficulty or is unconcerned with reaching it. For example, John L. Lewis, in presenting his case for pay increases before a congressional committee, remarked that many miners' families suffered from malnutrition. In view of the fact that average mining wages were then about $250 a month, one member of the committee called him a liar. But the real question to ask was not how accurate Mr. Lewis' data were but how much money the union had spent in the last ten years on teaching its members proper food habits. Unless a man knows how to spend what money he has, higher pay will probably not help him much. Persons who deal with children know that a spoiled child can suffer from malnutrition in the midst of riches;

and primitive or ignorant people, thrown into a machine culture, may do the same. Such conditions are frequently the real source of the discontent manifested in union action. Yet union leaders tend to dismiss them as "welfare boloney." Why this should be so, we shall shortly see.

A second factor in the appeal of the union movement is its partial satisfaction of the moral vacuum in modern culture, and the yearning for "purpose" which distinguishes the modern man. Thus Dr. Robert S. Lynd speaks of the "deep emotional need of all us little people in a big world to feel that we, and what we are building, are good and worth going on for," while George Albee writes of "the exaltation of identity with a worth-while cause," and adds:

What we need—all we need—is a program of aims which are demonstrably worth while. We need William James' "moral substitute" for war. . . . If, in our new economy of abundance, we can make it unnecessary for . . . Americans to spend so much of their time merely earning a living, and give them more time for projects of interest and dignity—and supply the projects—our world tomorrow will be enriched by a comradeship which, until now, we have known only in rare and precious moments.*

Much of this is correct. But is the only worth-while project the union? Should we not examine closely a point of view so open to the idea that the way to have peace is to start an industrial war? As we saw in discussing the basic weakness of democratic progress, it is ironically easy to associate the satisfaction which one gets in working toward an end with the end itself. Yet in fact working toward almost any other end (or type of social change) might often have furnished the same creative satisfaction, and escape from deeper thought. Many a man runs away from himself by trying to run others. Before we decide that "cooperative" collectivism is the only solution we must consider its effects both upon democracy and upon creativeness. Certainly we can end (active) conflict if the minority is kept afraid to fight.

* *Labor and Nation*, April-May 1946. By permission of the editors.

But the "peace" derived from pure collectivism of this sort is often scarcely distinguishable from the peace of death. Mr. Albee's point of view can easily be perverted into a masochistic and servile demand by modern men who have lost a sense of personal purpose in life that the state, or the union, intervene in monolithic style to impose values upon them.

On the basis of similar considerations Will Herberg of the International Garment Workers Union sums the matter up as follows:

Democracy means pluralism if it means anything at all—the wide distribution of power and responsibility, with various organizations embodying and championing the multifarious interests of men in social life. The idea of one great over-all organization representing the total interests of its members is essentially totalitarian. It cannot escape anyone how closely the formula "Everything in and through the movement" parallels the notorious formula "Everything in and through the state." *

But emphasis upon competition and the transfer mechanism must not be taken as pointing toward a policy of unadulterated "laissez faire" or "freedom" of contract in the labor field. Where one great buyer (the employer) "competes" against numerous small sellers (labor) the discrepancy in bargaining power easily becomes so great that collective bargaining is necessary to maintain a fair balance. Scarcely anyone disputes this today. Yet, if the transfer mechanism needs to be reenforced by the union, the union needs to be checked by the transfer mechanism. The type of union consistent with democracy is of the moderate "wages and hours" type, also concerned, though by no means exclusively, with protective and fraternal features; and designed, in any case, to supplement rather than supplant the competitive order. Syndicalism and democracy cannot be combined.

Such a conclusion requires that we work out standards of "reasonable" wages, permissible union objectives, forms of organization and forms of action. A few very elementary suggestions will be made later in this chapter. What we are primarily concerned with here, however, is the foundation for an approach

* *Labor and Nation,* April-May 1946. By permission of the editors.

to the problem; for, granting the shortcomings and frequent vagueness of the academic theory of "distribution," I cannot help feeling that the real objection to it, in the minds of many, is not its technical insufficiencies so much as the clear indication it gives of the possibility of some undemocratic and oppressive action by the union—oppressive, that is, of the "working class" itself. It is simply not true as was recently stated by Dr. Kittleman, economist for the International Association of Machinists, "While unions may also be an aggrandizement against the community, they represent such a large part of the community that the community, in a sense, shares the aggrandizement." Many working people now cannot get houses—not only because of the "real estate lobby" but also because of the building trades. Increases in coal prices and transit fares hit at the lower income groups, and other instances could also be given.

Many writers on wage theory and union policy, however, either are still thinking of the union as always the underdog (disregarding Professor Slichter's reference to it as sometimes "overdog") or are concealed or subconscious believers in some species of guild syndicalism; or else hold such a narrow view of profits as almost to approximate the Marxist doctrine of labor's "right" to the "whole product"—overlooking the work of the dynamic entrepreneur. With ideas like these, whether avowed and consciously realized or not, such men are not really interested in working out objective standards consistent with competition and economic democracy. Instead emphasis switches indiscriminately from standard to standard—however mutually contradictory they may be—provided only that in the particular instances they offer plausible justification for one more "raise." Even if the subject were not already difficult enough there would certainly be no chance for a solution in such an atmosphere. What is really being sought is an absolute privilege and immunity for union action.

Yet few men ever announce with glee that they must "inevitably" die tomorrow, and abject surrender to an alleged "trend" means either thoughtlessness or, more often, concealed approbation of the so-called inevitable. It is for this reason that the earlier chapters of this book were written. If they are correct, and if the competitive market and political democracy are closely associated, then no absolute privilege for any group is possible. If that be accepted, then we may begin to work on a solution. In case it is not, there will only be continued confusion.

The truth therefore must be realized that, just as business action and business motives may be perverted into monopolistic restriction, so also union organization and union motives may be perverted into restrictive, or into revolutionary and totalitarian, action. Either way, the basic distorting forces may be much the same: on the one hand, the "security motive"; on the other, the will to power. In dealing with business monopoly we discussed only the more "rational" and "economic" motives. But such a procedure is too narrow. Not only must we reckon with rational expectations of gain, or prudent provision against deflation. There is also simple megalomania; and this is true of the union as well.

The fact seems to be that the role of the union merely as a protective organization within the framework of the competitive order is not absorbing enough, once unionism has become established, to contain the energies of the true leader type. Walter Reuther, for example, would appear to be much the sort of imaginative and energetic leader who under other circumstances would have made an excellent businessman of the entrepreneur species. The writer would find nothing earth-shaking in the discovery that Mr. Reuther's suggestions on business policy, for example, were as wise as the ideas of the management. Yet, whatever their merits, Walter Reuther as union leader is not the man to be making them, under existing conditions; and the reasons for this, as we shall shortly see, are not pure nonsense. Yet the values of such men would probably lead them to regard entering management themselves as treachery to "the movement." Prisoners of their own values, but naturally desirous of doing a type of work for which they are, or feel themselves to be, peculiarly well fitted, they are almost inevitably forced into an antagonism toward the legal structure of industrial competition which excludes them from control.

Once the battle is joined, welfare and other considerations tend to be important primarily as weapons for harassing management or consolidating power; and otherwise become matters of secondary concern. The movement takes on a restrictive and revolutionary character, and industrial relations are proportionately embittered. In a recent article Merlyn S. Pitzele asks whether American labor can "defeat the communists." One comment which might be made is that it can do so only if it ceases to borrow such a large proportion of the communists' vocabulary. The truth is that the union movement only makes sense either as a protective movement or as a revolutionary one. If union leaders, avowedly capitalist in conviction, use consistently inflammatory language to consolidate their position, they must not be surprised if the rank and file go on to something more drastic than they really want to offer. For example if nearly all profit is "exploitation" and if all competition is evil, mere wages-and-hours unionism cannot meet the difficulty. Similarly if the union adopts, with however good intentions, a policy which prevents investment and hamstrings the capitalist economy, it is paving the way for action from the unemployed more revolutionary than mere trade unionism. And finally if the union denounces monopoly but at the same time uses tactics which increase it, it may not only be making itself strong, but also may be ushering in more extreme movements. Simple self-preservation requires that the unionist make up his mind under what system he really wishes to function.

In the remainder of this chapter I shall criticize certain union policies from the point of view of competitive democracy. Such criticism will of course be beside the point to the (conscious or unconscious) revolutionary, but I beg that those who really wish to keep democracy will consider them carefully. The totalitarian pressures of modern society are so great that only by the most intense effort of all men of good will can democratic collapse be avoided.

Despite a wide variety of points of view, and specific demands, within the labor movement itself, modern social thought and to some extent union action seem to contain a basic trend toward the advocacy of "cooperative" management by labor and business. The case for "democracy" of management so called has been examined in a number of places in this book. We have already given reasons why a mere vote *per se* is not an adequate cure for the psychological problems of size. Such questions aside, one of the most important objections to cooperative management is that it makes the work of the entrepreneur or innovator—as distinguished from the mere "manager"—almost impossible. We said in the last chapter that large-scale private business which still had the stimulus of interproduct competition, and which was still under vigorous direction, would probably be more efficient than either the state trust or the various National Recovery Administration and syndicalist suggestions. The reason for this is that the vested interests arising within the firm from the security motive would not have so much opportunity to assert themselves. Would this be true, however, if there were cooperative management?

We have made little specific mention of empirical data in this book. But it was not written out of thin air. And there are not many places which would furnish better instances of security sabotage, of the inadequacy of the elective method, and of the decline of the self-perpetuating group than the labor movement. Almost alone among New Deal administrators, Thurman Arnold was able to pierce the fog of "right" and "left" terminology to recognize those labor unions which were monopolies for what they were. The reader is referred to his *Bottlenecks of Business* for specific examples; but many more can be given. I do not doubt the reality of much which Robert R. Young has to say about monopoly in railroad management. But whether "banker control" has had any more influence in stagnating the railroad industry than the operating and jurisdictional rules of jealous unions, or as much influence, may well be doubted. One important task of the union, to be sure, is to see that technical change and reorganization are not carried through in disregard of human values. It is always difficult to draw the line. But the slogans of unionism, especially if backed by the idea of cooperative management, easily lead to a program not of cushioning the impact of change but of preventing it. The trend of modern development is to put even the most energetic businessman under three masters: the directors and stockholders of the corporation; the union;

the government. Their mutual "checks and balances" increasingly drain away the energy which has gone into the constructive change upon which rising living standards depend, and the executive is more and more reduced to a mere manager obliged to follow the line of least resistance—the sabotage of invention. Here is one of the most important reasons why thoroughgoing unionization is so often associated with technological stagnation.

Many people like to resolve economic life into a struggle between a fluid mass called "labor," all of whose members have identical interests, and another homogeneous group called "management" whose members likewise have identical interests. Few pictures are more misleading; and until we have gone beyond such simple divisions we can never understand the full oppressive potentialities of a unionism which has allowed itself to become distorted by the security motive, or by the will to power. In truth there is not infrequently a closer common interest, not merely in theory but in fact and conscious action, between employers and employed of one group, and employers and employed of another, than there ever is between all employers as such and all employed as such. Convenient myths of the class struggle, or onslaughts upon "business" as opposed to "labor," may be good propaganda tactics, but behind such masks as these some of the worst distortions of union motives occur.

As background to the full understanding of this problem it is necessary to stress once more the importance of the transfer mechanism as a supplement to the elective method. Unless the worker already has a modicum of economic independence, his bare vote in a large political electorate, or large union, will not protect him adequately; and this economic independence is closely related to the ability to change jobs.

During the past ten years government has done a great deal to remove economic barriers to transference, as we have seen; and it should do a great deal more. Social security, unemployment benefits, employment exchanges, vocational reeducation, relative stabilization of aggregate employment, and so on, all furnish promising avenues of approach. Such a regime renders transference so much easier that an arbitrary employer may soon find himself losing valuable men and be forced to reconsider his position independently of the organized strike. If he does not adjust himself he will have to take the consequences in declining efficiency of operation; and it is doubtful that he can pursue his policy indefinitely. Still more important for democratic freedom, the employee, under these conditions, who remains with such an employer will be himself largely to blame. If he stays because he loves a particular town, is he a "slave" to his employer or a "slave" to his love for the town? Frederick Wakeman in his blistering exposé of the advertising industry, *The Hucksters*, is almost alone among modern intellectuals in recognizing this point. The monstrous executive portrayed by him prostitutes the lives of his sycophants not so much because they cannot help themselves as because they love money more than self-respect.

But the more expensive and the more difficult it becomes to transfer, the more inapplicable becomes our analysis. Particularly if a whole industry is brought under one rule, and if transfer involves elaborate retraining, the power of the union leadership may become almost overwhelming. Thus, if the locals of a union are so "integrated" as to be mere rubber stamps of a central directorate, and if employers in their turn are forced into a single cartel, it is useless to talk any longer of transference, or of competition. Union policy which brings about these results is the antithesis of democracy, and under such circumstances labor itself becomes a frequent exploiter of labor.

The monopolistic and "self-exploiting" possibilities of distorted union action can be worked out in two ways: first, as it affects the weaker worker; and second, as it affects the weaker firm. Few if any American unions take the extreme position that all profit is unjustified. Virtually always the cry is "reasonable" profit. But what is "reasonable"? We have discussed this point in earlier chapters and will return to it later. For the present it is enough to realize that one of the prime slogans of union action is the reduction of profit margins to a "reasonable" figure.

Some orthodox economic theorists imply that the union cannot "squeeze" the "surplus" profits out of industry without severe repercussions upon labor itself; but this cannot be stated as a universal proposition. In static, well entrenched, "monopolistic" firms a considerable part of the proceeds of special privilege may be diverted to the union members. The result, however, is that the union becomes in effect a silent partner in exploitation of the general public; and we will trace the effects later. But no responsible economist should deny that a militant union can sometimes squeeze a considerable part of the "loot" from entrenched "monopoly."

Yet, though in favorable circumstances this may not have adverse effects upon employees who are already union members, there is almost always a narrowing of the opportunities of many other workers, and frequently of the union members themselves. The difficulty lies in the fact that large-scale money-wage increases aimed at the profit margin nearly always also make profitable the introduction of "labor-saving" devices which otherwise would not have been used. For example, a raise in the wages of elevator operators may be demanded to benefit the worker; but we may find instead that promptly many automatic elevators have been installed, cutting down the number of jobs. Those workers who still have jobs benefit, but many others will be permanently excluded from elevator work. People think of the "ousting of men by machines" as a perfectly accidental and automatic process. They do not realize how often excessive wage demands give it a special impetus.

It is true that the "substitution" of machinery for men may lead to an artificial demand for the products of the machine industry. But in practice this works chiefly for the benefit of a small group of highly skilled workers in machine plants. It does not help the mass of semiskilled men who are excluded. In any society one would expect to find some highly paid jobs for skilled labor, some medium-paid jobs for mediocre labor, and some poorly paid jobs for unskilled or incompetent labor. Pushing wages too high in the middle ranks may "split" the wage structure. When full effects are considered certain groups of labor benefit by very high wages; but the substitution of machinery for hand work, plus restriction of union membership, tends to force others down into lower-grade occupations. The "increases in productivity" so often urged as an argument for higher wages have frequently an ominous meaning. Sometimes they reflect a genuine gain in efficiency from larger volume; but often they may also be the result of unnecessary mechanization. Total labor income may be unchanged—possibly even somewhat increased; but its distribution among laborers may be increasingly unequal. "Disguised unemployment" crowds farming and other low-yield subsistence occupations. If manufacturing wage rates were only 50 per cent higher than agricultural wage rates thirty-five years ago, they now average more than double.

The point of view just expressed rouses much opposition, and numerous statistical studies have been undertaken to refute it. These, however, have succeeded only in establishing what most economists were already prepared to admit; namely, that there is a considerable zone of indeterminacy in the wage bargain. But the role of high money wages in inducing mechanization that otherwise would not have been undertaken, and the fact that labor is frequently a partner in monopoly, remain incontrovertible.

Let us restate the point of view put forward here. We do not deny that money-wage increases paralleling the spontaneous increases of productivity in society may be valuable and desirable for the whole community. Nor do we deny that certain groups may, in any case, benefit from wage increases even though society as a whole does not. However, indiscriminate attempts by the union to seize profits supposed (correctly or incorrectly) to be excessive, often set a wage so high as to cut off opportunity for weaker workers, to increase technological unemployment, and to foster monopoly. For reasons such as these many English socialist theorists have long conceded that the best way to capture profits in fact excessive (by whatever standard is involved) is through appropriate income taxation—not wage increases.

Turn from the weaker worker to the weaker firm, and it is often the case that, after a union has forced giant corporations to "cut it in" on the gains of special position, it will try to force the weaker concerns to meet similar wage demands. These concerns may be of several types. They may be older and less efficiently managed, beginning to run downhill. They may be smaller, with less favorable locations or contacts than the industrial giants; or they may be young and vigorous firms, potential sources of renewed competition and technical change, but still struggling to build up business connections and overcome the economic barriers which protect established corporations. In any case these firms "on the margin" furnish a prime guarantee of transference, democracy, and competition.

Now it is not always true that "marginal" firms pay lower wages than the leaders of the industry. Some of them, especially in areas where labor has been particularly scarce, may pay higher. But for the most part it is probable that their wage rates are somewhat lower than those which can be extorted from the strong, established corporation. Yet the smaller firms often enjoy an advantage in the labor market. Because they are small they can be made pleasanter places in which to work, with a stronger sense of personal contact and of "belonging"; and many laborers prefer rather lower wages in a small firm to the rush and anonymity of a large one. These advantages, however, will not appeal to the Napoleonic labor leader bent upon creating an industrial army responsive to his sway. He will raise the cry of "sweat shops," "exploitation," and either by a series of strikes or more likely by "industry-wide" bargaining will try to force a wage rate that is appropriate to the specially privileged concern upon competing concerns that are at the verge of solvency.

Yet, if such demands are pushed through, one of two things is likely to happen. Either prices to the public will be raised (which will probably increase once more the profits of the stronger concerns and start a new round of strikes); or the smaller concerns will be forced out of the industry, and one or two large firms will be left facing an all-embracing union. The margin of transference and competition will largely have disappeared. It is not surprising that under such conditions even some trade unionists themselves admit, "The ordinary rank and file union member frequently enjoys less freedom in relation to his own leader than he does in relation to his employer."

Behind this problem of the new or the "marginal" firm there often lies the problem of fundamental change and development.

We have seen that a well organized union can make itself a partial beneficiary of monopoly. But if this is the case a situation develops which the "liberal" who allows himself to think only in terms of an army of workers with identical interests, facing an army of capitalists with identical interests, will be powerless to understand. For while the entrenched union is digging itself in, a large population of farmers and farm workers remain at a much lower standard of living. Even if such underprivileged individuals try to move to industrialized areas they are likely to find that the established union does not, save in the emergency of war or at the top of a boom, welcome a "flooding" of its market by newcomers. Under such conditions the remaining hope of the agricultural laborer who wishes to go into industry will be the establishment of new plants, in new areas—in other words, a geographical decentralization of industry. Furthermore, unless monopoly is airtight, or unless other restrictive policies are overwhelming, businessmen will soon be found to take advantage of the opportunity.

Under such conditions, the unions in the favored areas might be expected to welcome increased industrialization and higher living standards for their "brother workers" in the corn and cotton fields—New York looking with approval upon the expansion and industrialization of Kansas, Texas, and Mississippi. Unfortunately, this is not always the case. Though a good part of the expansion in agricultural states represents a net gain for the whole country, and though there can be no doubt of the long-range benefits in cultural unity and better living conditions from a more widely diffused industrialism, nevertheless some of this growth is bound to be at the expense of the favored areas—and not merely at the expense of favored owners but of favored workers as well. In other words breaking the grip of private Eastern vested interests does not merely hurt the "monopolist." In the short run at least, it also hurts the unions that have participated in the proceeds of monopoly. Wage rates, or employment, or both, in the former favored areas will begin to feel the pressure from outside.

It is not surprising, therefore, that employees as well as employers in the regions, industries, or firms which are losing ground should try to hamper the development which affects their special interest. And the private vested interest of management finds the union an invaluable ally, or cat's-paw, in the struggle. For the union can throw a banner of noble purpose and high-sounding altruism over what is in essence largely a sordid battle to retain special advantage. Under such circumstances it is neither unusual nor impossible for entrenched privilege to "sic" its union upon the rising new firm or new region which is threatening their mutual power. Such an attitude is scarcely democratic yet the emphasis of American liberalism is becoming increasingly urban, and it is more impregnated with Marxian ideas of the "class" struggle than it realizes. In consequence the activities of the union win wide toleration. Henry Wallace, for example, says much about the role of business "monopoly" in holding back the expansion of the Middle West. But he has said relatively little about the role of union "monopoly" in doing substantially the same thing.

There is one question which we must ask ourselves if we want to get our ideas clear, and that is: What is a sweat shop? Many people seem to think it any concern which does not pay wages as high as any special group happens to think right. But so wide a definition is meaningless. A true sweat shop is a concern which employs very young, very old, very sickly, very crippled, very ignorant, or otherwise helpless people and, taking advantage of their helplessness, pays them so little and works them so hard that they become even more sick, helpless, ignorant, or crippled. The state and the union are amply justified in putting an end to such a process. But the concept, as we have outlined it, is a matter not merely of wages but also of sociological conditions. If the unions are really democratic they have to face the fact that there are degrees of skill and knowledge among laborers as among other people, and that many workers are capable of earning a decent and self-respecting, if simple, livelihood but are not efficient enough to be employed at top wages. If we insist upon top wages for all employees, we exclude these people from opportunity which would have been theirs and often leave them no remedy but relief.

When therefore the cry is raised that such and such a new or marginal firm is paying "sweat-shop" wages, we should go beyond the wage scale and ask what sociological conditions accompany it. If raw and ignorant workers are being given a chance to go into industry, under conditions which give them an opportunity to better their social and economic status, are we justified in interfering to throw them on relief, or back into rural slums? If a firm under a geographical or other disadvantage pays lower wages but gives good working conditions, should the union prevent the laborer who prefers small size to dollars from making his choice? If the transfer mechanism works as well as we could make it work, the healthy worker who is genuinely "sweated" will not be sweated long. But we shall not overcome the difficulty democratically by creating a number of entrenched labor empires separated from one another by restrictions of all sorts.

The basic plea of this chapter is that we must not let artificial slogans of "horizontal" class distinction blind us to the frequently far more severe and bitter "vertical" struggles between groups and occupations within a "class." As Lord Keynes has said in his *General Theory of Employment* *—almost the bible of American liberalism: "The struggle about money-wages primarily affects the distribution of the aggregate real wage between different labor groups. The effect of combination on the part of a group of workers is to protect their *relative* real wage. The *general* level of real wages depends on the other forces of the economic system." Still more explicitly he has alluded to the unions as "once the oppressed, now the tyrants, whose selfish and sectional schemes need to be bravely opposed." On such high authority, the analysis we have given cannot be dismissed as reactionary; nor can its correctness be successfully denied.

Complete survey of the restrictive and unstabilizing effect of perverted union action would require an excursion into monetary policy and into the role of equalitarian and syndicalist bias in American postwar inflation. Monetary problems, however, will be deferred to a chapter on the specific problem of planning. The question we must ask here is: Granted the recurrent abuses whose possibility we have shown, what can be done? We have seen that the union bureaucracy may sometimes oppress and exploit the union's

* Published by Harcourt, Brace and Company, Inc.

own membership, and that bargaining and other policies frequently work to foster monopoly. The disrupting potentialities of large-scale strikes in our highly integrated economy need little demonstration. But again, what is the proper solution?

Many labor leaders as well as employers talk as if the problem of strikes would be settled by more "responsible" union organization. Frequently the leader is able to get employer support for more "discipline" inside the union. Such a trend of development is essentially authoritarian. It fits in well with the fundamental dislike of competition and decentralization so often displayed by the Napoleonic labor leader. Yet the argument, like the argument for "monopoly," appeals to some business people. The chief reasoning behind such measures is the short-run gain in "efficiency" usually promised. But the most completely efficient organization from such an approach would be a chain gang. Perhaps some "wild-cat" strikes are prevented. But what is gained by the worker if he is taken out of a moderately strict control by the employer and put under far stricter rule by the union leadership? The idea is essentially undemocratic. From the point of view, also, of simple self-preservation, the businessman who supports it is as shortsighted as the businessman who supports the "monopoly" or cartel. Once the union leader creates an ironclad, all-embracing industrial army, the employer will soon be treated as a supernumerary. But for the worker under such circumstances it will merely be a change of masters—and by no means necessarily for the better.

Similar objections apply to proposals for direct government regulation of the union. As one writer puts it: "Nor would the conversion of the unions into quasi-governmental bodies necessarily serve to protect the masses of members from abuse by union officials. On the contrary, the probabilities are that this process would actually increase the arbitrary power of union officials. . . . Such at least has been the experience hitherto, for every extension of the quasi-public character of unionism under recent New Deal legislation has brought additional authority and power to the trade-union officialdom." *

Another method recently applied with apparent success is gov-

* Will Herberg, *The Antioch Review*, Fall 1943.

ernment seizure followed by the use of legal injunctions and fines. This also cannot be justified as a long-run democratic solution. From the point of view of the union it opens the way to every species of political blackmail. From the point of view of the public it is utterly unreliable, for its application is entirely dependent upon the character and discretion of the man who chances to be in office as President or governor. Finally, from the point of view of democracy it gives rise to an intolerable degree of arbitrary personal power. One cannot rule out the emergency powers of the executive, but their promiscuous exercise is very nearly if not quite as bad as unjustified strikes.

Two other suggestions popular today must also be mentioned: compulsory arbitration, and profit sharing. The essential weakness of compulsory arbitration is that the board often would be called upon to "arbitrate" not a wage dispute but the fundamental legal, political, and economic structure of the United States. This is too much power to be exercised piecemeal, and without guiding standards, by any group of conciliators. For example, suppose the issue is one of forcing the employers to submit to industry-wide bargaining, or of sharing control in the management. The naïve assumption that there is always a solution which can be reached by "men of good will" "sitting around a table" by no means always follows when basic political-economic philosophy is at stake. Even in "simple" wage disputes the problem can soon turn into government regulation of profits and wages. We may be forced into something like this in a few semipublic utilities, but it certainly is not an aid to competitive democracy. Finally, there is the question of enforcement: Will not compulsory arbitration in some cases lead to "involuntary servitude"?

Before making a general approach toward constructive policy we must discuss the idea of "profit sharing." This is proposed less as a direct remedy for strikes than as a means of creating a better psychological climate. Despite the apparent validity and simplicity of the idea, it does not seem to be an adequate solution. It does not per se overcome the psychological problems of size; nor does it meet the problem of unionism perverted by the will to power, the security motive, or the desire to create a syndicalist world. If we begin in an atmosphere of fundamental economic and personal hostility, there can be just as much dispute over the percentage of profit which is to be shared, as over the wage rate which is to be paid. Furthermore, what is "profit"? How much shall be deducted in allowances for obsolescence and replacement? How much for advertising? How much spent currently for new equipment? Of what type? Profit sharing looks simple; but it can easily become cooperative management in another guise, with all the restrictive tendencies which this implies. For though the management (and even some union leaders) may be convinced that the introduction of a new machine would increase profit certain groups of workers could quite possibly lose more in wages by the change than they gained in their share of profit. In the same way it still might pay to strike if the hoped-for gain in wages were greater than the expected profit share. It is at least likely that profit sharing would create more causes of friction than it would eliminate. One must be slow to assume that because a given firm uses profit sharing and has no strikes the profit sharing *per se* is the cause of the lack of strikes. On the contrary such firms are usually smaller ones under a particularly intelligent management striving to create good feeling and good working conditions in the shop. It is the size and the management—not the profit sharing—that are apt to be the prime factor in the situation.

But, again, what are we to do? The first requisite is that we decide once for all what role we expect the union movement to play in our economy. Do we want a syndicalist regime of cooperative management? Do we want planned monopoly, or do we want competition? The argument of this book leads to the conclusion that the "cooperative" ideal of a world free from rivalry is unattainable even in theory in an industrial interdependent economy; and that attempts to introduce it in practice lead to restriction and social stratification. Therefore we maintain that the role of the union in a competitive democracy is as a protective supplement to the competitive order—not a substitute for it.

We cannot expect to retain a democratic system and have no strikes. Some conflict is inevitable from the mere fact of freedom. What we must aim for, therefore, is rather a policy which keeps the strikes from becoming a national menace. A fundamental requirement of such a policy is that management do everything it can to mitigate the psychological friction of size; that not only the union but the company foster athletics, recreation, and so on, and help to bring about more decent welfare conditions. It is important also that all this be done honestly and with a minimum of company interference. Napoleonic union leaders are not the only Caesarian-minded people in the industrial field. Oppressive paternalism can be just as irritating as oppressive neglect.

In the same way the industrial worker, so far as possible, must be kept from feeling himself "lost." He ought to be able to feel that he has a fair chance of crossing the line into management, and the social line should be removed as far as possible. There will always be good reason for giving many higher jobs to more highly educated men. But the company would do well to consider a program of scholarships for abler younger workers. In general the worker must be considered as a human being and not as another cog in the machine.

One must not suppose that such a policy will *ipso facto* end industrial conflict. The militant unionist will ridicule the whole idea. The Marxist will call it a cream-puff policy to divert the workers from their fundamental "exploitation" and persuade them to be "traitors to their class." Relations may frequently look hopeless. But while the policy suggested is not enough in itself to bring about good industrial relations in a large firm one can be certain that without it there is no hope of long-run good relations.

Assume, however, that all that can be done to alleviate the psychological frictions of size has been done, that wages are fair throughout the country (not neglecting the interests of the weaker worker and the new firm), and that sweat shops (properly defined) are outlawed. Assume further that there are still crippling strikes and pressures toward monopoly. What are we to do? Such strikes would ultimately trace back to the will to power, the security motive, or movements aiming at supplanting the competitive democratic order. Can nothing be done?

Many people seem to feel that the matter can be left to the "self-restraint" of the unions. This is rather like the idea popular in some circles in the 1890's that the trust problem could be settled by leaving it to the "self-restraint" of the businessmen. The idea of "freedom of bargaining" commands today much the same emotional and uncritical adherence that the idea of "freedom of contract" commanded a generation ago. The hypothetical clergyman who remarked in the nineties that "we should leave the economic life of the country to the control of those great and good men to whom God has given the wealth" could be closely echoed in some modern implications that we could leave it to those "great and good labor leaders to whom God has given the votes."

Maintenance of liberal democracy, as I see it, requires that we treat the large predatory union on the same basis as the large predatory business. The large union may be a natural response to the large business. But neither is desirable *per se,* and neither should receive emotional encouragement in restrictive or predatory activities. In other words, both should be under reasonable and impartial antitrust laws. There is, of course, no such thing as an absolutely impartial law, or any other human act; but, as said before, there are distinctions of degree, and these are the differences men live by. Here again, regarding antitrust laws, there is need for careful thinking; and here again the fundamental obstacle is refusal to face the problem at all. The still occasionally surviving conservative dogma that there should be no unions, and the union dogma that there should be no union restraints, meet to produce chaos. As far as strikes go, the quasi-public character of certain industries may have to be recognized in definite rules for compulsory arbitration preferably of the limited sort recently proposed by Professor Slichter. This, however, seems to be an unmitigated evil, unfortunately sometimes necessary. It is to be hoped that the unions, awake to their own interests, will manage to avoid it.

Finally, behind any specific program there are two fundamental requirements: (1) that the unions accept the essentials of a democratic-competitive profit system—which means high risk-profits for new investment; and (2) that the public come to regard the large unions with the healthy suspicion now reserved for the large business. There is no chance for common sense if all strikes are to be regarded as a conflict of angels and devils—never mind which side one thinks the angels or devils happen to be.

These suggestions, it might be said, are counsels of perfection. But are we justified in ruling out intelligent and democratic understanding? And the rank and file of unionism may well ask itself if it really will be any happier under a regime which seeks to prevent inflation by reducing saving, to increase production by reducing incentive, to foster opportunity by encouraging monopoly, and to stimulate invention by giving unlimited power to the industrial vested interest.

In conclusion I should like to stress once more that I have made these criticisms and pointed out these possibilities not to show that labor is any worse than business, but that it is no better. The sins of business are committed within a framework of explicit "self-interest" which, if anything, exaggerates the predatory nature of business policies, and makes criticism extremely easy. But the sins of labor occur under a banner of noble disinterestedness, and those who think only by labels are easily misled. Yet, were we to accord to business the same fantastic tolerance frequently demanded for the unions, it is by no means clear which side would come off better in the final judgment. I have therefore stressed the abuses which are hardest to detect. It is much easier to deal with a wolf, than with a wolf in sheep's clothing.

· X ·

Economic Isolationism and the Capitalist Future

OUR ECONOMIC theme in this book, like that of many radicals, is the conflict of technical progress and the vested interest. But unlike many radicals we have not placed ultimate responsibility upon "absentee ownership" or other capitalist features alone. Instead we have tried to present the clash of science and security in the broadest possible institutional context, and to show the rivalry of the inventor and the artisan as a universal characteristic of human society. Certain aspects of the manner in which this conflict, and its resulting maladjustments, work to choke off industrial production within a nation have been shown in the two chapters preceding. Now we must trace the same forces at work in international life.

The title of the present chapter is "Economic Isolationism and the Capitalist Future." More properly it should be "Democratic Future"; but "Capitalist" emphasizes the extraordinary conflict frequently existing today between conservative aims and conservative policies in the United States. Economic isolationism, however, is no monopoly of any faction. The great danger to the perpetuation of a democratic world at the present time is that, while political isolationism now appears to be dying in America both on the right and on the left, neither the American liberals nor the American conservatives have entirely caught up with the twentieth century in their economic thinking. We are still largely preoccupied with the conditions of 1933.

In order to show the problem in proper perspective we will reverse the usual procedure and begin outside the United States. Prior to the Second World War there were three great "machine makers to the world": England, Germany, and the United States. Russia

153

was an embryonic fourth, with various secondary powers such as France, Japan, and Sweden helping to make up the total. The war largely destroyed Germany and Japan, temporarily at least crippled Russia and France, and seriously damaged England. So far as Germany is concerned we thus far appear to have decided to continue as a matter of peacetime policy the destruction brought on by war. We thus find Europe devastated at the same time at which a large part of her capacity for reconstruction has been removed.

Even before the Second World War, however, the standard of living of most of the world could not have been considered high by any American or British ideas. Thus, aside from what the German army did to Russia, it would still have been necessary for the Russian people in 1939 to multiply their capital equipment many times over in order to approach the prewar productive standards of the United States. By very generous estimates the national income per person of British India, the wealthiest nation of continental Asia, does not exceed $200 a year; and it has sometimes been set as low as $20. And so the tale goes.

Between world wars, to be sure, it would have been superficially plausible to argue that China, India, Africa, and, to a less extent, South America were largely "satisfied" with a handicraft standard of living, and that therefore they should not be counted in estimating the industrial needs of the world. But all such contentions ring hollow today. There runs now throughout the world a great stirring of handicraft peoples. Nations which for millennia have been content with a peasant economy are beginning to demand an industrial standard of living. All the countries of the world have been jostled together, and the resulting cross-fertilization of ideas has superimposed upon the wants of ruined Europe a gigantic and worldwide cry for "More!"

Pressures toward scarcity, moreover, are not exhausted in listing the devastation of Europe and the growing demands of the "backward" peoples. Even in nations still relatively wealthy, the quantities of money poured out by the belligerents to finance the war have raised consumption habits higher than ever. Almost everywhere today the age is one of want, inflation, and starvation.

These circumstances might have been expected to fill the United

States, the one great power whose industrial plant is unimpaired, with pride and confidence, and to make it redouble its efforts at production. Instead the American reaction is one of doubt and confusion: many conservatives shiver at the thought of "cheap foreign competition," while nearly all the liberals still talk of shortages of demand.

Throughout this book one question has been raised again and again: Is saving useful? We have seen that a prime argument for redistributive taxation has been that the well-to-do have a tendency on average to save too much. And we have also seen that an opposing school of thought argues that the competitive-capitalist distribution of wealth is justified because it is the best method of getting an adequate flow of saving without the widespread starvation and repression of Russian methods. Like most disputes, the argument has a time dimension. Certain pessimists used to maintain that immediately after V-J day there would be several million unemployed. They say very little about that now. But today the argument has been shifted into the future, and it is maintained that over the long run—say ten years—saving will prove excessive.

The writer has never shared the short-run pessimism regarding demand which many postwar planners displayed. Nevertheless, over the long run there does appear more of a problem. If we consider the continental United States alone, and if we try to confine our investment to our own territory, then it seems at least doubtful whether, on average, all our investment can be absorbed once the postwar backlog is made up. There are certain theoretical arguments concerning the "boundlessness" of human wants, and the effects of continued price and wage reduction whose abstract validity we have already conceded. But these arguments, by themselves, do not furnish reliable guides to practical policy. As Lord Keynes put it:

The object of saving is to release labor for employment in producing . . . goods such as houses, factories, roads, machines, and the like. But if there is a large unemployed surplus already available for such purposes then the effect of saving is merely to add to this surplus and therefore to increase the number of the unemployed. Moreover when a man is thrown out of work in this or any other way, his diminished spending power causes further unemployment amongst those who would have produced what he can no longer afford to buy. And so the position gets worse and worse in a vicious circle.*

In the last three chapters we have shown the manner in which hostile taxation and security sabotage, by conservative and left-wing forces alike, discourages new investment and holds back economic growth. Many economists would put the whole responsibility for such stagnation as Keynes has talked of upon obstacles like these. However, if the continental United States alone is considered, it is doubtful whether the entire blame can be thrown upon sabotage and taxation. We will not run over the "political arithmetic" on which the argument is based, and which has been so widely discussed in recent years. Suffice it to say that, despite present shortages and inflation (which the writer predicted), there are still valid reasons for supposing that over the long pull our savings will be excessive if we try to invest them in the continental United States alone.

But why should investment be thus circumscribed? This question reaches the core of the problem. The basic choice facing the United States in her *long-run* saving and investment problem is between redistributing wealth or seeking a margin of foreign investment. This is the issue which so many Americans of nearly all political creeds are desperately trying to avoid. For whichever choice is made implies serious embarrassments both for the conservative and for the radical. The first choice—redistribution—I will call, more or less figuratively, medieval "Japanese." It implies a determination to confine ourselves to home activity as much as possible. The second choice—foreign investment—we may call "Elizabethan." It is a policy of world-wide constructive action. America is not the first nation suddenly to be pushed into world affairs. Let us try to outline our choices with some reference to historical precedent.

Japan in the sixteenth and early seventeenth centuries carried on a lively trade with the European "barbarians." Europeans founded many trading posts, converted many Japanese to Christianity, in-

* "Essays in Persuasion" by John Maynard Keynes. Quoted by permission of Harcourt, Brace and Company, Inc.

troduced the large-scale use of money, and, in general, set in motion numerous forces profoundly disrupting to the customs and habits of Japanese feudalism. Rather than adapt themselves, the Japanese adopted a policy of economic isolation. All ports were closed save one, the Christians were persecuted and almost eliminated, the population was kept stable by infanticide, and every effort made to maintain the *status quo*. Japan became a hermit nation.

The results, however, were not as happy as the ideas of many modern anti-industrial medievalists would lead us to imagine. Despite every effort it proved as impossible then as it has always done to eliminate completely by law the impact of new ideas and new institutions. Foreign commerce was abolished, even to the general destruction of ocean-going ships; but the use of money and the rise of a commercial class continued, with disruption of feudal mores. In addition, even in the large areas substantially removed from commercial change, the "great peace" of the two hundred years of Japanese isolation was scarcely tranquil. Population, though severely limited, yet pressed close upon subsistence. There were no fewer than seven great famines in which thousands died though quantities of food were at hand in Korea and China. Worse yet, even within Japan, the means of communication were for the most part kept so crude that food could not be moved from district to district. After two hundred years of decay, disturbance, and retrogression the "barbarians" came again—this time from the United States and in force—and Japan was "compelled" to abandon her isolationist experiment. But the evidence indicates that even without Perry's ships the nation was ripe for change.

Contrast Japan with another small island country, England, during the same era. Instead of repelling change the English welcomed it, and began a tremendous expansion of world trade. By the middle of the nineteenth century, when Japan was finally abandoning her isolation, England was the richest and strongest nation of the world. Lord Keynes wrote in 1930:

The value of Great Britain's foreign investments today is estimated at about £4,000,000,000. This yields us an income at the rate of about 6½ per cent. Half of this we bring home and enjoy; the other half, namely 3¼ per cent, we leave to accumulate abroad at compound interest. Something of this sort has been going on for about 250 years.

For I trace the beginnings of British foreign trade to the treasure which Drake stole from Spain in 1580. . . . Queen Elizabeth . . . out of her share . . . paid off the whole of England's foreign debt, balanced her Budget, and found herself about £40,000 in hand. This she invested in the Levant Company—which prospered. Out of the profits of the Levant Company the East India Company was founded; and the profits of this great enterprise were the foundation of England's subsequent foreign investment. Now it happens that £40,000 accumulating at 3¼ per cent compound interest . . . would actually amount today to the total of £4,000,000,000 which . . . our foreign investments now are. Thus every £1 which Drake brought home in 1580, has now become £100,000.*

The two examples just given cannot of course be applied in any sense literally to the present situation of the United States. In the first place it would be impossible for the United States to isolate herself now as completely as Japan did. This fact calls for a discussion of just how "self-sufficient" we really are. In the second place no democratic thinker would advocate solving the employment problem by launching a mere program of national piracy; and this calls for an examination of the differences between "foreign investment" on the one hand and "imperialism" on the other.

Nevertheless there are similarities. In order to get a clear idea of the question, it is necessary to disentangle "long-run" and "short-run" problems. As already pointed out, any responsible economist must admit the constant possibility of short-run "cyclical" collapses in any dynamic economic system. The present debates over economic policy in the United States, however, do not primarily concern temporary lapses from full employment. Such lapses are a serious social problem and must be provided for but they do not compare in difficulty with long-range unemployment. Shall we redistribute still more drastically, or shall we lend abroad?

Putting our choice so bluntly embarrasses many people, for, as will shortly be shown, there is almost no political group in this

---

* "Essays in Persuasion" by John Maynard Keynes. Reprinted by permission of Harcourt, Brace and Company, Inc.

country which can face the issue squarely without abandoning certain cherished features of its program. Putting the matter so baldly also raises a host of technical problems; for no man in his senses would imply that the job of re-creating any approach to a free world market could be carried through without encountering tremendous difficulties. We shall not discuss here the technical monetary problems, which shift from day to day, but put our emphasis rather on long-run problems, aims, and motives. Assuming for the moment that a relatively free world investment market could be re-created, let us see why it is that so many people are reluctant to take the necessary steps.

The first objection always made by adherents of a "Japanese" policy, whether they are radical or conservative, is: "Why should we build up foreigners when we have poverty at home?" This exceedingly plausible question must be examined at length. Most people who advance it, however, have one fundamental fallacy in mind. They assume extravagant figures for the benefits the poor would derive from their policy. In the chapter on "Redistribution of Wealth" we calculated that the gain per person from redistributing the entire margin of "net" new investment in this country—that is, the annual amount of saving and investment that could be diverted without causing the economy to run backward—would amount to not much more than $125 per person in 1940 dollars. But since few of the most ardent redistributors (save those pursuing equality for its own sake) would propose anything so drastic as complete elimination of net new investment, the amount should probably bet set considerably lower. Call it $100 per person. This is scarcely a tremendous amount.

But even $100 per person is probably too high an estimate, for such vast transfers of labor and resources cannot be managed automatically. Nor can we overlook the repercussions of the taxation entailed upon incentive. No idea is more deeply ingrained in the mind of the public today than that there is somewhere a vast store of "wealth" which the rich withhold from the rest of us. We have already shown, and could show still more conclusively, how extraordinarily this margin is exaggerated. But it is even more important to realize that at best such "wealth" is only potential. It has no physical existence at the present time. In so far as the capital wealth of the rich has physical existence now, it is in the form of steel mills, mines, and so on. But these do not directly increase consumption. You cannot eat a turbine or sleep in a smokestack. Again, so far as the atomic bomb and other inventions go, indeterminate years of experiment lie ahead before they will be useful to civilians. It is as if some clairvoyant in 1830 had foreseen (as T. B. Macaulay rather accurately did) the full results of the industrial revolution, and demanded in that year redistribution on the basis of the potential output of 1930. We cannot insist on the present enjoyment of the inventions of the next century—or even the next five years. Our tendency is to assume that demand automatically satisfies itself. Yet as large-scale redistribution increases the demand for consumption products it may also reduce the incentive to invest in making them. The odds are overwhelming that the government will have to fill the gap.

Government, however, has seldom proved very imaginative in the field of consumers' services. Vast public amphitheaters and baths were the Roman answer to the problem. Up to the present ours has primarily been battleships. Perhaps we can do better in the future. But one may well be skeptical of the amount of personal satisfactions which will actually be derived from a redistribution program. And when we remember the effects of redistribution taxes in stratifying society, and decreasing competition, it is reasonable to assume that the rate of introduction of new inventions will be greatly retarded. Thus even if some net investment still be permitted, great pressures toward technological stagnation are set in motion which cannot easily be reversed. The redistributive solution is not merely one of economic isolation. It will probably be one of cultural stagnation also. The notion of a vast surplus of undistributed wealth, like most popular notions, derives from a definite fact. It took shape in 1933 when the western world was indeed suffering from an unnecessary scarcity, and there was "poverty in the midst of" relative "plenty." But those days are past, and if we have any regard for our own interests, as well as for the welfare of the world, we shall begin to think once more in terms of scarcity and of production.

If, then, treating the problem of long-run "over-saving" by

redistribution makes for a great reduction in the dynamic nature of our economy, it must be realized that the twentieth century United States can afford even less than seventeenth century Japan to adopt a semistationary cultural pattern. For the mere maintenance of our present standard of living—quite aside from its improvement—implies the importation from abroad of many vital necessities. Our machinery, for example, cannot keep its quality if numerous foreign-mined alloys are not available. Tin, rubber, sugar, coffee, quinine, and hundreds of vital drugs are mostly brought in from abroad. Many of these products and drugs, it is true, could be replaced by substitutes made here—but only at much greater cost. It would take a book in itself to describe the readjustments needed for a self-sufficient United States. It is enough to realize that, though we could continue to live, we could not live well by any modern standard. Yet if, in order to maintain even our present level of well-being, we must import many things, and if we adopt a program which results in a failure to keep up with the development of technique, then a day may come, as it has already come for England, in which—inconceivable as it may now seem—our old-fashioned goods may be at a disadvantage in the world market, and we may find ourselves not merely with a stationary but with a slowly falling standard of living.

This possibility will probably seem farfetched, and indeed it is. For there is another and much more immediate danger. Low though our present average standard of living may seem to be in the light of what we have been taught to expect, it is supreme luxury compared to that of most of the world. If we refuse to help the rest of the world attain a higher standard of living—and by "help" I mean not charity but a chance for self-respecting expansion—can we expect to be allowed indefinitely to enjoy relative riches, and to occupy a great continent which by Asiatic standards is still undeveloped, without being attacked? Japan was allowed to remain a hermit nation for two centuries because she had relatively little which other nations desired. But we have what all nations desire—the greatest industrial plant in the world—and if we cannot use it in peaceable partnership with the rest of the world, then sooner or later some hungry and vigorous tribe of raiders will attempt to seize it from our complacent hands. Self-preservation, as well as altruism, points the way to world employment of our investment industries rather than their drastic curtailment by redistribution at home.

Before we discuss the many obstacles to the foreign investment solution, let us summarize once more the alternatives available for supposed redistributive gain. There is undoubtedly a short-run conflict of interest. That is to say, in the short run the gain in incomes to the lower income groups from redistribution might be more than their gain through expansion of general national income by foreign investment. But this gain is much smaller than is usually supposed, and, once it is realized, little more will be forthcoming. The rate of growth of national income will be tremendously reduced, and all sorts of pressures will develop toward technological stagnation—to say nothing of antidemocratic tendencies in social life. Perhaps a quantitative statement will help to show the problem, though all figures in this connection are bound to be little more than guesses. Net new investment at full employment in this country usually amounts to about 10 per cent of gross national product. That is the maximum proportion which could be redistributed and converted to consumers' goods. But the average rate of growth of output per head under capitalism, over the past century and a half, has been about 2.5 per cent a year. Thus we should gain at most 10 per cent (and probably a good deal less) and thereafter should have relatively little more to expect, while, on the other hand, once foreign investment were well started we could gain in less than "four" years as much as the total benefit from redistribution, and rapid growth of the national income would still be continuing—to say nothing of increased chances for world peace. Of course under modern conditions some growth is possible from "replacement" alone—supposing inventiveness and productivity not to decline; but for reasons already given it is most probable that so drastic a redistribution would be accompanied by social arrangements and attitudes of mind likely to reduce tremendously the effective rate of invention.

The calculation just given is stated merely to put the argument in more concrete form. It is at best an approximation. Nevertheless though many liberals clamor for present foreign relief, their lukewarmness toward a long-run foreign-trade solution arises from the fact that any intelligent consideration of the problem soon points clearly toward the need, if anything, for more rather than less saving—and this is closely related to the distribution of wealth. Of course one cannot say that it is impossible for a socialist state to produce as high a proportion of saving as capitalism, or even a higher proportion. Russia proves the contrary. But such a result would probably be obtained only by the harshest repression. To give an example of what would be needed, we might estimate equal income per family in this country on average at about $2,400 a year (in 1940 dollars). In order to obtain a capitalist ratio of saving, every family with this small income would have to save about 20 per cent, or $480, a year. But families of that income today, on average, save hardly anything at all. Perhaps the whole problem of saving under socialism could be taken out of private hands and managed through government taxation and government investment. Yet taxation necessary to finance such a program even on a capitalist scale might seem unbearably high. In Russia the government has tried to force savings of over 30 per cent. But liberal socialists scarcely advocate the methods she has used, and we have yet to see how much of this ever becomes effective in higher living standards. In the light, then, of world conditions, the desire for peace, and our own self-interest, it is difficult to resist the conclusion that, if we value rising living standards at all, and do not wish to grind our people to a subsistence level, the welfare and peace of the world would be much better served by releasing the full productive powers of capitalist incentives and capitalist saving than by largely destroying them.

Let us now, however, see why some conservatives might still be opposed to the "Elizabethan" policy. There are two reasons. First, though the long-run logic of the foreign investment solution ought to call for renewed emphasis upon saving and so on, many liberals and a majority of more extreme elements in this country use foreign needs as an argument for the reimposition of all sorts of controls to "prevent inflation." We shall come back to this problem later. The second reason for conservative dislike of the foreign solution, however, deserves to be treated first, and concerns the problem of imports. Despite all that has been said concerning the disadvantages of redistribution, and the need for American capital expansion if we are to have world peace, a considerable part of American capitalism is reluctant to face "foreign competition." The trouble lies in the fact that if American loans abroad are to remain solvent we must buy from our debtors at least enough to pay a large part of the interest on the loans. This, however, means lower tariffs, and lower tariffs mean some readjustment of American industry.

Senator Robert A. Taft has put the protectionist argument substantially as follows: "We cannot afford to lend foreigners enough money to buy the best machinery in the world on credit, use that machinery in connection with cheap foreign labor, and then send the finished product back to compete with our own men." The surface plausibility of this argument is striking. Nevertheless it will be found to rest ultimately upon the fallacy that every country —and by equal logic every state, every town, and (why not?) every household—must make everything it uses for itself. Suppose that one "country" raises cattle while another slaughters and packs the meat. Does labor in the meat-packing country put labor in the meat-raising one out of work? Yet what is the difference between this example and the country which specializes in machine making compared with countries which specialize in machine using? Do they put each other out of work? The adoption of a program of foreign investment and substantially lower tariffs might mean that, on balance, some American "light" or consumers' goods industries would in the long run cease to grow as fast as they have grown, and in a few instances might be abandoned. But it would also mean a tremendous increase in the market and in the prosperity of heavy industry and of the country generally. The opposition to freer trade is simply one more example of the age-old conflict of the individual and the general welfare, of security and progress. Nationalist feeling is to many businesses what "security" is to many unions—the banner behind which a special industrial "vested interest" may be protected.

It is neither just nor correct, however, to lay the shortsightedness of American industry regarding the tariff to simple venality plus stupidity or ignorance. The truth is that it is often simply a cultural lag. When American industry was still in its infancy the tariff made a certain amount of sense. It was to be sure a very expensive and divisive method of subsidizing infant industry; nevertheless nearly all economists have conceded the "infant industry" exception to the doctrine of complete free trade. They have always distrusted it, however, for three reasons. First, the infant is seldom willing to admit that he is grown up. Second, some infants are stillborn—that is, no amount of encouragement will ever enable them to stand alone. Third, all that the tariff can do can be done much more cheaply and effectively by subsidies—as is also the case with industries whose skeleton one wishes to preserve for war purposes. And since (as industry well knows) subsidies are far more difficult to justify publicly than tariffs, the chances are that they will be sooner abandoned when genuine industrial maturity has been reached.

Theoretical issues aside, there have been various occasions—for example, after the War of 1812—in which mature and still vigorous English industry deliberately set out to destroy our newly developing industries. The infant New England textile industry was saved only by a tariff put through (ironically enough) by John C. Calhoun of South Carolina. All this, however, is past history. To call the modern American industrial colossus—glowing in the first flush of vigorous and lusty maturity—a helpless infant is ridiculous. The only thing infantile about it, one may sometimes think, is its political brains! So far as industrial efficiency goes, we compete almost too well.

This brings us to a reverse argument. It is sometimes said that the United States can make everything so well that it cannot possibly buy back enough to keep its foreign loans solvent. It is admitted that such imports as we do buy now are vital to our system, but pointed out that their money value (as distinct from their technological importance) is relatively so small that they give very little help to the foreign credit situation. Reenforcing this argument is the frequent assumption that we must collect from abroad in a relatively short time the full capital amount of our loans, and writers such as Professor N. S. Buchanan ridicule the idea that the United States could possibly manage the net collection of say thirty or forty billion dollars in a year or so.

The capital repayment dispute, however, is largely based on misunderstanding of the investment process. Save in time of panic and profound maladjustment, the prudent investor does not try to call in all his loans at once. He invests and reinvests, and, though individual loans are repaid, the money is usually re-lent. The same is true of the national economy. The reader is referred to Lord Keynes's account, earlier quoted, of the history of English foreign trade, from which it will be seen that the value of actual goods imported by England as a result of servicing her loans was only half the interest upon them—in her case 3.25 per cent. Thus, if the principal of American foreign investments comes to equal some thirty or forty billion dollars in seven or eight years, we shall not suddenly have to reimport goods of that amount. Professor Buchanan is probably correct in saying that such a vast movement would be impossible. But with any reasonably intelligent management, the imports necessary will run not to thirty or forty billion a year but to say 3 or 4 per cent of that amount, or about one billion a year. There may be a great deal of shifting about of securities— say from government to private hands and *vice versa*—but the net real imports need not greatly exceed the figure indicated.

In the light of such considerations we can see the import problem in much better perspective, and it must be realized that there is in this country a large potential demand for semiluxury handmade goods of all sorts. Our high tariffs have for over a generation largely excluded from all save the wealthy the imported silks, carpets, laces, wines, glass, toys, china, clothing, spices, and art objects which our people would gladly buy were foreigners once more permitted to build up their demand in this country as the American producers now do. Such imports do not mean any general lowering of American wages or American industry. Our comparative advantage in machinery and heavy industry is so great that we would do much better to expand those lines rather than waste labor making, let us say, imitation oriental rugs. On the other hand, freer trade, like all industrial progress, means that certain protected vested interests will suffer. If we demand that no American producer, however high his costs, shall be ousted by a foreign competitor, then we can never hope for freer trade. But by the same token—let there be no mistake about this—we cannot hope to solve our long-run employment problems save by greatly retarding the growth of our industrial output, or by gradual socialism, or most probably by both together. Nor, far more important, can we have any further hope of a more peaceful or a more democratic world.

Full of the consciousness of their own abstract good intentions toward the world, and sublimely unconscious of the practical effect of their economic policies upon other nations, the American people have to this day not the slightest approach to an adequate conception of the role they played in the economic ruin of Europe and the bringing on of the Second World War. But the fact is that we, be it ever so unintentionally, were nearly as responsible as Hitler for the debacle.

Whether the German and Japanese cultures were so inherently militaristic that they would have fought anyhow, is a question concerning which the writer has no expert knowledge. Therefore we will put it to one side. But even from the most superficial acquaintance with international economics we can say without a doubt that if the German and Japanese peoples had really desired peace, had honestly and sincerely worked for it, they would not have received the slightest ray of hope from the American government, until long after it was too late. When the children of light have nothing to offer, men will turn to the children of darkness. And the American people, through Congress, saw to it that men of good will in Japan and Germany were never able to offer their people any chance of better things.

Let us begin by discussing the Japanese problem. Japan, be it remembered, was industrialized as the sequel to an American naval raid which reopened her ports. Thereafter under the pressure of western ideas the population, which, as we saw, had been kept stable largely by infanticide, was allowed to grow rapidly, and Japan, like England, became unable to feed itself at home. This point is of the utmost importance. Lack of foreign trade to us would mean a lowering of our standard of living, but lack of foreign trade to Japan meant death.

Despite this basic vulnerability the Japanese were able to maintain a standard of living that was rather high for an oriental nation. They bought raw cotton—largely from the United States—processed it at home, and shipped the finished cloth over the whole world. They were thus among the best customers of the American cotton farmer and among the chief rivals of the American and English textile manufacturer. Unfortunately for them, the manufacturers had the greatest political influence.

What follows may be reviewed not in terms of right and wrong but simply in terms of facts. When depression hit the world in 1929 all countries began to increase their tariff barriers against Japan. We did more. After 1932 we not only maintained our barriers against her but also raised the price of our cotton, thus further squeezing her economy. Now it must be remembered that the effect of this on Japan was not merely inconvenience, it was starvation. She had the choice of quietly submitting to the throttling of her economy by the western democracies or trying to fight her way out. Eventually she took the fighting way.

It cannot be disputed that Japan, ever since her westernization, has had an arrogant military caste patterned on the Prussian model. These men despised efforts toward peaceful commercial cooperation and sought to establish a regime of imperial conquest; but the point is that they were a minority, and that they gained their power only as it was made increasingly clear that Japan had no hope of being admitted to world trade on equal terms. The American public saw none of this. The United States gratuitously and unnecessarily insulted her in her own eyes, by excluding Japanese yet nominally admitting African immigration; and followed this by a series of economic measures, all of which, however unintentionally, were directly aimed at her economy. During the most crucial years our Ambassador was a member of a textile family, Mr. Grew —with all his moral excellence of character, unfitted by interest and by training to understand the situation. He thought the rise of Japanese militarism—which, to do him justice he clearly foresaw—merely the result of a lust for conquest and was of the opinion that no economic concession would have reached the real problem. By the time a more intelligent understanding came, it was too late. Perhaps it was always too late, from the time we forced the Japanese ports open. But certainly between world wars no adequate effort at understanding was ever made. Take next the case of Germany. German reparations after the First World War were in fact collected for and by the United States, since the governments of England, France, and Italy merely forwarded to us, in settlement of inter-Allied war debts, the sums Germany paid to them. But Germany itself did not at first make any great effort at repayment. Instead American dollars borrowed by individual Germans and German cities and corporations were collected by the German government, forwarded to the Allies, and by them repaid to us. Frequently the whole matter was handled by a series of bookkeeping transfers in New York.

After 1929, however, we began to make fewer loans and the Germans were obliged to pay reparations by building up a surplus of imports into this country. But what did we do then? Just when it was most important that Germany be allowed to import to us to maintain her payments, just when the Nazi menace first began to rise, and the thing which might have stopped it was some relief from the ever growing depression, we permitted deflation to spread at home, and at the same time raised our tariffs. The anti-Nazi German government strove desperately to help the situation by a program of drastic enforced price cuts. German labor, like Japanese, worked harder and harder, for longer and longer hours, at lower and lower pay, to sell something over the American tariff barrier. Finally the frantic masses turned to Hitler. Nor were the effects of American policy confined to Germany. They hurt England and France too. The Smoot-Hawley tariff had at least as much to do with the outbreak of the Second World War as the Munich Conference. But we remember the Munich Conference—that was British—while the international effects of the Smoot-Hawley tariff are forgotten. I do not wish to start another myth of innocent Germany (or for that matter innocent Japan) betrayed by a stupid or vindictive America. Other nations have suffered without turning bandit. The world has had enough of the whining self-justification of Germany. Nevertheless simple honesty requires that we too admit our guilt in manly fashion, and remember our mistakes as we start to build anew.

We have sketched the cases of Japan and Germany to give some idea of the consequences, not merely in dollars or social reorganization but in the blood of our young men, of permitting a minority of American vested interests of capital and labor to hold back the national welfare under a slogan of patriotic protection. Surely we will not again believe that we can erect a lasting peace if we amend Owen Wister's slogan "Let the best man win" to "Let the best man win—provided he is a white (?) American." The American fear of foreign competition combines the ridiculousness of a female wrestler afraid of a mouse with the meanness and greed of a miser disputing the last crust of a dying man.

It will be seen that I feel strongly that the "Elizabethan" internationalist policy is the one which we should strive to adopt. Yet there are tremendous problems to be met both at home and abroad. Strangely enough, however—and to me this is a hopeful fact—if the United States adopts a reasonably generous attitude toward loans, and maintains a trade policy of sufficiently low tariffs and relative freedom from other restrictions, the remaining obstacles are nearly all moral and ideological rather than technical. The world wants some approach to an American standard of living. America wants a continued rise in its standard of living. If these are, as I believe them to be, the basic drives of the present time, and if there is any sort of political intelligence left among the people of the world, then the fundamental forces at work lead inevitably to the eventual reestablishment of some sort of freedom of trade and of investment. Let us, however, see what are the present ideological obstacles.

Anyone who has studied the technical problems knows that under present circumstances a good part of our loans have to be government loans, or at least government-guaranteed. Nevertheless, the policy for which we are arguing here is not one of indefinite American government charity, nor is it even one of perpetual intergovernment trading. And the reasons we have urged for thinking that the internationalist solution would in the long run give the greatest productivity for all countries concerned, including America, are all based upon the idea of relatively independent investment, and a relatively free market. Probably the greatest obstacle to the reestablishment of such a market, however, is the fact that both in this country and abroad there are many people to whom the idea of private trading is *ipso facto* immoral. American authorities of this persuasion will seldom state such a viewpoint unequivocally. They are apt to take refuge instead in the "inevitability" argument, and say that the reestablishment of private foreign investment is impossible because the Europeans are too impregnated with socialism to tolerate it. Another argument sometimes heard among Europeans, especially the more radical Europeans, is that there is no reason for making concessions to the United States since the United States has to lend abroad anyhow in order to avoid a depression; and therefore foreign nations are doing America a favor by borrowing from her.

This second idea is entirely incorrect. Though it may sound strange in view of our earlier arguments, the United States does not have to lend abroad in order to prevent unemployment. It can, if it wishes, absorb all its "excess" at home. That is to say, the resources absorbed by European loans could be used for American government outlay, and so forth. We have already argued at length that such a policy would be an almost unmitigated cultural disaster not only for the United States but for the whole world, and that over eight or ten years or sooner the lower income groups within the United States would begin to lose by it. But our argument was based on the idea that investment controlled and planned by government, because of the decline of self-perpetuating groups and the power which such a system gives to vested interests of all sorts, would soon lead to cultural stagnation. If European and other foreign nations, by refusing to set up conditions under which competitive private investment can be made, reduce the choice merely to one of planning for government home investment, or planning for government foreign investment, then the argument for a long-range international program is far less convincing. For reasons of humanity we should still wish to give relief. But the resources available to America and to the world from a simple appeal to charity are enormously less than the potential wealth available to the whole world if the United States and other nations are able to cooperate in a dynamic program of competitive private investment and development. Within the next few years, I believe, the people of the world will discover that socialism and comprehensive planning cannot deliver enough wanted goods—and it is goods that they will want rather than control.

I have spoken of the power of the vested interest under a regime of comprehensive planning. This is well seen now in the condition of present-day (1947) Europe. Even such scanty resources as she has are frequently wasted because of trade barriers set up by the different controlled economies. Yet my experience has been that it is the socialists and near-socialists (and of course communists) that are most reluctant to relinquish controls over international trade. The reason is that a relatively free international market limits the discretion and the power of the planners in home affairs. Consequently they will tend to oppose it and to admit foreign trade, if at all, only under severe regulation.

Many Americans feel that a system of government trading is desirable for its own sake because intergovernment rather than interbusiness trading will help to prevent wars and make for better feeling. Undoubtedly, in the present semisocialist state of the world, exalting the word "government" *per se,* many foreign countries will be readier to accept United States government loans than United States business loans—if these are forthcoming. But whether this would really make for world peace is highly dubious. The United States would have to take direct moral responsibility for every mistake made, no matter how accidental. And in the event of any disagreement, justified or unjustified, the full resentment of the foreign nation would have a nationalist tinge. Moreover, however pure our own motives may be, the continuation of general intergovernment trading will mean the creation of enormous opportunities for oppression of small nations by larger ones and for endless ferment. The proposal appears to be one more example of our habit of taking the extreme extension of an evil for its cure. Because some private trade calls for government action, we will solve the difficulty by making all private trade call for government action.

European and other foreign writers who advocate control also forget the use Germany made of economic restrictions to penetrate other countries. The truth is that, if loans are made to a nation with the requirement that all funds be spent in the lending country, the borrower is largely at the mercy of the lender. It cannot buy in the best market but must take what the lending country chooses to give it; and the way is paved for complete economic domination. If we were really trying for economic domination as some Europeans charge we would not be working so frantically to reopen *general* trade among *all* nations, but would try to make it merely a two-way controlled proposition. The essential arguments for and against wholesale intergovernment trading are the same as those for and against comprehensive planning within a nation. Obvious and admitted gains in short-run stability must be balanced against the longer-run gains of spontaneity and freedom. Similar problems are found in fundamental political ethics. Do we gain much by substituting for a vested monetary and trade-union interest a vested love of power? Veblen of course was fond of saying that commerce, piracy, and war were essentially the same thing. We have seen that this argument contains a grain of truth in that all technical development produces some form of conflict. But to lump together, indiscriminately, rivalry in economic bargaining and rivalry in an atomic war is to obliterate all those distinctions which make up the prime realities of life to everyone save the mentally adolescent.

We have mentioned earlier, as one obstacle to American public support for internationalist policies, the use which certain groups make of internationalism to reimpose government or monopoly control. Here we must distinguish between the short-run and long-run problems. Although in the long run the writer believes that there might be a problem in finding investment outlets for all our saving within the continental United States, this has not so far been the case since the war. On the contrary, as everyone now realizes, we have had inflation. But will continued exports abroad be the whole story on any further inflationary tendencies which the economy is likely to show? The writer does not believe so. The present Marshall plan, for example, is intended to maintain the existing rate of export—not to add to it. It would take a very brave man to say that without foreign aid there would have been no inflation in the United States. On the contrary a tremendous increase in the money supply, great wartime scarcities, a huge rise in consumption levels, constant increases in money wages, tax policies deliberately set to penalize saving and, in fact (though not quite so intentionally), to reduce the incentive for private investment, all have played their part.

Yet now it is asked, as a matter of emergency, that we reimpose controls. These controls are said to be only "partial." But one at least is the rationing of steel, and whoever "rations" steel plans the whole economic system. Determination of the relative growth of every factory, farm, and town, will be involved. Food rationing indeed is far less dangerous. The question is one of good faith. There may be short-run emergencies in which rationing and price control will help; but the fundamental problem is to get production and reduce purchasing power, and when both political parties show no real willingness to meet these issues it may well be questioned whether their proposals are made in good faith. Worse, if possible, and completely indefensible from the point of view of this book is the suggestion that anti-trust laws be relaxed. Before we adopt business or government regimentation, let us insist that some sign be given of a real intent to meet the long-run problem. This implies, at the very least, a tax policy encouraging saving and discouraging consumption. For example, some have said that private investment cannot be revived because it is "too risky." But certainly the present "Heads I win, tails you lose" tax policy of the American government gives people small incentive to run risks. A world market cannot be reestablished by American vested interests who desire protection at all costs. But neither can it be reestablished by admirers of government planning for its own sake, however keen for immediate relief they may be, of whom it may be said that in terms of the long-run needs they are far better haters of the uncontrolled economy than lovers of their fellow men.

Turning now to a very different set of obstacles, we find the greatest remaining difficulty to be the attitude implied in all the associations which cluster around the word "imperialism." Much modern American discussion tends to treat foreign private investment as virtually synonymous with "imperialism"; but, Veblen to the contrary notwithstanding, there is a difference. The distinction can be best put in a historical parallel. Foreigners may well ask whether America proposes to develop them in the way Europeans developed nineteenth century America—or in the way nineteenth century Americans "developed" the American Indian.

Our convenient national absent-mindedness has enabled us nearly to forget that the United States was built up largely by foreign loans from England, France, and Germany. Up to the First World War the United States was still a net debtor to Europe. It may be said, indeed, that the Europeans sold us our country to fight the First World War, and their countries to fight the Second. Yet in the long period from 1790 to 1914, when a great proportion of American capital was foreign-owned, we did not feel "enslaved," nor was there overwhelming resentment of "foreign domination." Some of our original railroads had their entire line and rolling stock shipped out from France or England. Yet, though there was a certain amount of grumbling and plenty of joint native and foreign corruption, the people of the United States on the whole welcomed the aid toward more rapid expansion which Europe gave them.

The relative absence of nationalistic friction in the building up of the North American continent—particularly as compared with equivalent happenings in many South American countries—deserves special examination and furnishes a clue to two factors which must form the basis of any foreign policy we undertake. The first is a policy of loans rather than direct control. The second is the relative absence of race prejudice. Of the two, the second is probably the more important.

Because of the substantial cultural unity of North European lenders and North American borrowers, the Europeans (by no means always justifiably) found it relatively easy to entrust their funds to companies managed by native American businessmen. Thus, even though a company was in fact owned abroad, we did not feel that opportunities were denied to us in our own country. In the second place, foreign capital frequently was held in bonds rather than stocks, and in any event in nominally "American" concerns rather than branches of foreign ones. Contrast this with the condition of Mexico under President Diaz. It is true that foreign investment was then rapidly raising Mexican national income, but at great social cost. For not only were most of the foreign enterprises mere branches of foreign concerns, but even within Mexico a definite policy was followed of excluding Mexicans from executive positions. The same has been still truer of China. To be sure, foreign nations cannot expect to get adequate investment if they insist on padding the pay rolls of American-financed concerns with untrained local citizens. Yet even if it costs more, and even if industrialism is somewhat delayed, the American investor would do well to train foreign citizens to direct his investment so far as this is consistent with its safety. "Non-economic" resentment of exclusion within one's own country is a far more potent source of ill feeling and insecurity than dozens of problems concerning the exchange rate.

Race prejudice is one piece of baggage which competitive capitalism must promptly discard if it is to survive at all. Either we live up to our professed standards and put an end at the earliest possible date to Class B citizenship—whether in Manchuria or in Mississippi—or else we stand forth as hypocrites and liars to the rest of the world. More radicals are created daily by race prejudice and pretentious snobbery than by dozens of economic problems.

If the United States obtains the cooperation of the democratic nations of the world to achieve a higher standard of living combined with greater economic freedom than communism can, and if it lives up to its other values, then it need not fear Marxist infiltration. Appeal to the victims of racial discrimination is the one remaining card which communism has. If this appeal is largely hypocritical, the Asiatic has no way of telling; and, faced with the choice between a full belly accompanied by the restoration of the sahib attitude, and relative poverty accompanied by a fighting chance for self-respect, he will almost certainly take poverty.

Racial discrimination, tariff barriers, undue tenderness for American vested interests—these are the obstacles which are most likely to defeat American foreign economic policy. With the nations abroad the problem is a preference for government action for its own sake. Yet in the last analysis the people of the world appear to value rising living standards more than special kinds of government. What is needed is that we live up to our own values. We denounce the British Empire preference system and praise free trade, but our own Export-Import Bank makes no loans unless the proceeds be spent in this country. Temporarily we have removed many tariff barriers, but still many maintain that the reciprocal trade agreements are to be managed so that no American industries will suffer. Let us not deceive ourselves. Freer trade, like all industrial progress, is bound to mean that some people will lose something of their special positions. Unless we are prepared to face up to the conflict of general progress and the vested interest—abroad as well as at home—we may soon see the suicide of capitalism. So much for the conservatives. But, more than that, we shall also see the collapse of democracy.

· XI ·

Three Plans

A POLICY half right may give results entirely wrong. The first five chapters of this book outlined general political and social standards of democratic progress. The next five made a number of criticisms and suggestions regarding various specific economic problems. Now it is time to bring our conclusions together and apply them to the principal types of policy current in the United States today, to see whether any of them fully meet the standard outlined. In order to do this we shall discuss two main points of view now prevailing—the "conservative" and the "ultraliberal." After examining their merits and demerits and relating them to our standards, we shall offer certain suggestions of our own. It is not maintained that anyone completely conforms to the "party lines" which we distinguish; nevertheless the two policies given represent clearly marked streams of tendency to which many people in general adhere.

The first line of policy to be discussed is the "conservative" one. Conservative policies embody several elements of great value which we shall develop later on; but the conservative point of view has three outstanding weaknesses which render it inadequate as a long-run solution: frequent undue tolerance of private monopoly, an indiscriminate emphasis upon economy in government at all costs, and an advocacy of high tariffs and other forms of economic isolationism. As long as these three features are retained, without modification, the conservative policy fails to make sense—even on its own terms. So far as economy goes, reduction of expenditure is highly desirable during a boom and during a period of inflationary pressure. But we have seen that a capitalist society, from the very fact that it is free and is technologically creative, is always exposed to the risk of recurrent depression. If the government is to pursue a policy of unyielding economy, whether in depression or in

178

boom, then the chances of stabilizing the durable goods industries are almost nil. We shall come back to this point and the problems which it implies.

A second point concerns economic isolationism. In the last chapter we decided that ultimate solution of the problem of long-range stagnation, to say nothing of the problem of world peace, is likely to depend upon a continuous program of American investment abroad. But while this program may be pursued for a number of years in the face of a high tariff policy, without encountering serious difficulty, it will break down sooner or later unless we permit a sufficient reverse flow of imports to meet at least part of the interest on the investment. Surely the United States will not allow the lessons of 1929 to go unheeded.

But the dangerous thing about the conservative policy is that circumstances may enable it to be pursued, as in the eight years following 1921, without apparent difficulty long enough for the public to forget most of the lessons of previous decades. Since the fundamental pressures at the present time are primarily inflationary, indiscriminate economy, even though it may aggravate short-run cyclical collapses, may be adhered to without immediate disaster; and in the same way, as long as we are willing to lend indefinitely today to pay interest on what we lent yesterday, everything may seem to be working smoothly, as in the 1920's. Such a period of apparent security would be a prime test of the political and economic sagacity of the American people. Will they have the forethought to realize that their apparent prosperity is based upon an unsound foundation, or will they, as in the twenties, thoughtlessly pursue a policy of economic isolationism without regard to the ultimate consequences?

The second general policy approach to be discussed in this chapter is the "ultraliberal" one. Without meaning to attribute to any specific individual all the views which we shall outline, the approach may nevertheless be fairly well exemplified in such names as Henry Wallace, William H. Davis, and Robert R. Nathan. It has been called a policy of "guided capitalism," and seeks to "preserve free enterprise" by numerous large-scale adjustments in price, income distribution, and production structure. In its more extreme forms it approximates the system advocated by Lord Beveridge in his *Full Employment in a Free Society.*

At first glance the ultraliberal policy, whatever its other defects, does not seem to run the risk of as sudden or as violent disaster as the conservative one. However, we must not be prematurely optimistic. If the danger which the conservatives run is deflation, then, paradoxical as it may sound in the light of present publicity, the great danger in the liberal policy is inflation. Furthermore, if inflation becomes too great we shall encounter possibilities of political and social disturbance quite as disrupting to the whole fabric of democratic society as deflation ever could be. In addition, and even if the system is otherwise well administered, the ultraliberal policy contains within itself a strong bias toward the creation of a self-perpetuating group and of eventual technological stagnation.

We shall not repeat here the arguments regarding the decline of the self-perpetuating, noncompetitive group, the inadequacy of the vote as sole protection for the individual in a large electorate, the likelihood of simultaneous political tyranny and economic stagnation where competition disappears. Here we shall merely show that the ultraliberal, no less than the reactionary, will release forces working toward aristocratic self-perpetuation and we then go on to discuss the various economic weaknesses which the system implies, regardless of political and social disadvantages. The ultraliberal policy contains two serious defects: First, there is the distrust of saving and the feeling that the distribution of wealth is the prime cause of most of our troubles. Second, there is the jealousy of profits. These two forces working together will produce serious economic maladjustments which can scarcely avoid eventual social dislocation.

In evaluating the ultraliberal position it is important to remember that it is put forward not as a means of supplanting the free enterprise system but as a means of "preserving" it. That, of course, is all to the good, but it can be shown that the policies advocated are not compatible with the preservation of anything more than an empty shell of the competitive-democratic order. Even if one granted for argument that saving is excessive in the United States, drastic taxation, raising demand, would have serious repercussions upon the inducement to invest. It is of course a cardinal principle with most writers of the ultraliberal persuasion that almost no profit is needed to induce business activity. The confusion here lies in thinking that because some people will do *some* work with very little hope of profit, all people will do *as much* work with very little hope of profit. We will not repeat here the earlier discussion of this point. Suffice it to say that the margin of venture capital is likely to be greatly reduced, and that a gap will appear which will have to be filled by government investment if prolonged unemployment is to be avoided.

However, drastic taxation to redistribute wealth is not a necessary part of a full employment program, even if it be assumed that savings are excessive. Professor Alvin Hansen, particularly in his earlier work, sought to evolve a compromise solution whereby the government would concentrate on borrowing excessive savings rather than taxing them, and thus avoid some of the stagnating effects of excessive taxation. In effect Hansen proposed to substitute for the private expansion demand, which he thought permanently reduced by prospective stabilization of the American population, additions to the government "welfare" industry which would absorb a flow of resources equal in value, on average, to about five billion dollars a year at the 1942 price level. If all Hansen's assumptions are accepted, and the foreign market is excluded from consideration, then this policy makes a certain amount of sense. But it is likely to be combined with other attitudes, and particularly with an insistence upon complete over-all security, which would have the effect of leaving very little elasticity in the economic system.

The course of thought among younger economists of this country, particularly those trained by Keynes and Hansen, may be summarized as follows: One group, fixing its attention entirely upon the maintenance of a completely stable national output, has concluded that freedom from economic fluctuation can be obtained only by comprehensive licensing and planning of the entire flow of investment. A less vociferous but equally numerous group, including the writer, grant nearly all that the ultraliberals maintain regarding fluctuation, but feel that the social and political consequences of 100 per cent planning of investment flow are so serious that it is better to seek a more modest goal. Our chapter on business cycles has shown that complete planned stability involves a very high degree of sabotage and retardation of production. Lord Beveridge, though scarcely by intention, makes the point even more emphatically. The little business which Henry Wallace and others seem to advocate is not the type of little business we have extolled for its role in technical progress and democratic freedom. A man who has no discretion concerning his price policy, his wage policy, the quality of his goods, or the profit which he is allowed to earn, is in no sense an industrial pioneer. Survival of a few limited property rights is not the survival of capitalism. The businessman under these conditions is no more than a hired foreman or manager who is allowed to flatter himself by saying that he "owns" a plant.

One final point in the ultraliberal policy must be considered, and that is its ideological instability. This aspect of the case is well summed up in an article by Ellery Foster in *Labor and Nation,* entitled "Think Fast, Intellectual,—or Else." His argument is that people cannot always be against something. In order to be happy, they must be for something. Constant criticism of the capitalist order and the profits it permits creates a spirit of intense antagonism—and labor groups will become so impatient of the residual property survivals embedded in the comprehensively planned state that they may disown it entirely. This is a point which writers who concentrate upon economic stability do not develop, but it is of extreme importance. Tell a man often enough that he is being gypped, and he will come to believe it, whether it be correct or not.

Turning from ideological to functional weaknesses of the ultraliberal program, we find these best exemplified in the current inflationary crisis. Present critical conditions cannot be understood without going back to the war itself and the methods by which it was financed. It is of course a cardinal principle of the ultraliberal point of view that, in the long run, purchasing power is insufficient, because of excess saving. This argument, however, cannot possibly be true during a war. Although the United States was unusually fortunate in having to reduce relatively slightly its aggregate pre-war output of consumers' goods, nevertheless the tremendous in-crease in money income due to reemployment of workers in war plants and general increase in output of war goods resulted in total money income vastly in excess of the civilian goods to meet it. In other words, relatively unchanged prewar output of civilian goods had to be shared among greater numbers of people having much larger money incomes. Such sharing inevitably meant that the standard of living of a large part of the nation would have to be lowered; and in no event could prewar consumption expectations be maintained.

It must be understood that there was not a choice between low-ering and sustaining the standard of living. The sole question was how it was to be lowered. This could be done through taxation, or through inflation. Theoretically, voluntary saving might have done the job; but no government in history has ever been able to finance a war solely from the voluntary contributions of its people. The trouble was, however, that reduced consumption had to take into account the fact that the great bulk of consumers' expenditure was by the very low income groups. Consequently a substantial de-crease in consumption had to be made, either by taxing the lower income groups directly, or by taxing them indirectly through in-flation. This again was no more than simple arithmetic.

Lord Keynes advised for England a scheme of war finance com-bining compulsory pay-roll taxes with the issuance of government bonds which might be cashed in after the war. The choice in effect was between lowering the standard of living of the workers by in-flation—which would leave them impoverished when the war was over—and lowering their standard of living by taxation, giving them in return capital assets which they would have as a backlog after the conflict was finished. Common sense and humanity alike called for the second solution. Experience indicated that a large part of the bonds would be held indefinitely. "Capital levy" pro-posals were not necessary parts of the plan. However, the adminis-tration rejected the compulsory savings plan for two reasons: First, it feared the political repercussions of taxation of the lower income groups. Second, it feared an eventual slump and preferred to build up an inflationary backlog in the hope that it would be absorbed in the ensuing depression. Attempts to control inflation were confined almost entirely to price control and rationing.

But the trouble with rationing and price control is that, if it is not reinforced by adequate taxation to mop up excess purchasing power, and if it does not command adequate public cooperation, it cannot succeed in the long run. As it turned out, the unwillingness of the administration further to tax the lower income groups prevented adequate financial cooperation, while the wage program alienated the support of large parts of the population.

Few public acts have been more disastrous than the adoption of the Little Steel formula. We must remember that the choice was not between lowering and sustaining the standard of living but between methods of lowering it. The Little Steel formula said in effect that wages must be raised enough to keep the standard of living unchanged. It would be difficult to imagine a stronger encouragement to strike; for the criterion of wage fixing was the achievement of an impossibility, so that there was no chance of really satisfying the demands of the workers.

A good part of the blame for strikes is to be placed on the acts of various economists and public administrators who consistently talked in terms of maintaining living standards, rather than on the shoulders of laboring men. Anyone who reads the discussions of the Little Steel formula is bound to conclude that maintenance of the standard of living was no more than labor's "right," even though there was a war. Yet every workingman knew from experience that his standard of living was in most cases not being maintained. Could any better recipe for labor unrest have been imagined?

As we all know today, gloomy predictions of unemployment as soon as the war was over were not borne out. Yet still it is maintained that a depression will shortly ensue, and nearly all the writers of the school we are discussing imply that, had the Office of Price Administration been kept, such a depression would never have arrived. In other words, almost the entire blame is placed upon the inflationary price rise following the removal of price controls. The chapter "Progress and Instability" has shown that some degree of eventual postwar slump is quite likely. But this would be true had OPA remained in force. The fact is that unstabilizing distortions of the structure of industry are almost certain to occur whenever a backlog of demand must be rapidly made up. Even a planned society with perfectly stable prices, which did not want to sabotage new inventions and keep the consumer waiting, would meet the same problem.

The main reason why the OPA was discontinued was that it had been diverted from controlling inflation to attempting a large-scale redistribution of wealth and imposing general planning upon the entire economic system. As long as the idea was one of equal sacrifice by all groups in order to win the war, the OPA commanded general public support. But with one particular sector of the economy—labor—appearing to receive constant favor while others were restrained, the rest of the people felt more and more unfairly treated. Had wages been stabilized, the Office of Price Administration might still be in existence.

Whatever the rights or wrongs of repealing OPA, there can be no doubt that the only way to overcome present inflationary conditions is by increased production and stabilized income. Yet a strong effort is being made to persuade the whole country that the danger is not in increased wages but is instead the work of "profiteers." One is reminded, however, of Lord Keynes's statement, "The profiteers are a consequence and not a cause of rising prices." A basic fallacy of the whole argument is the assumption that, if wage increases do not result in higher prices in the industry in which they are granted, they are not inflationary. This is quite unwarranted. Suppose a wage increase is given by the steel industry without an increase in steel prices. Will this avoid inflation? Not at all. The amount of steel or steel products bought by steel workers is only a fraction of their total expenditure, and a large part of the increased money income will be spent on other products, including food. Yet though farmers are among the least monopolistic elements in the American economy, expenditure of constantly increasing sums for their output will inevitably drive their prices up. Wage earners will then demand another raise, and so it goes. Increasing wages of industrial workers, even without higher prices of industrial products, will mean increased expenditure on farm products; and in a time of scarcity like the present that will mean higher prices for farm output. As a result money wage increases are largely neutralized by higher prices and a rising cost of living. The only way to break the vicious circle is by increased production and stabilized wages. Contrary to much union and ultraliberal propaganda, it is not the prices of the great industrial firms which have contributed most to inflation, but farm prices and prices of the relatively competitive nondurable goods field. Attacks on "big business" as the chief cause of inflation at the present time can scarcely be substantiated. Sometimes one wonders whether they are honestly made.

Nevertheless, there has been a considerable price rise over the whole economy, even though not a symmetrical one. Many people therefore point to increased profits as a main cause of inflation and a justification of industrial unrest. Space is lacking to explain fundamental wage theory here. We have already pointed out that all wage increases do not need to be translated into price increases. However, unless smaller firms are to be supported indefinitely by government subsidy, some increase in prices is inevitable when a large-scale wage increase has been granted. Furthermore, such increases at the "margin" are likely to have more than proportionate effect upon profits in the more favored firms.

How great, however, is the profit share? Much of the attack is couched in percentage figures in order to exaggerate the importance of the problem. For example, it may be said that wages have gone up say 8 per cent, while profits have gone up say 20 per cent. But it must not be forgotten that wages and salaries make up about 60 per cent of the national income, whereas profits are about 10 per cent; and 8 per cent of 60 per cent is a considerably more significant figure, as far as increases in income are concerned, than 20 per cent of 10 per cent. In absolute terms profits *before* taxes in 1946 were 2.1 times what they were in 1929. Compensation of employees was 2.2—a slightly larger ratio. Employees' compensation was 58 per cent of national income in 1929, but 65.9 per cent in 1946. Finally profits *after* taxes in 1946 were only 1.4 times what they were in 1929. Furthermore, a large part of profits is not caused by higher prices but is a result of them; and a good part of profit income is saved; therefore the increase cannot be treated as a prime cause of inflation. Other arguments equally popular among the ultraliberals ascribe the downturn of the cycle to the fact that with the rise of profits saving has increased. But an increase in saving should help to prevent inflation.

Behind the whole problem lies an unwillingness to face the relationship between risk, uncertainty, and profit. Demand may be high now, but risks also are great; and not the least of these is the risk of unexpected strikes. Thus many unions, at the same time that they attack high profits, adopt the policy which makes such profits necessary. I do not doubt that many of the members of the ultraliberal school are sincerely anxious to maintain the capitalist system. Though, for the most part, capitalism or "free enterprise" means to them little more than the survival of certain property rights, still there are undoubtedly some who have in mind a more comprehensive and accurate definition. Yet, whatever their good intentions, the attitude of mind which their publicity creates leads to constantly increasing demands for higher living standards while it makes for increasing reluctance to produce and growing industrial friction. Such an atmosphere does not give a hopeful outlook for the future of any society which contains it.

At this point people will object, "It is easy to criticize, but what would you do under the same circumstances?" And it is time for us to give more constructive suggestions. We have seen that the conservative policy cannot stand as a long-run system because of its twin defects, indiscriminate economy and economic isolationism. On the other hand, the ultraliberal policy contains a strong inflationary bias, and is likely to lead to great social friction. The question is then, What can we do?

It will be seen that the point of view of this book does not lead to great optimism for the future if we follow either of the policies that now prevail. Both have good features, but, in both, these features are neutralized by equally glaring inadequacies. What is needed, if democracy is to survive in the United States, is a policy which will combine the good features of both sides and omit their weaknesses. Whether we can obtain leadership capable of working out and inaugurating such a policy is one of the most important questions of the present time.

The general policy approach which the writer would adopt has been fairly clearly indicated by his criticisms, and cuts squarely across party lines at the present time. The relative weaknesses of the conservative and the ultraliberal approaches could be summed up in a fairly simple formula: The conservative policy is boom economics, and the ultraliberal policy is depression economics. Carrying the matter still further, we find each policy reflecting the crying need of the particular time for which it is intended. Thus the conservative policy emphasizes supply, and obstacles to production, while the ultraliberal policy puts all of its emphasis upon demand, and frequently seems to assume that demand will automatically satisfy itself. But, as everyone should recognize, both sides of the case have to be remembered. Production without demand will be self-defeating, and demand without production will be inflationary. A policy which ignores either side is bound to fail in the long run.

In the nineteenth century it was frequently said that if you wanted to train an economist all you had to do was to catch a parrot and teach him to say, "Supply and demand." Today it is rapidly becoming true that if you want to train an economist all you have to do is to catch a parrot and teach him to say, "Planning." In any debate the advocates of all-out planning have a great advantage because "by definition" their system, if perfectly administered, would be bound to give the results they claim, though even here there is the insoluble conflict between speed and stability. However, to say that planning will always work everything out, is like saying that socialism would be certain to bring good government because "socialist" people would always choose the right man. The danger of the word "planning," used indiscriminately, is that it appears to offer an automatically correct solution, while slurring over all the immense practical difficulties involved; whereas less drastic solutions immediately bring to attention some of the difficulties because they are bound to be more specific. Anything less than 100 per cent control, therefore, can never have the intellectual symmetry of all-out advocacy of planning; but it may well turn out that the theoretically easy solution is in fact much more difficult, while the apparently difficult compromise proposals, though superfically less convincing, are more workable. The policy which sounds smoothest in an argument may not be the one which is in fact easiest to administer.

As our chapter "Science, Democracy, and Capitalism" stated, everyone is in favor of planning today, if it means merely that disturbance cannot be allowed to get out of bounds; and we have seen that there are disturbances inherent in change and expansion which simply cannot be ignored. On the other hand it is not enough to advocate planning. It must be asked, For what purpose does one plan, and how? Accordingly, an outline of a specific approach must begin by stating the sort of world for which the plan is drawn. The writer believes the modern world to be a world of scarcity and of risk. Once we consider the needs of the rest of the world, as we must do if only from the standpoint of peace, then it is blasphemous inhumanity to say that our saving is excessive. The writer repudiates entirely the theory of secular stagnation. Accordingly, the primary aim of policy at the present time should be to encourage investment and production rather than increase demand through redistribution. This means that we should welcome increased savings and permit high profits in order to offset the great risks of the modern world. It must be remembered that, avowedly at least, the ultraliberal point of view does not use ethical arguments against the capitalist distribution of wealth. It says instead that that distribution must be changed in order to make the system "work." With this I disagree. I respect the ethical arguments for complete equality although I do not follow them, but the functional argument is the product of provincial shortsightedness and muddled analysis. As far as labor policy goes, it also seems to me that the ultraliberals substitute for an arrogant and privileged class of businessmen an equally arrogant and privileged union oligarchy. Is it anything more than merest common sense to say that the United States government will not tolerate unlimited privilege in any group? Both from an ethical and from a functional standpoint, the principle of union responsibility must be accepted.

It will be seen then that the writer adopts several elements of the conservative attitude: The taxation we need to encourage investment is far less drastically progressive than that which we now have. The principle of union responsibility should be accepted, and some measure of control may prove inevitable; but the growth of government is not desirable for its own sake. On the other hand the encouragement of investment involves certain policies which the conservatives repudiate, most important of which is a lower tariff. Without a willingness on our part to accept adequate imports, we do risk the likelihood of a long-range shortage of investment outlets.

So much for the conservative elements of our program. What of the so-called ultraliberal ones? First and foremost, the economic system is not self-adjusting in the short run. It is not inaccurate to state that our system is good because it is bad, and bad because it is good. Therefore, we must have adequate means for stabilizing the capital goods industries. Here, however, is a difficulty which can never be wholly overcome. Suppose that the particular shortage of purchasing power is due to the rapid supplanting of automobiles by airplanes. Under the orthodox system of pains and penalties, losses in the automobile industry would force men to leave it, while profits in the airplane industry would bring men in; but, as we all know, certain "short-run" difficulties may be encountered in the process. Yet if the absolute maintenance of income unchanged is our standard we encounter a curious paradox; for by paying the men in a dying industry as much as they received before, we give them little incentive to move and, on the other hand, by locating public works in areas in which there are already shortages of labor we aggravate the scarcity. There is no perfect solution for this problem, but a practical compromise can be evolved. The combination of social security, unemployment benefits, and judiciously distributed public works will give a degree of stability and security never before approximated.

In public works those which should be used all the time for their own sake must be distinguished from those which can be given a cyclical application. True democracy and opportunity, as we have already seen, involve large-scale government outlays on health and education at all times without regard to the cycles. But some such outlays may be postponed. A desirable policy is to set up a large-scale government welfare industry with a counter phase to the private demand for durable goods. Government investment would be invoked when private demand failed to furnish an adequate market for the durable goods industries. No other method short of complete socialization of investment can be absolutely relied upon to confine a depression within socially tolerable bounds.

Many people feel that the scope offered by public works and other projects in the United States is too small to stabilize our income at the present high level of production; but this attitude expresses a timid outlook. Suppose we undertook to rebuild the slums of every city. Would that not make a tremendous demand for durables and inject large amounts of purchasing power? The rebuilding might well avoid creating huge barracks enclosed by public parks, and rather spread the cities out over much larger areas with individual houses surrounded by individual plots of land. This of course would be more expensive; but after all it is the aim of our policy to create money income, and the social consequences of settling people in their own houses rather than crowding them into barracks, however shiny the gadgets, are certainly worth the higher bill.

Many conservative economists will object to this policy on the ground that it seeks to bring about full employment without removing maladjustments. But why should it be supposed that the two policies are antithetical? Why can we not adopt a policy which seeks simultaneously to create demand, and at the same time to remove obstacles to supply? The false choice now presented to the American people between price flexibility, let us say, and wholesale government expenditure is entirely uncalled for. There is no reason why we cannot proceed on both fronts.

A friend asks me to state specifically what I would do if a depression began tomorrow. The general outline of an answer can be very briefly given. First of all, we should not consider that the occurrence of a depression after the present postwar boom means that the entire fabric of capitalist society is about to collapse, or that long-range stagnation is inevitable. Therefore, we should not assume that it would be necessary to reduce the average proportion of saving. Accordingly, the first thing that we should do is to reduce taxes, not merely on lower income groups but all along the line. The distribution of wealth is not the ultimate cause of the business cycle. Nor is the profit lag. The ultimate cause is rapid expansion. Taxing the rich in depression is purely punitive. If, instead of doing so, we reduce taxes on everyone, we simultaneously increase both consumption and the incentive to invest. Next, we should not begin a movement for a general increase in money wages (real wages will be increasing spontaneously), and we should explore the possibility of wage reduction in those industries in which demand conditions are such that wage reduction would increase workers' incomes and employment. Next we should lower tariffs, and do all we can to stimulate foreign investment. Finally, if it becomes clear that large-scale price and income decline is likely, we should begin a program of public works. At first this should be made up of projects which can be easily discontinued. But if a really serious gap appears, large-scale projects of the type described earlier should be begun.

The policy thus outlined attacks the problem at both ends, rather than putting all the emphasis on investment or on demand. It combines the advantages of both extremes while omitting most of their defects. The danger is, however, that we may get a reverse combination: economy, punitive taxation, and continued barriers to foreign trade. Such an outcome could only spell disaster. As in the story of the beautiful lady who suggested to a genius that they might cooperate in the production of a superior being who would have her body and his mind, the reply might well be made that unfortunately the reverse combination is also possible.

From the conservative point of view, the weakness of the plan outlined is that it implies the possibility of a rising national debt. Here I have little to add to my debate with Professor Moulton in September, 1943, and my book *The Creation of Purchasing Power*. The issue is not whether the debt is rising in absolute terms but whether it is rising in comparison with the national income; and the real question is whether there is anything in the debt *per se* which would keep the national income from growing. The national debt does imply some burden, but if government expenditure is accompanied by reasonable policies in other respects there is no reason to suppose that government indebtedness will on average outrun production.

The conservatives' instinctive distrust of the national debt is not entirely wrong. The danger incipient in the policy here outlined is that it is so easily confused with a superficially similar approach that is based on quite different assumptions. That policy —the ultraliberal one—first hamstrings the incentive to invest, in the name of redistribution, and then declares government investment necessary to "save the system." In other words the ultraliberals, having seen to it that the private economy will not work, announce government investment as the means of "keeping it going." Such a policy, as we have pointed out, results in creeping socialism and, by our analysis, eventual creeping fascism.

But is the ultraliberal policy much worse in its effects than a policy which would expose the capitalist order to a repetition of the years following 1929? Is it worse than one which cuts off the flow of foreign capital needed to give us at once a peaceful and a prosperous world? Who would believe that the repetition of the 1930's could permit a survival of capitalist institutions? My feeling is that the conservatives in attacking the national debt mistake their enemy. Debt is not a cause, but a symptom of profound maladjustment. The basic cause of long-range stagnation is a distrust of the essentials of capitalist institutions plus the joint action of conservative and liberal monopoly groups. Our problem, then, is not the national debt but the forces that make the debt necessary. By an ideological reconstruction of capitalism that would show its connection with democracy and science and thus obtain the removal of many of the fetters now binding the system, and by limiting inflation and unemployment, the way would once more be opened to a wider freedom and a renewed achievement.

But will we adopt such a mixed program. Or will we forever stumble between choices concerning which it may be said that "each is partly in the right and all are in the wrong." The essential issue is ideological. Long practical and theoretical acquaintance with problems of public and business policy has convinced me that there is not nearly so much disagreement among economists in matters of analysis as they think. At least 85 per cent of the time, apparent disagreements of policy and analysis trace back to fundamental disagreements on ethics and social standards. And here I must again warn the reader that "conservatism" does not necessarily mean a belief in any genuine capitalism. On the contrary we find business groups today cherishing the naïve belief that restriction and red tape are somehow different because "voluntarily" imposed by business, instead of by government. The inflationary crisis is taken as the signal for demanding what is in fact the reimposition of N.I.R.A. If this system is adopted, it will be a long step toward economic fascism. Further it will eventually be found to have been a futile step. For as collusive control was no substitute for needed purchasing power in 1934, so also it will be no substitute for needed saving and production in 1948.

· XII ·

The Future of Democratic Progress

"A RACE preserves its vigor as long as it harbors a real contrast between what has been and what may be."

We began with this quotation, and we must end with it. Creation of a living democracy must always be "unfinished business." This is true not merely as a statement of fact, but also as a condition of survival. And though, in the last chapter, we confined ourselves to methods of stabilizing the competitive economy, a man would be very poor in charity and in imagination to suppose that mere relative economic stabilization was all that our society needed. Something must also be said of social frontiers ahead.

Our argument has been that the competitive economic market furnished the best framework within which democratic progress *could* take place. We did not say that, in itself, it was a guarantee of democratic progress; but we nevertheless maintained that without it democratic progress, under modern conditions, would be virtually impossible. In other words, the competitive economic market, though not a sufficient condition for democracy and progress, is an overwhelmingly necessary one.

The line of thought pursued has been as follows: The administration of a complicated interdependent technology requires a hierarchy of highly trained and responsible technical operatives, even if the political state has nominally "withered away." Also, simply to maintain this technology, leaving aside all question of improving it, we must cultivate in the population some desire—even when stated in the most altruistic terms—to do a good job by holding responsible office. Yet at the very least skilled technological control cannot be left to just anyone, so that some form of selection is unavoidable; and, granted the joint necessity of some

195

desire to hold position plus the need for selection among candidates, the inevitability of a degree of rivalry and disappointment immediately follows. The potentiality of rivalry and disappointment inheres in any form of integrated social life—if not, in fact, in all life. The relevant psychological approach for an interdependent society must run in terms of reconciliation to "legitimate" disappointment rather than preventing disappointment. Economic peace is a generally accepted code of emulation and selection. What is needed is both the discovery of a selective code and the general acceptance of it—which, while recognizing and regularizing the constructive conflicts inherent in creative activity, will restrict to a minimum those forms of rivalry and conflict which are merely predatory and sterile.

In popular discussion our modern equalitarian bias has largely obscured this whole problem of selective method. Either the question is shunted to one side, or there is a foggy suggestion that the entire matter can be handled by "elections." Nevertheless, behind much modern left-wing propaganda lies a confused, subconscious feeling that conflict would be reduced to a minimum, and society run more efficiently, if a regime of "comprehensive" planning were adopted. By this is meant a system in which much the greater part of economic activity, especially new investment, is licensed or planned in advance by some organized and integrated central group.

In the long run, however, such an organization would prove incompatible both with political democracy and with technological progress. The technical operatives would come to form a self-perpetuating group, for under modern conditions, having control of production and economic life and hence of the actual existence of the population, they would also be in a position—directly or indirectly, roughly or suavely—to control the elections if the political state survived, or the population directly if it did not. Democracy, therefore, as Mr. Herberg of the International Ladies Garment Workers Union says, means pluralism. The life of the individual, economic, social, and political, must be divided among many organizations—all to some extent in competition with one another. This in the modern world means a relatively competitive society, and competition implies technical change.

But do we really want technical change? Would it not be better to have a technologically and politically decentralized rural economy using almost no machinery, in which each family is virtually self-sufficient? The first answer to this question is that, practically speaking, we have very little choice. Most of the world today, especially England and Western Europe, could not raise enough food for its present population under such a system. This may, indeed, also be the case with the United States. Mass suicide of a large part of the population of many countries is implied, to say nothing of the immense task of persuading people to make an enormous change in their manner of living. But even theoretically the ideal of a static rural state does not seem to the writer to be one which would really satisfy a great portion of mankind, especially the active elements of the western world. It should be remembered that the system implies either infanticide or some other non-industrial method of birth control, and that it would probably also result in a great lowering of the status of women. But in addition, and most fundamentally, it involves a large-scale frustration of the creative urge of mankind. It would be a triumph of the artisan over the inventor.

The philosophy of life which the writer believes to be most fundamentally democratic, and the one hitherto most congenial to the modern man, is the philosophy of the artist—the searcher. The nineteenth century "utility calculus" slurred over most of the important things of life. Man is not merely a consuming machine. Nor for that matter is he merely a contemplating one. As Thomas Wolfe put it: "I suppose like so many other boys I pictured a future life of brilliant works crowned by success and fame and ease, and surcease from labor; but it does not work out that way at all. . . . As far as I am concerned there is no life without work—at least, looking over my own, everything I can remember of any value is somehow tied up with work." * This is an extreme statement. Yet our dilemma is that if we make men free they become creative, and if they become creative they are apt to create trouble for themselves. The joy of the sciences in discovery also reflects itself in the instabilities of the business cycle and the

* *The Atlantic Monthly,* December 1946. By permission of the editors.

terrific problems of the atomic bomb; but, were we to go back to the rural machineless age and yet keep our culture genuinely democratic and tolerant, some inquiring and ingenious person would soon begin to reinvent. Unless stopped by authority, the long climb to industrialism would commence once more.

There is another aspect of the modern problem which must be faced. We have said that democratic political freedom is closely tied up with the decentralization, alternative work opportunities, and limited control of the competitive economic market. But how much competition would there be left if interproduct rivalry were abolished? The quasi-immortal corporation is an inevitable and valuable incident of large-scale enterprise (not necessarily, be it remembered, the same thing as monopoly), but it makes possible a perpetuation of strategic position probably stronger than the Victorian personal firm. Without interproduct competition, political as well as economic ossification of society would be likely. Thus not only our technical progress but our political freedom becomes associated with continual independent technical change. What hope is there for the future, what ideal of progress shall we set up?

Our distribution of wealth—the competitive market method of selection, and of control of those selected—has been attacked for many reasons. It has been attacked because it is unequal, because it creates self-perpetuating privilege, because it is wasteful, or, alternatively, because it causes both unemployment and the business cycle. Most of these criticisms are mistaken, or based largely on a false premise. Some form of inequality is inevitable; some privileges are bound to be inheritable while the family survives. The left wing is scarcely consistent in attacking the well-to-do both because they spend too much money and because they save too much. "Long-range" unemployment is the result not of "oversaving" but of the frustration of investment by pressure groups. The business cycle is not the result of the distribution of wealth. One version of the charge alone can be granted: The high savings and creative invention of our society, taken together, do make for rapid growth, and the *rapid growth* makes for instability. Assuming therefore that the process of growth can be stabilized, or counterbalanced, within reasonable bounds—a question already discussed—the usefulness of our social system comes to depend upon the usefulness of the growth and change which it makes possible.

Now of growth and change, as of competition, it may be said that they are nearly always necessary but not sufficient conditions for genuine progress. Mere change and mere expansion are not inevitably good. Indeed, the arguments earlier in this book concerning the "boundlessness" or "insatiability" of desires could easily be converted into saying that growth and change are futile. But our philosophy has rejected such a criterion. We have spoken, instead, of "better" wants and "better," or more satisfying, forms of action. In other words, democratic progress must be judged by a qualitative standard. Can the quantitative rise in "output per head" be justified in terms of a qualitative improvement in the nature of men's lives? That is the real question.

Behind the idea that human wants are insatiable, and therefore progress is futile, lies a basic fallacy. Wants as a whole, or the activity of wanting, as such, may be taken as insatiable, or alternatively as "constant." But this does not prove that particular wants will not be substantially satisfied. Thus, as output per head increases, the *quality* of the new wants and activities substituted by growth may rise. Also we may remedy many of the evils which now distress us without stopping the whole process of growth.

A good example is democracy of opportunity. We have seen that, if society is to give a satisfactory approach to "equality" of opportunity (the equality can never be absolute), the state must intervene by large-scale outlays on health and education so that the less privileged will not be unduly handicapped. But we also pointed out that, because the pursuit of relative economic inequality was a prime incentive of competitive growth and economic service, there was always a conflict between the extent to which equality of income and inheritance could be forced and the extent to which we could have continued growth. Also we said that economic inequality was both a useful and a relatively harmless form of distinction in a world in which some form of inequality (for example, power) was inevitable. All these apparently conflicting ideals may be substantially reconciled within the framework of democratic progress. For neither the amount needed to give men good health, nor that needed to give them good education, increases with infinite speed. To put it differently, the basic requirements for a "fair" start (an equal start being always impossible) do not necessarily rise as fast as the national income. Absolute outlay on "equalizing" expenditures for health and education may be constantly rising even when proportional sacrifice is unchanged. And since the absolute requirements for a fair start are not "boundless," democracy of opportunity may become constantly greater without imposing so high a progressive sacrifice as to cut off, or seriously retard, continued growth. Thus the mere quantitative rise in output per head can, in this instance, work to give greater satisfaction of the qualitative standard of democracy of opportunity.

Democracy of opportunity, however, opens up many social frontiers besides educational and health expenditure. First of all, there is race prejudice. This is the greatest single blot on contemporary American civilization. Though not a result of capitalist democracy, it is present within capitalist democracy. If we do not work to overcome it, we cannot expect our fabric to survive.

Again, if we attain both adequate welfare expenditure and the removal of race prejudice, still democracy of opportunity requires something more—the retention of adequate independent competition. Here, as Professor Viner has pointed out, we need to work on two fronts. We need more competition of some sorts and less of others. In particular we need less "cost-raising" competition. Not all the evils of modern society result from "bad" impulses. Sometimes they result from "good" ones. The modern emphasis on "cooperation" and "rationalization" leads to a "live and let live" form of competition, in which technical costs and production are kept more or less stabilized, while tremendous outlays are made for advertising and false obsolescence. The Chinese do not like to patronize merchants with handsome stores, for they know that they must pay for the extra costs; but in America the condition seems to be exactly reversed.

Many left-wing writers jump to the conclusion that there should be "no" advertising. But this is a point which requires much more careful thought. In the first place many people really prefer the glamour of clean and cheerful merchandising, or their favorite radio program, to cheaper prices. In the second place, without advertising, how can the genuinely new product ever get a hearing? Would "the world" really "beat a path to the door" of the "better mousetrap" maker if it had never heard of him? Something may be done by law about false and misleading advertising, but the real remedy lies in the education of the consumer. This of course is the hard way. But it is the democratic way.

As we let our minds range ahead toward ideals of future conduct, we need not only think of a business world which is more competitive, though in a less wasteful way. We may also think of unions more interested in overcoming the psychological problems of size and less interested in inflaming them. The bus driver, almost entirely secured from dismissal by an embattled union, may think it a joke to run past the consumer waiting on the corner; but when he himself turns a consumer and goes to the grocery store, the movies, or the bar he does not find it a joke to be passed over. What we have today is a number of joint production relationships in which any part can stop the whole at any time. Consequently the way is open for the ruthless or shortsighted groups to exploit the rest of society. As long as such exploiting groups are few they score a net gain. But what a world we shall live in when every group ceases to be interested in the quality of its service, and grudgingly gives as little and takes as much as it can! I like to think of the possibility of a world in which this condition is largely reversed.

Here we find another great frontier of social action: study of the psychological problems of conflict and of occupational specialization. In this connection we need a less romantic approach. Many writers and research workers (though by no means all) attack the capitalist forms of competition as if they were the only forms. A great deal of writing has been done on the assumption that our goal should be an absolute right to self-expression. Shall we extend this right to the sadist? Let the psychologist and sociologist face the fact that any society implies a structure of duties as well as rights, of rivalry and inequality as well as cooperation. True, they may grant this and yet prefer other methods to our own. But they would at least have seen the problem.

Suppose that by policies such as we have outlined a free and rapid growth of output continues. What then? Democracy of opportunity is not the only qualitative standard whose relative satisfaction is made possible by quantitative growth. As a country grows richer it can become less ugly and more healthy. It can afford to insist upon the incorporation, within the structure of private costs, of certain social costs hitherto unheeded. It can insist, through taxation and regulation, that private competitive calculations include the prevention or amelioration of smoke, of fumes, and of pollution. Our cities can once more see the sun, our rivers become less like sewers, our highways less filled with oil fumes and Diesel smoke, our railways less covered with dirt. In a world of poverty it can at least be argued that the need for more production is greater than the aesthetic criterion; but with increasing output per head the aesthetic becomes more attainable.

And so we come to the final problem: the rediscovery of qualitative standards; of moral sanctions, of aesthetic appreciation. Our quantitative progress makes possible all these things, but it does not automatically give them to us. It may give us more leisure, for example; but many of us have almost forgotten how to play. The good life is a balance of qualities. The creative impulse has many sides. We need to learn to put more emphasis, even in our leisure, on doing things and being things rather than simply buying things. A nation of mere dial twiddlers will always be psychotic. The dials may be all right in themselves—but we must be willing to add something more from our own personalities to give real satisfaction.

At the end, therefore, not merely as a hope for the future of our society but as an absolute condition of its having any future at all, we must shift part of our energies from the increase of physical science to the study of social values. Modern man is a drunkard in a high-powered automobile. How deeply we have been impregnated by the scientific spirit, and how perverse the resulting reactions may be, is well seen by the atomic bomb. Many of our universities and great foundations have taken the bomb as a signal not for redoubling work in government, history, psychology, social study, and art, but for more atomic research. Do we benefit the drunkard by making his car still faster? I do not say that modern man should not have more rapid discovery. But unless he is to wind up in irretrievable sudden ruin he must spend more time learning how to manage his discoveries.

In time of bewilderment the call to action is the only one which really strikes home. We have named some of the possibilities within our society in order that we may see that competitive economic democracy is not merely a passive gospel. Still within the framework of our society there are great possibilities. The Statue of Liberty can still be one of liberty enlightening the world, rather than liberty defending New York harbor. It is extraordinary how unfailingly the modern emphasis on law, on "planning," and on regulation turns our attention away from the solutions which, though difficult, are the only democratic ones; and directs it instead toward pseudo solutions which do not really solve the problem but only end it. The challenge which faces our society today is not to give security and stability. That could be easily done. The challenge is to give relative security and stability while retaining creativeness and freedom. Such a challenge is not met by simple stagnation.

In the light of standards such as these one soon recognizes the reactionary and conservative nature of the modern radical and ultraliberal. There is nothing new about planning or centralized power. They are two of the oldest ideas in the world. If cultures are to be judged by majority vote, the "natural" state of man is planned and regulated despotism; or oligarchy and caste, reenforced by iron custom. For a brief two hundred years, however, mankind has sought to realize a dream of better things: freedom of opportunity and expression as wide as the population; a world in which men might rise on independent terms; a world of tolerance and impartial law. An English anthropologist calls the United States reactionary because most of us still adhere to that dream, because we still cherish the ideals of the eighteenth century. Is the suggestion, then, a world in which the son seeks only to repeat his father's trade and families continue the same unchanging round? Many modern suggestions approximate just that. What a perversion of terms is here when this is hailed as progress! Fascism is not dead—it has only changed its name and turned left. But let us see democracy and the democratic market as the vigorous and surging thing which it could be, and we need not despair for the future.

Yet, if despair is unwarranted and dangerous, foolish optimism is equally misleading. No one can deny the magnitude of the present crisis. The outlook for the survival of the type of liberal, competitive, democratic society which we have in mind depends upon the actions and attitudes of two groups: the censor class and the businessmen. The censor class may wreck the system by creating an atmosphere of intense ethical antagonism. The business community may wreck the system by refusing to permit measures of reform and stabilization needed if the system is to keep going at all. An examination of the attitudes and outlook of both these elements of our society is necessary if there is to be a chance for the survival of democratic progress in the modern world.

The basic choice now facing the censor class has already been outlined. Shall they continue to function as critics within the framework of the present system, and largely by persuasion—or shall they act as revolutionaries attempting to seize power themselves? Though the influence of the intelligentsia upon social life may seem to be very slight in the short run, the ideas of those who train each succeeding generation are of immense importance and, over a period of fifteen or twenty years, become a prime influence in shaping policies. One may, for example, mention the economists as one small segment of the intelligentsia. The writer would certainly concur with Lord Keynes's famous statement: "Madmen in authority, distilling voices from the air, are often the slaves of some defunct economist."

There are many factors which would tend to turn the censor class toward the revolutionary rather than the critical role. Some of these are rooted in the most disinterested and noble motives. Others result from the special conditions under which most members of the intelligentsia are now compelled to live. The truth is, there are many reasons why the members of the censor class should be particularly dissatisfied at the present time. Whatever their original status, they are all now members of the white-collar class;

and the white-collar class, for reasons independent of capitalism but closely related to democracy, is undergoing a rapid loss in economic status and prestige.

Some twenty years ago Professor Thomas Nixon Carver pointed out that universal education, plus restrictions of immigration, would soon bring about relative equalization of earnings between the different occupations in this country. The special position of the white-collar class today is largely a survival of the days in which a peculiar sanctity hung about the man who could read and write. It is not so long since the mere ability to write was enough to keep a man in England from being hanged. Under present conditions, almost everyone can read and write, whereas the highly skilled manual trades are becoming more and more valuable; but the white-collar intellectuals are likely to feel the resentment of any group which is losing ground in the process of adjustment to change, and, like all economically declining groups, they are apt to lay the discomfort which they feel not to the values which they profess, but to some mysterious defects in the "system." The fact is that the rise of the manual worker in relation to the white-collar class is no more than should be expected on grounds both of capitalist competition and of democracy. The fundamental ethical concept of equality of opportunity, when implemented by public education, is bound to operate on a restricted population so as to readjust relative economic rewards. This does not mean greater equality of individual incomes, but it does mean greater equality between callings. For intelligent young men will not prepare themselves for underpaid work when opportunity is open for better. The war has accelerated the movement of middle-class families into manual work in industry, and the trend may be expected to continue with increasing force in the years to come. The result will be an increasing democratization of our social life.

But though the rising social status of the worker may be viewed as one of the prime achievements of American democracy it involves a number of very serious sociological repercussions that fall with particular weight upon the intellectual white-collar type and, in any case, entail large-scale readjustments in social life. For, as Professor Carver pointed out, one consequence of equalization will be the nearly complete disappearance of servants from the home. Servants are a vanishing species in America, and this would be true were there never a war, a union, or a Minimum Wage Act; and it will remain true no matter how prosperous we become. Those who expect an eventual return to prewar conditions in this regard will be grievously disappointed.

The social implications of this fact might at first seem to be negligible. Relatively few Americans have ever had servants, while for those who were servants there is no doubt that shifting over to industrial and other occupations often means a stronger family and an increased home life. However, in addition to the relative disappearance of servants, there has been a change in the external surroundings of most families. In the patriarchal farm establishment, even without help, there were usually many members of the group among whom the care of children and the aged could be shared so that it was not a crushing burden on any single individual. But in the small urban or suburban modern family this is not the case.

The real significance of the "servantless world," when combined with the shift to urban life, arises from the fact that until very recently nearly all our conventional ideas of leisure, beauty, and "good form" came from aristocrat-and-slave or near-slave civilizations where the elite led lives of leisure surrounded by dependents. There is no servant problem at Shangri-La, nor was there much at the courts of the Renaissance. In other words, many of our ideas of the "good life" are based upon a social environment which no amount of democratic progress can ever give again. Norman Douglas in *South Wind* maintains that only a civilization with slaves could know real art or leisure. Now, after a situation temporarily aggravated by wartime shortages of the usual labor-saving devices, some people say that only with servants can there be leisure and a home. The latter doctrine is probably as false as the former; but certainly without servants the members of the middle class cannot maintain the kind of homes they have had. Our art, our manners, and our architecture must be overhauled. Every well-to-do household in the United States must eventually reorganize itself, and the most important aspect of this adjustment is its repercussions upon the lives and status of women.

What we are seeing today is a redistribution of leisure quite unrelated to and independent of equalization of money income. Though relatively few American families have ever had servants, the ideals appropriate to the feminist movement and to middle-class intellectuals are appropriate to a servant culture. Of the feminist movement it might be said that the late Victorian upper-class woman, having decided to limit the size of her family, found herself bored with cutting roses in the garden and went in for ballots and a career. To her period we owe not merely the career woman but also the vast mass of public-spirited good works and political interest manifested in such organizations as the League of Women Voters and the Junior League. But active participation in such organizations means for young women, unless they are endowed with extraordinary energy, either few children or none—or else enough servants to keep the family going. Furthermore, nearly all American women, of whatever economic group, are coming to feel that they are entitled to the highly active public life which was formerly possible only to the wealthy. There is therefore, as Mrs. Cyrus points out, a profound conflict between a woman's instincts as a mother and homemaker and her ideals of participation in political and economic life. The small urban family and the rapid disappearance of servants makes ever more acute the choice between children and a career.

To many people the only solution of this problem is thoroughgoing communization of home life in which children are reared primarily by the state. Such a solution would indicate virtual abandonment of the family as a separate institution. Yet it is in the family that much of our social training now takes place, and in which so many of the minority points of view continue to exist. Some authoritarian-minded writers see a great gain in the wiping out of individual traditions. They rejoice that it will be easier to eliminate ancestral "prejudices." This thoroughly undemocratic point of view runs counter to our whole emphasis upon pluralism and variety. No one has ever succeeded in answering John Stuart Mill's famous dictum, "First: the opinion which it is attempted to suppress by authority may possibly be true."

However, the collectivist solution is not the only one. Compromises can be worked out which make home life and child rearing possible without complete destruction of the family or the establishment of socialized beehives. Development can proceed on three lines: the nursery school; residential apartments which include restaurants, play schools, and nursery service; increased mechanization and redesigning of individual homes. To these may be added special hotel-nursing homes designed for old people. It may be asked, of course, How do these solutions differ from the collectivist one? Superficially they appear much the same. They differ, vitally, in the facts of competition, transfer, and choice. Instead of living in a state housing unit which they can leave with difficulty or not at all—a unit, let us say, in which the menu and the nursery discipline are determined by majority vote—families have a choice among various "competing" nursery schools and various places to live. The significance of choice immediately appears if we turn back to the arguments in our discussion of competition and political democracy, and of the inadequacy of a vote, without the transfer mechanism. Even though many costs are economized or shared, it will still be possible under our suggestion for the members of the family, within limits, to determine the manner of upbringing of their own children. We achieve the economic advantages of collectivism without abandoning the framework of competitive democracy and the freedom which it implies.

All this of course cannot come about at once, nor need it ever come about entirely. I have spoken of the restaurant-plus-nursery apartment house as one extreme. But, if the present trends of mechanization of the home plus organization of outside services continue, so drastic a solution will not be necessary. The individual home, supplemented by the nursery school, the apartment hotel for the aged, and so on, can easily survive. The main danger to home life, therefore, will lie more in the disruption of service efficiency by business and labor pressure groups. If the machinists and machine makers do to labor-saving devices what the building trades and construction industry have already done to housing, and the railroads and railroad workers to train transport, then the horizon for the family becomes extremely dark. But, if we keep pressure groups within control, then the home and the servantless world can be reconciled.

It must not be supposed, however, that considerable emotional friction would not be involved. Judged by our previous folk ways and ideals, the modern home cannot be as completely satisfying. A whole saga of American life is summed up in the idea of the family reunion. But such vast patriarchal (or more usually matriarchal) affairs become increasingly difficult. Yet it is not enough merely to be pessimistic. After all, nineteenth century upper-class parents went many hours without seeing their children. It is easy to overstate the contrast. Children, furthermore, if properly reared, become once more something of an economic asset in the home. Of course the modern spoiled child who is accustomed to having the entire family prostrate itself before him is of no earthly use in the carrying on of domestic life. But if he is trained to consider himself as a part of a social unit, and to work within the unit, then in a servantless world children past infancy are once more of great help to their parents. This furthermore can be accomplished without any serious encroachment upon their freedom and play time. Another result of the servantless world may be the bringing together of the generations now so badly split. Until extreme age or invalidism, old people cease to be a drag on the family and, by their mere presence, are often a boon to young parents anxious to escape occasionally from domestic cares. Of course much friction may result from conflict between the authoritarian tradition of the older generation and the resentment of the young. But as time goes on this attitude may be expected to change, and a more cooperative system of mutual respect to spring up. Thus a servantless world could produce a stronger rather than a weaker family. And since woman is no longer compelled to depend upon her husband for support the family unit should be more democratic.

However, two types will probably be unsatisfied by this solution, and both are strongly represented in the censor class. First, there is the militant feminist. One of the most undesirable forms of adjustment to modern living conditions is the two-child or one-child family. The career woman can give physical birth to one or possibly two children without excessive damage to her career. Whether she will be a mother in any other sense of the word is a matter of temperament. But the clash is readily apparent when it is recalled that many sociologists consider that it takes from three to four children to give a well balanced home and maintain the population.

The second unsatisfied type is the man or woman—businessman or intellectual—who is intensely absorbed in outside work or a career. One possible good result of the servantless world is that the father will once more become a part of the American home. Conditions will often force him to take a more active part in the rearing and management of the children. On the other hand a different type of man or of woman might become completely separate. The academic writer, for example, who does his work in his spare time is unable to help in the home to the extent that other fathers may. And the artist, male or female, is at a particular disadvantage as the head of a family. Their outlook may thus have a bias toward communal planning which will lead them to push radical and authoritarian solutions rather than those more favorable to the family and the home. There is grave doubt whether women can continue to have children in a servantless world and maintain all their present career aspirations. It remains to be seen whether the race will survive the desire for a type of living incompatible with home and children, or whether the sterile type of hotel life often now fashionable will herald the decadence of our society.

One technical economic point should be mentioned. It is sometimes said that without servants there will not be as great a demand for capital because people will no longer want as large houses. This is not correct. A tremendous investment field is opened up in the realm of labor-saving devices, and very large amounts of capital may well be absorbed in this manner.

So far we have been examining the personal and ulterior motives which would make the members of the white-collar intelligentsia dissatisfied under modern conditions. We have tried to show that their problem springs not so much from capitalism as from certain fundamental ideals and processes of democracy itself. Now we must turn to other factors that also make for dissatisfaction, but spring from noble and disinterested motives. The truth is that the American censor class is justly alarmed at the general decay of moral and aesthetic standards throughout the country. "Moral standards" need not designate a particular code but simply the willingness of an individual to sacrifice his personal interest to an ideal, even when there is no fear of detection. Man may argue as to which scheme of morals should be adopted; but no society can exist without some code of morals. Democratic progress, we have said, comes through persuasion. But if there be no ultimate community of values how can one persuade? We have seen that the modern intellectual tends to blame the competitive system for the increasing demoralization of social life, and we have tried to show that this blame is not warranted. In effect, what is needed is a good (that is, presently convincing) reason for leading the good life. The truth is that democratic morality, in the sense of sympathy and willingness to sacrifice personal advantage for the sake of an abstract standard of right and wrong, is much older and more imperative than any of the conventional sanctions usually urged for it. The reasons come and go—the necessity remains. A man may be right for the wrong reasons. "Every man is not a proper champion for truth," said Sir Thomas Browne. "Many from . . . an inconsiderate zeal unto truth have too rashly charged the troops of error, and remain as trophies unto the enemies of truth. A man may be in as just possession of truth as of a city, and yet be forced to surrender." But in our society, unless a course of action can be justified in "scientific" terms, it is held to be wrong; and we are inclined to forget it need not follow, from the fact that a man is talking nonsense, that he is acting it.

Yet, where are the sanctions to which the modern man can appeal? "Be good and you will be happy"? The wise man knows that this is true, but only in the sense of a special interior quiet. "A quality of mind steady in its reliance that fine action is treasured in the nature of things." The Philistine translates it as saying, "Be good and you will be rich or powerful"—and laughs at it. Again, "Be good or you will go to hell"? Our agnostic generation discards such an argument at sight. Finally, "Be good for the sake of your family and your children"? Many modern liberals are doing everything they can to undermine the family motive. Yet, having discarded the three sanctions hitherto most used—the ethical, the religious, and the family—many intellectuals now feel the only hope lies in substituting a remaining sanction: "Be good for the good of the state." This can never have a driving force equal to that of the family or the religious sanction, because it is less directly personal. Self-love will help to keep a man from wanting to go to hell. Love of family may lead him to try to transmit a good name, but love of country tends to be too remote. What it really is, in most cases, is love of home or friends or fear of public scorn. This, of course, is only an opinion. But, whether love of the state can be made an adequate personal sanction or not, it brings overwhelming tendencies toward centralized, controlled uniformity of opinion, which is the antithesis of democracy. Furthermore, in order to be directly effective, it almost always has to be supplemented with a war psychology.

The writer suggests that the liberal's rejection of the family solution for agnostic morals is due to the essentially romantic tone of modern intellectual life. The romantic is impatient of any form of restraint, and he is particularly apt to resent the family since that is the type of restraint with which he first came into contact. Extreme romantics like Rousseau or Alfred de Musset seek even to escape from the requirements of ordinary prudence and health. The influence of the nineteenth century utility calculus in this connection is also important, because it leads men to seek happiness not so much in performing function as in getting thrills.

But there is another element which is both creditable and discreditable to those who espouse it. A great part of the emotional drive behind redistributive taxation is inverted snobbishness and resentment of the family motive, not so much in its economic aspects as in the ideal of building up and transmitting a distinguished name. The liberal is peculiarly ungrateful in taking such an attitude. For where could one find more outstanding examples of the family motive as a social force than Franklin Delano Roosevelt and Mr. Justice Holmes? If it is not open to every man to be a descendant of distinguished ancestors, it is nevertheless open to everyone to become in some degree an ancestor himself, and there can be no question as to which is the nobler role. As Booker T. Washington put it, "Years ago I resolved that because I had no ancestry myself I would leave a record of which my children would be proud, and which would encourage them to still higher effort."

It is unfair, however, to ascribe resentment of the family motive solely to inverted snobbishness or resentment. There is also a noble love of liberty and the desire for absolute equality of opportunity. But, as we have shown earlier, absolute equality of opportunity is forever unobtainable. And, in trying to remove those last inequalities which our society still retains, we may find that we have gone over to a condition of entire despotism. Impatience with the secondary inequalities of the competitive system, and the family motive, may well place us under the fundamental inequality of despotic government.

We turn, then, from the censor class to the business community and ask what attitudes of mind are likely to be found in it. We have seen that the censor class is subject to many influences working for hostility to the capitalist order. But the business community contains an adverse bias also. The essential psychological problem may well prove to be that the capitalist (like the Platonic guardian) is unable to function without his "myth"—but that the nature of the capitalist myth is such as to prevent the businessman from advocating the measures needed to keep his system going.

One of the principal psychological advantages of socialism is that it is very easy for the individual worker to justify his position. However mistaken in fact he may be, he can always say that he is working for the public good because he is working for the state. The businessman, on the other hand, always finds it difficult to justify himself, and feels that in order to do so he must refute the charge that he is working solely for his own selfish interest. Therefore it is natural that when he is bitterly attacked, as he is today, he should instinctively turn for comfort to Adam Smith's doctrine of the "invisible hand." The famous misquotation from Adam Smith, "Every man working for his own selfish interest is nevertheless led by an invisible hand to promote the public good," furnishes an immediate means of justification to the businessman and an answer to his critics.

Of course, if the myth is literally accepted, it is hard to see why intervention by the state should ever be needed. Unfortunately, however, the pure doctrine of laissez faire has never been literally true. Even Smith himself did not state it so dogmatically; he actually said "in many instances," which is a very different thing from the "always" which the misquotation implies. If the capitalist clings to the dogma of laissez-faire economics, however, and tries to justify his system by saying supply and demand automatically always insure adequate social stability, he can never be really convincing. One of the principal obstacles which the believer in capitalism encounters in discussion is that he is nearly always assumed to say that the system will automatically adjust itself. Because this ability always to adjust within tolerable limits is domonstrably untrue, the defender of capitalism on such a ground is defeated before he has ever begun.

Yet, probably because of the psychological appeal of laissez faire already discussed, intelligent conservatism, recognizing the problems of effective demand, frequently does not attract business elements in the United States today. Rather we find an economic fundamentalism which seeks to overcome our problems by denying their existence. The trouble with the "modern" analysis is not that it is necessarily radical but that it is uncomfortable. The capitalist, as we have seen, does not want, indeed may not be able, to face the fact that competition and "supply and demand" will not always and automatically ensure either justice or stability. But since hardly anyone (certainly not the writer) would be willing to return to a regime of laissez faire, and since such a regime will inevitably be discredited by recurrent crises, inability or unwillingness of the capitalist world to adapt itself may well destroy the system. If conservatives prove unable to accept the valid elements of modern criticism, they cannot hope to refute the mistaken policies strangling the system. In such a case we may never get the relatively stable, free, democratic capitalism which lies within our grasp but rather some socialist or fascist hybrid. At the present time American capitalism bids fair to destroy itself through its own ignorance and, more important, lack of desire to learn.

We must be on our guard also for a different reason. The breakaway from blind adherence to laissez faire may bring another, and perhaps even greater, danger. For many businessmen who discard automatic adjustment consider that they are thereby free to discard the whole body of established capitalist thought. The results of this were particularly marked between world wars in

Great Britain where a program of planned monopoly attracted the adherence of the most divergent groups. Large-scale labor and large-scale industry combined to throttle the new man and the new idea. If the philosophy of this book be accepted, such a program was neither more nor less than incipient economic fascism, and it was sometimes referred to as the conservative "corporative" state. Yet our business groups now play with the same idea.

We hear a great deal today of what business must "plan"—what it must do to give jobs. Over and over again we learn that business must have a "new attitude" in its work. But the individual firm is in no position by itself to do much toward full employment. Unless a business is to be run at a loss and the pay roll loaded down with useless employees, the businessman as a businessman has very little room for policy in this connection.

When a group of businessmen are gathered into an association, there is a little more leeway—but then the action taken is frequently harmful. It is easy to seek to prevent depression by tracking down "unfair" or "cutthroat" competition—too easy. Unfortunately, ideas of this sort do not furnish a sound analysis of the cause and cure of the business cycle. The root cause of cutthroat competition is usually the jerky expansion which is an inevitable concomitant of rapid change. Trying to prevent it will not solve the distortion of the structure of industry and the consequent shortage of demand which underlies the depression. All too often, instead, the "prevention" is merely the cloak for comprehensive monopolization. It is rather by acting as an intelligent citizen that the businessman makes his most valuable contribution.

One of the paradoxes of modern radical criticism is that it often makes a businessman feel better as a monopolist than if he were conducting his business on more individualistic lines. There is unfortunately no necessary connection between the actual value of a man's work and the nobility of his avowed aims; a man may frequently be a better citizen if he sticks to trying to make money in the usual way than if he attempts to plan and "trade for the public good." But in the present state of public opinion, by assisting in essentially monopolistic restriction, he often obtains a public approval that is denied him if he takes what is in fact the more useful line of behavior. The easy coalition of the right-wing idea of unfair competition and left-wing ideas of planning or "cooperation" into a near-fascist regime of controlled monopoly is one of the chief dangers of our time.

There would appear, then, to be four main types of policy advocated in the modern world: (1) blind adherence to laissez faire at home and to economic isolationism abroad—which can only lead to eventual collapse; (2) planned monopolistic combination and log-rolled stagnation by business, labor, and government—a margin of otherwise unemployed must usually be occupied in armaments; (3) full-fledged socialism or fascism, which may be obtained either by direct seizure or by the more subtle hamstringing of the capitalist economy, public investment being used indefinitely "to fill the gap"; (4) removing barriers to investment and production so as to give the utmost freedom to the capitalist machinery, while standing ready to forestall disastrous deflation by the injection of purchasing power. Surely there can be little doubt as to which of these any believer in democracy and science should prefer.

There is, however, another aspect of the capitalist myth and the competitive market method which requires particular comment and justifies careful thought before interfering in economic affairs. It is characteristic of the competitive mechanism that it can never be standardized and reduced to routine without losing a large part of the energy and variety which are its most valuable attributes. Profits must be at the least proportional to risk, and risk is subjective rather than objective. Furthermore, the off chance, the one-in-a-hundred possibility, of supernormal profit is among the great impelling forces of investment. History shows that the extraordinary returns on investment rarely survive longer than a generation, and that labor's average real wages have persistently risen with the rise of the national income. The share of "capital," in the long run, has been remarkably constant. But if the attempt is made to limit the maximum expectation of the businessman, *in advance,* to "normal profits"—if, for example, he knows that as soon as he manages to increase profits his union will immediately strike—what reason is there to exert himself?

Competition in hope of supernormal profits is the force which gives both growth and realized normal profits. By limiting the hope to normal profits we cut off not merely the "excess" profits but the growth. The "purely competitive" ideal of the economic theorist is static and makes little or no allowance for dynamic investment. Yet the tendency of the human race is to demand absolute gospels and simple slogans. Selective codes such as hereditary right, seniority, or nose counting, employ objective standards easily appealed to. The competitive doctrine can never have comparable simplicity. Therefore it will always be less satisfying to those who believe in it and more vulnerable to adverse criticism.

Yet, come what may, there must be leaders under any system, and such leaders must be allowed to do their work and be protected from the jealousy of those not in power. So a new myth must be evolved. All wealth, it will be said, belongs to "us." The new privileged aristocracy are "our" servants, and we pay them well in money or titles or power, because of their great services to "us." For most people, differences in salary are always easier to rationalize than differences in profits or interest. But will this new myth be more literally accurate than the old? Will it make for more personal freedom, or less?

After all, "social myth" is but a euphemism for social lie. Adam Smith intended his myth merely as a convenient rough approximation. It is as pointless to object that it is not literally true as to object to the literal verity of Plato's myth of iron, brass, and golden men or the modern communists' myth of the labor theory of value. Is not much of our criticism of capitalism, when stripped of its verbiage, nearly as obvious as that there isn't any Santa Claus? Capitalism is not to be judged by mathematical "pure" competition but by alternatives in fact available. Rightly we do not trust Smith's doctrine as far as once we did. But will the new myth prove much more reliable? Can personal and economic freedom survive the end of change and business competition? That is a question which our children or grandchildren may well see answered.

It might appear that this book, isolating so many adverse currents, would have to close on a note of entire pessimism. That, however, is not the case. Perhaps the hope that modern America can see its own best interests will prove unwarranted. Perhaps arguments such as we have used will be suppressed in the totalitarian ages which now so gravely threaten. Even so, there still remains a feeling of comradeship with the unknown men who from the nature of free governments must rediscover these truths whenever and wherever democracy reappears. These are the problems of democracy. These are the requirements of economic peace.

Yet, easy as it would be to end on a pessimistic note, I cannot feel justified in doing so, even on purely neutral and scientific grounds. The present crisis is not the first in which hope for American democracy has seemed lost, and it may not be the last in which fears for the future are triumphantly overridden. If we have found tremendous forces working against democratic progress, we have also found great opportunities waiting to be grasped. The one overwhelming fact of the modern world is that all the nations desire an American standard of living and that only western—especially American—investment can approximate that desire. The oriental would do well to study the facts of western achievement rather than the economic criticisms of recent intellectuals. England was not comprehensively planned when mistress of the seas. The American standard of living, the rise in labor's standard of living, was not achieved by the omniscient state. The Orient has had regulation, hierarchy, absolute power, and a noncompetitive philosophy for a thousand years, but it has produced no such results as our two hundred years of competition. In the Occident the Empire did not build up Rome. The Empire was merely the slow smothering of the creative energy of the Roman Republic.

In the light of world conditions it is difficult to escape the conclusion that capitalism once more makes economic sense. The present book is concerned more with democracy than with capitalism. But in so far as the apologetics of capitalism versus socialism is concerned, we have needlessly weakened our case by putting aside the argument of simple material progress. By the current standards of many socialists, it would be easy to make out a winning case for capitalism. Do we want to prevent inflation? Then saving is needed, and capitalists have always been savers. Do we want production? The capitalist system has been among the most productive in history. Do we want opportunity? It is the system which has had the most open pattern and the widest access to the top.

Governments, it has been often remarked, can only stay in power by the means by which they achieve it. Yet the left wing today does not promise the people a regime of secure poverty. That would be the promise which they could keep. They promise instead an economy which will grow and change as fast as capitalism, and yet be more secure. This is a promise which, in the nature of things, is impossible of performance. If we really wish to set up a static culture on our present level of machine technology, we must forget democracy and teach the masses not to want higher living standards. We should furthermore begin to think about training a new aristocratic governing elite in the paternal, aristocratic *noblesse oblige* which would be the only means of keeping such a system tolerable. But the American left wing combines constant propaganda for "more" with policies and ideologies eminently arranged to frustrate production, feeding us an irritant poison advertised as its own cure. As for *noblesse oblige* and the self-restraint and balance needed for successful government, it is difficult to think of anything more foreign to the romantic outlook of many ultraliberals. Theirs is not even a policy for stable fascism. It is a policy for utter disaster.

Some persons will object that the fundamentally optimistic approach of this book is unrealistic. Their criticism may be taken in two senses. First, it may mean that the writer does not know the practical problems. But personal experience in government and in business, and close connection with many economic and political executives during the last twelve years should negative this contention. However, "unrealistic" has a second application. The meaning may be that it is unrealistic to fight against an apparently overwhelming trend. With this attitude the believer in democracy must forever disagree. It is not more than three years since the apparently overwhelming trend was toward immediate fascism. How much better to take courage instead from another believer in democracy, T. B. Macaulay, who was confronted as we are with short-run crisis and long-run hopes. Macaulay wrote in 1830:

"The present moment is one of great distress. But how small

will that distress appear when we think over the history of the last forty years; a war, compared with which all other wars sink into insignificance; taxation, such as the most heavily taxed people of former times could not have conceived; a debt larger than all the public debts that ever existed in the world added together; the food of the people studiously rendered dear; the currency imprudently debased, and imprudently restored. Yet is the country poorer than in 1790? We fully believe that, in spite of all the misgovernment of her rulers, she has been almost constantly becoming richer and richer. . . .

"If we were to prophesy that in the year 1930 a population of fifty millions, better fed, clad, and lodged than the English of our time, will cover these islands, . . . that machines constructed on principles yet undiscovered will be in every house, that there will be no highways but railroads, no travelling but by steam, that our debt, vast as it seems to us, will appear to our great-grandchildren a trifling encumbrance, which might easily be paid off in a year or two, many people would think us insane. We prophesy nothing: but this we say: If any person had told the Parliament which met in perplexity and terror after the crash in 1720 that in 1830 the wealth of England would surpass all their wildest dreams, . . . that stagecoaches would run from London to York in twenty-four hours, that men would be in the habit of sailing without wind, and would be beginning to ride without horses, our ancestors would have given as much credit to the prediction as they gave to Gulliver's Travels. Yet the prediction would have been true . . . We cannot absolutely prove that those are in error who tell us that society has reached a turning point, that we have seen our best days. But so said all who came before us, and with just as much apparent reason. . . . On what principle is it that, when we see nothing but improvement behind us, we are to expect nothing but deterioration before us?" *

Are we justified in allowing the fascism of the left or the "voluntary" monopoly of the right to bury the new century of democratic progress before it has begun?

* T. B. Macaulay, review of *Southey's Colloquies.*